802.1X Port-Based
Authentication

802.1X Port-Based Authentication

Edwin Lyle Brown

CRC Press
Taylor & Francis Group
Boca Raton London New York

CRC Press is an imprint of the
Taylor & Francis Group, an **informa** business
AN AUERBACH BOOK

CRC Press
Taylor & Francis Group
6000 Broken Sound Parkway NW, Suite 300
Boca Raton, FL 33487-2742

First issued in paperback 2019

ISBN-13: 978-1-4200-4464-5 (hbk)

ISBN-13: 978-0-367-38967-3 (pbk)

Library of Congress Cataloging-in-Publication Data

Brown, Edwin Lyle.
   802.1X port-based authentication / Edwin Lyle Brown.
      p. cm.
   Includes bibliographical references and index.
   ISBN 1-4200-4464-8 (978-1-4200-4464-5 : alk. paper)
   1. Computer networks--Security measures--Standards. 2. Computers--Access control--Standards. 3. Computer network protocols. I. Title.

TK5105.59.B765 2007
005.8--dc22
                                                2006030999

Visit the Taylor & Francis Web site at
http://www.taylorandfrancis.com

and the CRC Press Web site at
http://www.crcpress.com

DEDICATION

I dedicate this to several of the special women in my life: my mother, Bea Webb; Mary Nevin; Della Bonnette; my daughters, Jennifer, Rachel, and Erin—and most of all to my wife, Pam.

PREFACE

I have heard that there are a couple of rules to be followed in writing a "good" piece of nonfiction. The first rule is to make certain that all the "w's" are covered. The second rule is to tell the reader what is going to be written, then write it—and, finally, tell the reader what was written. To a certain extent, this seems a bit silly. But it has merit, and I will follow all of these rules in this book.

The first rule regarding the "w's" means that the text should always identify the what, who, when, where, and, in some cases, the why regarding the author's subject. I suppose in a news article, "why" becomes speculative and should not be included. However, I am not a reporter. I am a technologist, probably not a good enough one to qualify as a true geek, but I am a technologist nonetheless. And this book will cover some of the realm of why. As for the other "w's", I will also attempt to explain those as well—even when.

As for the second rule, this book is portioned into three distinct chapters. The first chapter will present an overview with the intention of developing a baseline or performing a level-set. Therefore, this chapter is intended to ensure that everyone has the same fundamental knowledge that is necessary to understand the subsequent chapters and their individual sections. The second chapter of the book discusses technology; the third discusses design, implementation, and troubleshooting issues in a Cisco environment. To further abide by the second rule, each chapter begins with an overview of the subject being covered. Then, each section begins with a Section Summary that varies in length depending on both the size and complexity of the particular section. Because I have spent far too many years in the consulting world, this will look like an "Executive Summary" to many people. Each summary is followed by a body of text that addresses the subject of the particular section. I ignore part of rule number two by not including additional verbiage to recap the particular section. In short, each section tells what it is going to cover and then proceeds to cover it.

So what is this book about? That is the question that everyone will ask when they pick this up. This book is about one aspect of network security. A friend told me that I needed to identify what network I was talking about.

Is it a television network? Or a collection of highways? No, this network is a means of connecting computerized devices to allow them to communicate with one another. To a certain extent, the physical method of connection is moot. It can be a series of wires or it can be wireless. In fact, both types of mediums will be explored. The aspect of security that is associated with that network and is encompassed by this book is called port-based authentication.

What is port-based authentication? It is a concept, or perhaps a premise, that a particular device should be evaluated prior to being allowed to communicate with other devices located on the network. Actually, that is a slightly more restrictive definition than is deserved. The definition of port-based authentication will be expanded to be something more on the order of: The credentials of the device, or of the individual using that device, must be evaluated to determine what type of access, if any, should be allowed. This book is about how that definition can be applied—and the effect of its application—to the majority of computer networks in existence today, by using something commonly called 802.1X.

802.1X sounds quite cryptic. Actually, 802.1X is a particular network protocol established by the Institute of Electrical and Electronics Engineers (IEEE). The use of the term 802.1X commonly encompasses much more than what is covered within the specification of the protocol. The protocol, itself, is only a small portion of the port-based authentication process. If I were to continue explaining all of that right here, this would become the body of the book, rather than the preface. At this point, I'll simply say that the subject of this book is port-based authentication with a primary focus on the protocol 802.1X.

That covers the "what," as far as this preface is concerned. The next question in my mind when I pick up a work of nonfiction is whether or not I will find it useful. This question relates to "who"—or is it likely that I will understand what the author has written? That does not beg the question of whether the style the author employs is enjoyable to the reader, but, instead, it boils down to the question of whether the content of the book is directed toward the reader's sophistication and prior knowledge of the subject. Just like Goldilocks with the porridge, is this book too hot, too cold, or just right?

To answer that question, *802.1X Port-Based Authentication* is written for a broad audience. I have assumed that the reader has a general-to-complex understanding of computer networking, Ethernet, and configuration and troubleshooting knowledge of Cisco devices in particular. The last section of the book uses examples derived from the implementation of 802.1X on Cisco devices. The content is explicitly directed toward that environment, but much of what is presented is useful in environments utilizing other vendors. There is a section of this book that specifically addresses the configuration parameters associated with Cisco devices. It should be able to be leveraged to a varying degree with non-Cisco equipment, as well.

I have assumed that the reader does not have an advanced knowledge of port-based authentication and 802.1X. Hopefully, the content here will be as useful to individuals with a moderate understanding of that topic as it will be for those with little prior knowledge of the subject. This book is written in such a way as to lead the reader from a minimal level of sophistication in the subject through an increasingly complex investigation of the topic. Simply stated, the presentation of each topic will assume little prior knowledge or experience and progress through some complex discussion. The entire book is presented in that fashion. Basic and fundamental information, prerequisite knowledge, if you will, will be presented prior to moving on to the next subject. Although the ordering of some sections in the book is arbitrary, in the sense that the subject of one section may not be dependent on the topic covered in the immediately preceding section, the nature of a book still requires some physical sequence. However, prerequisite knowledge for any section of this book will have been presented earlier in the book.

THE AUTHOR

Lyle Brown has been professionally involved for the past 30 years in one form of information technology (called data processing when he began) or another. He obtained a batchelor's degree in computer science in 1975 from the University of Southwestern Louisiana and worked as a programmer on DEC PDP-8 computers for a year before spending more than 20 years working for the state of Louisiana. During those years, he became interested in LAN and WAN technologies and developed some of the first implementations for various state agencies. After leaving state employment, he worked for various companies designing, developing, and implementing Cisco-based local and wide-area networks. He obtained a variety of certifications, most prominently as a Cisco Certified Internet Work Expert (CCIE). Lyle is currently employed by BearingPoint as head of the Global WAN, LAN, VPN, and Wireless Technologies Architecture group. He and his wife reside in Louisiana.

CONTENTS

CONTENTS

1

OVERVIEW

Amazingly enough, the title of this chapter explains what it is all about. This chapter is intended to provide a basic foundation in the subject of Port-Based Authentication that will be sufficient upon which to build a deeper understanding. The way in which I will accomplish that is to provide three sections in this chapter.

The first section will contain what is anticipated in a first section. It will provide a fundamental description of 802.1X—Port-Based Authentication: what it is, how it functions, and why it is important. The amount of detail is minimal in this chapter. It is intended to ensure that a basic level set of information has been established. Subsequent sections of the book will provide most of the detailed information of how and why 802.1X functions in a specific way in a given circumstance. This section identifies the three network components and the various protocols involved in an 802.1X authentication.

The second section may seem a little out of place. It is a discussion of the history of the standard and the technical documents published. Many books will begin with the history before proceeding to a discussion of how it works. I am not certain that the history of 802.1X is unique, and because of the entities that were involved in the development of the standards, it probably is not. The history of 802.1X is convoluted and complicated because of the interactions of standards over time. The history involves at least three distinct sets of standards and two organizations. Understanding what is being developed at a particular point in time, and roughly how the pieces fit together, helps to clarify the current status of the standards. Also, the history is so brief that both sides of technology implemented at an evolutionary point in time are still present in many networks. Both pre- and post-evolution changes in technology exist in current networks. This means that understanding when a particular product was created will imply certain capabilities or the lack thereof in any given network.

The final section in this chapter is really a bridge into the next chapter. It provides the details of the connections among the three network components. The various conversations that can take place in the authentication process are diagrammed. Detailed information is provided on what can occur in each exchange and under what conditions.

1.1 WHAT IS 802.1X AND WHY SHOULD I CARE?

1.1.1 Section Summary

As this is the first section of the book, it will provide the basic information necessary to proceed to more complex subjects. So what is 802.1X? It is a common belief that 802.1X is some kind of security. Some may think that it is an authentication process employed when a device connects to a network. There is also a conception that wireless authentication, and all of the issues with secure communication over that medium, is 802.1X. All of those beliefs are at least slightly inaccurate. Strictly speaking, 802.1X is a language that extends the Extensible Authentication Protocol (EAP) over a Local Area Network (LAN) through a process called Extensible Authentication Protocol Over LANs (EAPOL). This protocol is employed to transport credential information between two devices. Thus, the actual definition in the standards is much more limited than the commonly held beliefs. Rather than attempt to enforce the stricter definition, I will use the term 802.1X very loosely and allow the concept of 802.1X to be roughly equivalent to Port-Based Authentication. Wherever a strict interpretation is required during the course of this book, I will emphasize that situation.

Port-Based Authentication actually leverages three components to accomplish its mission. 802.1X is probably the largest piece of the three, but could not effectively function without the other two. Those other two components are the Extensible Authentication Protocol-Methods (EAP-Methods) and Remote Authentication Dial In User Service (RADIUS). Again, 802.1X is the protocol employed to allow two devices to communicate. The protocol is called EAPOL. EAP-Methods is actually the data field of the protocol EAP, and EAPOL is a special case of EAP—which will be discussed shortly.

802.1X is an extension of the IEEE 802 protocol and, as such, it operates at Layer 2 of the Open System Interface (OSI) model. This is the Data Link Layer and is present in both a wired and wireless LAN. 802.1X employs the protocol EAPOL to prevent a device attempting to connect to a network from doing so until it has provided credentials that can be validated. Credential information is encapsulated in EAPOL by a device attempting to connect, and then sent to another device that is part of the infrastructure of the network, usually a switch or wireless access point. There, it is decapsulated and sent to a RADIUS server for validation. If successful, the RADIUS server tells the switch or access point—and the device wishing access is allowed to fully connect. If the validation is not successful, the switch or access point is notified, as well, and no access is allowed.

Thus, there are three parties involved in the process. The first is the device wishing to connect, known as the Supplicant. The second device is the one to which the Supplicant wishes to connect. This device is part of the local network infrastructure and is known as the Authenticator. The third device that houses the credential information is usually a RADIUS server and is known as the Authentication Server. The Authenticator sits between the Supplicant and the Authentication Server. No direct communication is ever allowed between those two entities. The Authenticator is always the recipient of any communication and always will repackage the content of the communication before forwarding it. The Authenticator usually will not be able to translate the content of credential exchanges, but must be able to repackage the content from either the Supplicant or the Authentication Server and forward it to the intended recipient. By inserting itself in the process in this fashion, the Authenticator can guarantee that the Supplicant cannot communicate with any other device.

EAPOL is a very simple protocol that is used only in Port-Based authentication between an Authenticator and a Supplicant in an 802 LAN. The basic communication consists of two types of packets. The Authenticator sends Request-Identity packets to the Supplicant. The Supplicant sends Response packets to the Authenticator. Based on notification from RADIUS concerning the validity of credentials supplied by the Supplicant, the Authenticator will send either Success or Failure packets to the Supplicant. There are a couple of additional types of packets that will be discussed, but the basic protocol consists of these four types of packets.

The Port-Based Authentication process does venture into the realm of Authorization to a certain extent because the VLAN in which a device is placed is variable. The VLAN can be a Guest VLAN, the Authorized VLAN associated with a port, or even a dynamic VLAN associated with the credentials. The assignment of a VLAN within Port-Based Authentication is very robust.

Why is this becoming more important in local networks? There are two situations that are influencing this. First, electronic access to information is becoming a basic function of many jobs, and, second, it is becoming more common for attacks on networks and theft of information to occur. Port-Based Authentication can be one mechanism employed to help both situations. Port-Based Authentication can help ensure that only people who are supposed to be on a network are the ones on it. This reduces the population that must be inspected to a level that is at least controllable. Yet, this is the first level of security, not the only one that should be implemented.

1.1.2 What Is 802.1X in Detail?

The first place to start is to discuss the term Port-Based Authentication. What is Authentication and how does it differ from Authorization? Authentication is the process of identification. Frequently the process makes use of a username/password combination. Authorization is the process of granting certain privilege based on identity. Authentication provides assurance that a person is who he or she claims to be, but says nothing about what access should be granted. Thus, the process of ensuring that someone is who he says he is must take place at a "port." The port in question is a Layer 2 connection. In the wired environment, this is a physical port on a switch. In a wireless environment, it is an "association" with an access point. The implication of Port-Based Authentication is that a device attempting to connect to a network will be challenged at the point of connection before communication with any "authentic" devices already resident on the network is allowed.

802.1X defines a set of protocols to support a methodology to answer the question: Is this an authentic user or device that is allowed to connect to a network? In the Section 1.1.1, this was identified as a Data Link Layer (Layer 2) mechanism. Very simply, 802.1X is a Layer 2 protocol used to support the determination of whether or not credentials supplied by a device wishing to attach to a network are sufficient to allow the connection.

From a physical perspective, 802.1X consists of three entities: a device attempting to connect to a network, a second device that houses the desired connection point, and a database containing credential information used to validate the connection. These devices are called a Supplicant, an Authenticator, and an Authentication Server, respectively. These names will change somewhat depending on which particular specification is referenced, but these names are the commonly used terms. No matter what name is used the functions are the same—a rose by any other name, so to speak. Figure 1.1 illustrates the three entities.

These three devices execute three different logical conversations to conduct an authentication. Two of the conversations are physical exchanges and can be seen in packet captures. These physical conversations are shown in Figure 1.1. One conversation is entirely logical and cannot be seen in

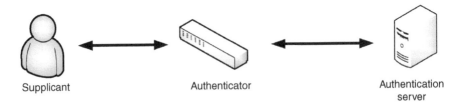

| Supplicant | Authenticator | Authentication server |

Figure 1.1   Basic 802.1X Communication.

packet captures. The Supplicant and the Authenticator have a physical conversation, and the Authenticator and the Authentication Server have a physical conversation. Both of these conversations can be seen as data transfers. The physical conversations actually support the exchange of credential information between the Supplicant and the Authentication Server. This is the entirely logical conversation. The key point here is that the Supplicant can converse only with the Authenticator. Thus, the Authenticator actually acts as a translator between the Supplicant and the Authentication Server.

This means that there are several protocols implemented to support this authentication system. Each of the conversations, either physical or logical, must be supported by at least one distinct protocol. The three conversations—and all the protocols employed—are commonly called 802.1X; but, in truth, only the physical conversation between the Authenticator and the Supplicant is 802.1X—EAPOL. The physical communication between the Authentication Server and the Authenticator is conducted using the RADIUS protocol. The logical conversation between the Authentication Server and the Supplicant is conducted using EAP and EAP-Methods.

What is EAP? EAP was created to be implemented in the Point-To-Point (PPP) protocol. PPP is a protocol used for communication taking place on a serial link—usually a leased telephone line. At first glance, it would seem that a serial protocol and a LAN protocol are entirely different animals and would not have much in common. Generally, this is true. However, the specifications for EAP are almost philosophical in nature and only require the topology be a Point-to-Point connection. If you look at a single connection on a switched LAN, or an association in wireless environments, then you will see that they have strong Point-to-Point characteristics. Point-to-Point characteristics are fundamental in the concept of EAP. As long as those characteristics are present, then it is relatively simple to utilize EAP. This can be accomplished with a Layer 2 encapsulation—EAPOL—in a switched LAN. The result is 802.1X.

What is an EAP-Method then? An EAP-Method is the way in which a particular authentication is conducted. In a sense, an EAP-Method is an authentication. Parsing EAP-Method into EAP and Method makes it a little easier to understand. It is a particular Method used to execute an authentication utilizing EAP as a transport mechanism. EAP-Methods are defined for various ways to authenticate. There are many methods that have been defined. Some utilize certificates, others use Username/Password, and some are methods of tunneling information between the Supplicant and the Authentication Server. However diverse they become, each and every one will always be encapsulated in EAP between the Supplicant and the Authenticator.

EAP, again, is a protocol defined to function within the PPP suite. 802.1X leverages the topology of PPP and assumes a simple architecture of a single device connecting to a single port on a network. A single Supplicant connecting to a single port on an Authenticator looks much the same as the PPP environment. Thus, 802.1X looks like PPP, functions at Layer 2, and is operable prior to allowing any communication over the port except for traffic directly related to the authentication of the Supplicant. As noted previously, it can function on either wired or wireless media. While switched Ethernet and 802.11 (Wireless) are the most common implementations, the specifications include virtually all 802 types, including switched Token Ring and FDDI. Why a switched environment? Because a switched environment is the closest a LAN can come to a one-to-one relationship for a device connecting to a LAN, and that one-to-one relationship is the primary topology for EAP in PPP.

To recap: Port-Based Authentication, commonly called 802.1X, is conceptually a simple thing. It consists of three physical entities in its current implementation: the Supplicant, the Authenticator, and the Authentication Server. The Supplicant is a device wishing to connect to the network. The Authenticator is the device housing the "port" that the Supplicant is attempting to use. The Authentication Server has the ability to validate credentials supplied by the Supplicant. The Authentication Server may or may not contain the database used for validation, but it is responsible for the actual validation. The EAP defined for PPP is leveraged in the 802 LAN environments to transport credential information between a Supplicant and an Authentication Server. The credential information and the way in which it is used is defined as an EAP-Method. The particular EAP-Method will define what data is used and how it is used. This information then will be transported as a block of data within the EAP protocol.

802.1X or EAPOL is utilized as the protocol for conversations between a Supplicant and an Authenticator. The Authenticator and the Authentication Server use the RADIUS protocol for conversations between themselves. The EAP-Method is the logical exchange of credentials between the Supplicant and the Authentication Server.

1.1.3   How Does It Work?

As stated earlier, the Supplicant and the Authenticator converse, and the Authenticator and the Authentication Server converse; but the Supplicant and the Authentication Server never converse directly. This is a fundamental concept. The Authenticator is always the recipient, translator, and man-in-the-middle for all conversation between the two endpoints. 802.1X is effective because it does not allow a Supplicant to communicate with the network prior to authentication. Actually, there is one situation in which a non-authenticated Supplicant can communicate with a device on the network. That situation has to do with reporting environmental conditions and will be discussed in later sections. For all practical purposes, no communication is allowed from a device attempting to connect until the authentication process has been completed. There is an awful lot of waffle in that statement, but it is correct.

Each endpoint, Supplicant or Authentication Server, speaks only to the Authenticator, and the Authenticator forwards the information from one to the other. When the Authenticator and the Supplicant converse, it is strictly within the EAPOL protocol at Layer 2. This precludes the Supplicant from doing anything but conversing with the Authenticator and using anything but that protocol to do it with. Anything the Supplicant attempts to do outside of that protocol is ignored. It is possible to configure the authentication process to allow very specific traffic from the network to the Supplicant in one specific instance. This is intended to allow a Supplicant to be "nudged awake" by another device resident on the LAN and cause the Supplicant to fully participate in the 802.1X process.

Because 802.1X is a Link Layer protocol, it should make sense that everything kicks off when link is established. As soon as link is established, the Authenticator demands identity credentials on the link that came active. It uses an EAPOL frame called a Request Identity. If there is a Supplicant at the other end of the link, it will respond with a Response packet. The Authenticator will accept the Response, repackage it, and forward it to the Authentication Server using the RADIUS protocol. Nothing will be allowed to be transmitted from the Supplicant—at least, the Authenticator will not respond to anything but EAPOL packets from the Supplicant. The Authentication Server will respond to the Authenticator using the RADIUS protocol. The Authenticator will repackage the data from the Authentication Server and forward it to the Supplicant using an EAPOL protocol packet—a Request Identity. This type of conversation will continue until the Authentication process completes. At that time, the Authentication Server will notify the Authenticator of either success or failure. The Authenticator will pass this information along to the Supplicant, but will also act on it. It will either allow the Supplicant into an authorized VLAN or it will not. It is possible to put unauthorized Supplicants, or devices that do not have Supplicants, into a special VLAN called a Guest VLAN.

There are multiple possibilities for the assignment of a VLAN to the connecting device. First, there is a VLAN that is associated with the port. This VLAN is defined in the port configuration in the same way that a port without 802.1X enabled has a VLAN configured for it. This is what is referred to as the Authorized VLAN because it will normally allow access to some form of corporate resources and is often the VLAN to which an authenticated Supplicant will be assigned. The authenticated Supplicant can also have a VLAN assigned to the credentials in the RADIUS server. This VLAN is dynamically applied upon successful authentication. The Guest VLAN was identified in the previous paragraph. It can be configured on a port that has 802.1X enabled. Thus, there are several possibilities regarding VLAN assignment for a device attempting to attach to a network. They range from no VLAN at all to one specifically chosen for the particular user.

The logical conversations between the Supplicant and the Authentication Server are pretty much meaningless to the Authenticator. It acts like the kid in the classroom sitting between two classmates who accepts and passes notes between them without reading the notes. That is: until the Authenticator finally gets a message from the Authentication Server indicating success or failure. If success is indicated, then the Authenticator will perform some activity based upon the success message and authorize the port to a specific VLAN. If failure is indicated, then the Authenticator will tell the Supplicant to go away and keep the port in an unauthorized status. In some implementations, it is possible for a Supplicant that cannot be authenticated to be placed in a Guest VLAN.

Conceptually, that is really all there is to 802.1X. It is a simple and clean concept of how authentication can be implemented at the time a device attempts to connect to a network. During a practical implementation, there are significantly more questions and potential situations that require consideration. But ultimately it boils down to three devices, three conversations, and at least three protocols.

1.1.4   Why 802.1X?

Why implement something that will undoubtedly complicate the LAN environment? Perhaps the answer is: life around here has become dull. We really need something for everyone to get involved with—and securing the environment will do that. Certainly, there are some individuals who, in their deepest souls, believe that is the answer. However, the answer that provides the most justification is something like: unfortunately, not all people respect privacy—and they are willing to steal proprietary information or cause trouble for the sake of causing trouble. This statement is both true and frightening.

For a long time, the common belief was that the perimeter of a network was what must be secured. The general belief used to be that the employees of a corporation are trusted, valued resources dedicated to the success of the company and their co-workers. No company intentionally employs malicious, jealous, angry, frustrated people—but there are some in almost every company. The internal network that exists to provide the type of access to information the loyal employee requires is also available to provide the same type of access to the disloyal employee or even an outsider. On the one hand, the network must be the vehicle that supports the activity of the enterprise, allowing access to confidential and proprietary information. On the other hand, it must ensure that this same information is not provided to the wrong individual.

The original networks that were developed never really had security as a premise. They were developed to expedite access, not protect it. If you could plug into a network port, you usually had access to everything on the network. Some sensitive information probably was protected where it resided, such as a server, but the transport of the information across the network was not. That became the foot in the door, and for a creative, unscrupulous person, that was all that was needed. Thus, protecting access to a network port has become increasingly important. Historically, many mechanisms have been implemented to restrict access. Each and every one has certain shortcomings. 802.1X has its share as well. It is doubtful that there will ever be a solution developed that will not have at least a hole or two.

Port-Based Authentication provides one leg of a multi-legged beast intended to lessen the vulnerability of a proprietary network. 802.1X enhances the likelihood that everyone attached to a local environment is authentic. That statement is important. In fact there are two parts to that statement that are important: local environment and authentic. 802.1X may be implemented in a worldwide enterprise with hundreds of sites and thousands of ports, but it is ultimately concerned with only one port at a time. The local environment is reduced to the scope of one device attempting to connect to the network. That is the first part. The second part is that 802.1X is intended to ensure that the one device attempting to connect is actually authentic—or authenticated.

It is difficult to separate authorization from authentication. Frequently, the question becomes, "Is this user allowed to access this resource?" rather than "Does this user have credentials that verify that he is who he says he is?" Look at the first question. It presumes that the second question has been answered. Should not a user first prove he is who he claims to be before he is authorized? Viewed in this manner, authentication is a prerequisite for authorization. Ultimately, the two functions must work together, and 802.1X provides a mechanism to ensure that only authenticated users or devices are allowed on the network.

1.2   THE HISTORY AND TECHNICAL DOCUMENTS

1.2.1   Section Summary

It may seem somewhat unusual to present the history of a technical subject in this much detail, but, in the case of 802.1X, it is useful in understanding why the state of 802.1X is what it is today. As discussed earlier, 802.1X is a protocol that carries credential information utilized in the authentication process. The authentication process, itself, leverages several different components: 802.1X, EAP, and EAP-Methods. Furthermore, RADIUS is implemented to house valid credential information. Each and every one of these components was developed and enhanced at several different times by different groups. While each of these groups was addressing a particular topic, it would, attempt to integrate or support the other related initiatives as they were in existence at that time.

To use an analogous environment, such as our world, we would need to develop a view of evolution through a continuum containing multiple creatures. Each of the creatures is impacted by—and has an impact on—the other creatures in the habitat. Each of the creatures would change, somewhat, based on the characteristics of the environment around it. In turn, the environment, itself, would begin changing based on the new impact of the changed creature.

In the timeline discussed in this chapter, our creatures are 802.1X, RADIUS, EAP, and EAP-Methods. Each of these entities has developed a symbiotic relationship with the others. Each has evolved and, in evolving, has caused further evolution in its symbiotic partner. This is important to understand. The history of Port-Based Authentication is very short. Effectively, it is still possible, even probable, that the reader can utilize what was in existence at a particular point in this evolutionary process in his or her current production network. The entire history of this subject spans only five to ten years. The most current "leaps" in evolution took place in 2004. This is the dividing line between modern and ancient history for Port-Based Authentication. It is reasonable to assume that many networks have components necessary for Port-Based Authentication that were created prior to 2004. These components will have capabilities concurrent with the state of evolution at the time they were created. It is not reasonable, therefore, to discuss this subject from only the perspective of what is the current state of evolution. All the capabilities at various points in time must be considered.

Understanding the importance of the state of each of the components at various points in time is necessary to fully interpreting what is happening in various networks that utilize components created/implemented at different times. Sometimes a network can be confusing because various devices support different levels of functions, based on when they were created or implemented.

The world of Port-Based Authentication is based on EAP. EAP began formal life in 1998. It did not leverage any of the other components, but did plant the seeds for both 802.1X and EAP-Methods. Documents formalizing EAP-Methods began to be created almost immediately after the publication of standards for EAP. 802.1X was formalized in 2001. It specifically leveraged EAP. Without formal EAP specifications, the formal documents for 802.1X could not exist. 802.1X specifically leveraged EAP into EAPOL. During this period, RADIUS existed, but was only formally incorporated with Port-Based Authentication in documents published in 2003. In a very short period of time in 2004, the formal documents for both EAP and 802.1X were significantly revised. The basic content of the old specifications for each remained intact, but each was significantly enhanced.

At the time of the writing of this book, EAP, 802.1X, EAP-Methods, and RADIUS have all recognized one another and have melded into a fairly comprehensive set of formal documents. However, the evolutionary process is not complete. There is significant work being currently conducted to extend the evolutionary process—especially in terms of wireless security.

1.2.2 When Did All of This Come About?

Although the formal history of 802.1X is fairly short, it is somewhat convoluted. The interaction of various IETF RFCs and IEEE Standards makes for a confusing discussion. The various specifications were developed separately over time and then fitted together. They fit well, but exactly when each part came into being and how it interacts with the other specifications is a bit dry.

The first documents—standards—were published in the late 1990s. It was not until early in this decade that significant interest caused a flurry of written activity. Realistically, the past couple of years is the true time frame during which much of the current implementation of 802.1X was defined. As stated in Section 1.2.1, the "modern" history of these standards really began in 2003–2004.

Figure 1.2 shows the timeline regarding the publication of some of the material.

It is obvious that a significant amount of activity has begun to take place in the past couple of years. Beginning in 2004, a number of new or revised standards regarding EAP, 802.1X, and 802.11i have been published. The use of 802.1X is a fundamental concept in much of the continuing work concerning the initial authentication process for many 802 media—especially wireless.

1.2.3 The Technical Documents

To get a fundamental understanding of why 802.1X is implemented the way it is, it is best to review the various technical publications from an historical

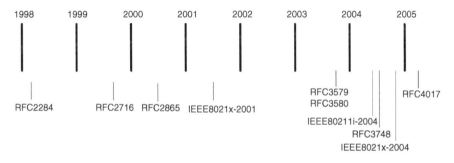

Figure 1.2 802.1X Timeline.

perspective. There are three tracks of specifications and two standards bodies that are involved in the authentication process. EAP-Methods tend to be concerned with encryption of transmissions and the process of validating credentials. We will treat EAP-Methods as a special case because many of the specific methods implemented are proprietary and not formally documented. This is beginning to change, and if this book were published five years from now, it probably would contain more references to formal EAP-Method documents.

The Internet Engineering Task Force (IETF) controls two sets of the specifications: those pertaining to EAP and RADIUS. These documents are all known as Request For Comment (RFC) publications. The Institute of Electrical and Electronics Engineers (IEEE) controls documents pertaining to LAN specifications—specifically 802.1X. Those documents are known as IEEE Standards. The IEEE numbers their documents and that is why the protocol we are concerned with is 802.1X. The actual title on the cover of the specification is Port-Based Network Access Control.

In some cases, the same people have been involved with the development of more than one of the tracks and that has probably helped to establish continuity. Although it is not technically true to consider the evolution of the documents as an integrated process, this book will tend to present them as such. The next few pages will attempt to present both the evolution within a particular track, such as EAP, and across all three tracks. Again, while it is not technically correct to call the entire process 802.1X, that is the common perception and, to a certain extent, this book will continue to follow that precedent.

Let us start with the early history of EAP. EAP began formal life in 1998 with RFC 2284, entitled PPP Extensible Authentication Protocol (EAP). Of course, significant discussion took place prior to the publication of this document, and it may be that years earlier the beginnings of EAP existed in the foggy thoughts of some unknown individual. Yes, there will always be someone who is credited with the thought, but who really knows what conversations actually may have sparked the proposals?

It is interesting to note that EAP is founded in the Point-to-Point Protocol (PPP). PPP is essentially concerned with serial connections, not with LAN connections such as Ethernet or Token Ring. EAP was created to formally describe how those serial connections should and must occur. The first formal document related to PPP is RFC 1134, which was published in 1989. The first main standard for PPP is RFC 1171, which was published in 1990. This standard has been modified a large number of times and a large number of peripheral standards have evolved from it. One of the three primary components of PPP is the definition of a Link Control Protocol (LCP) that defines how two devices should connect at Layer 2. LCP describes how this link should be established, maintained, and terminated. Imbedded in this definition, but not fully described, is an Authentication Phase. RFC 2284 describes that Authentication Phase as EAP. Remember: EAP is the main protocol leveraged in the 802.1X authentication process. Thus, the real birth of 802.1X can be established with the publication of this RFC.

This document is pretty small. Compared to most published standards it is almost trivial in size. The reason for this is the fact that Link Control was already defined and implemented. This simplified the construction of RFC 2284. The content of this document fits into a small niche within the PPP suite of definitions and standards, and leverages all of that previous work. But do not be fooled by the size of the document. It may be just a few pages, but the content establishes the foundations for everything that is now happening in the world of 802 authentication.

There are exactly two "technical" sections in this RFC. The first is only a few pages long and describes the protocol itself. This section roughly describes the flow and carefully avoids a definition of how authentication, itself, takes place. It describes three entities: a peer (known as the Supplicant), an Authenticator and an optional "backend" (called the Authentication Server). The gross flow of information between the Supplicant and the Authenticator is defined in this section.

The second section of the RFC is not much longer and further describes the structure of EAP packets containing authentication information. It does not describe how this information is to be used or the complete flow of packets required for that authentication. It does define a limited number of types necessary for the process to function, including Identity, Response, and NAK. Within the specifications, only one mechanism is required to be supported for authentication. That is MD5-Challenge. The RFC allows for user input and the support of One Time Passwords and Generic Token Cards.

Thus, RFC 2284 is really just a tease. It extends PPP, at the Link Layer, to allow for authentication prior to the initiation of higher layer services, but does not describe how that authentication is to take place. This is not a hole in the RFC, but, instead, a forward-looking approach that allowed a robust authentication environment to develop. The authors of RFC 2284 may or may not have anticipated the direction and impact of EAP, but they appear to have been wise in excluding a stringent definition of the authentication process while simply defining a mechanism to support the process. In this RFC, the actual transport of credentials was defined with an encapsulated protocol called EAP-Methods. As expected, several different approaches to actual authentication have been developed using EAP-Methods. Many are proprietary, but one, EAP-TLS, has become a standard with formal specifications.

In summary, the original specifications for EAP-Methods identify only six EAP Type codes, 1 through 6, with the first three being Identity, Notification, and NAK. MD5, which is Type 4, is also required by the RFC. Provisions are made for One Time Passwords, Type 5, and Generic Token Cards, Type 6. Now, in 2005, there are almost fifty codes that are assigned as EAP Types. Some types are established in published documents and some are not. Some are proprietary and detailed information on their workings is not readily available. More information on the specific techniques used for authentication by various EAP-Methods is included in the Technology Section of this book. But, in general, this book is not intended to discuss the details of various methods or identify the cost/benefit associated with any individual method.

In 1999, RFC 2716, EAP Transport Level Security (EAP-TLS), was published. It extends RFC 2284 by describing the exchanges required to cause authentication to occur. In the case of EAP-TLS, there is a mutual authentication through the use of certificates. The use of smart cards for remote access authentication requires the implementation of EAP-TLS as the EAP-Method. The EAP-TLS exchange of messages provides mutual authentication, integrity-protected cipher suite negotiation, and secured private key exchange. There are a large variety of other defined schemes.

At this point it would be wise to discuss the backend. This term is used in the RFC to identify a container for the database used to authenticate credentials. The backend has come to be known as the Authentication Server. RFC 2284 does not require a backend Authentication Server, but allows for it. However, EAP-TLS assumes a backend server and begins to discuss a RADIUS server as such. By 1999, the optional backend was becoming a distinct device. In fact, a RADIUS backend server is currently assumed and required by many Cisco products. This server performs two functions. The first is obviously the role of being the authoritative source for authenticating credentials supplied via EAP. The second is that of modifying the behavior of the Authenticator based on information associated with credentials supplied for authentication. It is possible to associate a specific VLAN or a set of filters with a specific user—or a set of users—and then supply this information to the Authenticator upon successful authentication.

Now that a brief look at the ancient history of EAP has been presented, and a connection to RADIUS has been established, let us look at that history. By 1999, RADIUS was the accepted backend referred to in the first specifications for EAP. There is one RFC that fully describes RADIUS: RFC 2865. This RFC is entitled Remote Authentication Dial In User Service (RADIUS). It contains a variety of information pertinent to 802.1X. The most important is a discussion of authentication mechanisms. It does not, however, discuss methods in terms of actually describing the EAP-RADIUS functions. It does specify that a user name and password must be supplied, and then allows for a variety of methods to perform the authentication. Because no strict mechanism is required by either 802.1X or RADIUS for authentication, the exact specification of logical process, in documentation such as EAP-TLS, is essential.

This definition of RADIUS contains additional information that is fundamental to the current implementation of 802.1X. All of the "attributes" available to describe the user are defined in the document. Forty-four different attributes are defined in a lengthy manner, but only a small fraction of them are really pertinent to 802.1X. A subset of the attributes defined in the RFC can be passed back to the Authenticator if the authentication process is successful. As discussed above, these attributes are used, then, to modify the characteristics of the actual connection between the Authenticator and the Supplicant.

RFC 2865 also contains additional information that is fundamental to the current implementation of 802.1X. All of the attributes available to describe the user are defined in this document. Again, forty-four different attributes are defined at length but only a small fraction of them are pertinent to 802.1X. At the time of this writing, well over 200 attributes have been defined. A subset of the attributes defined in this document can be passed back to the Authenticator if the authentication process is successful. These attributes will be used, then, to modify the actual connection established with the Supplicant.

There are a number of additional RFCs that discuss aspects of RADIUS in more detail, notably RFC 2866 through RFC 2869. These are supplementary and clarify behavior. Most of the information presented in these documents is not specific to a discussion of 802.1X, but is useful and will be discussed in later chapters.

Moving forward in time, but remaining on the subject of RADIUS, late in 2003, the use of the attributes defined in RFC 2865 was formally clarified in RFC 3580: IEEE 802.1X Remote Authentication Dial In User Service (RADIUS) Usage Guidelines. This document discusses each of the RADIUS attributes and the applicability within the 802.1X authentication process.

Thus, around the turn of the century, both the EAP and the RADIUS tracks had been established and had begun to develop a linkage. Up to this point, there was no definition of using EAP in a LAN environment. This was where the IEEE stepped in to begin the 802.1X track. Now step back in time—to 2001 from 2003. In June of that year, the LAN/MAN Standards Committee of the IEEE approved 802.1X as a standard in IEEE 802.1X-2001. Remember, the original RFC, RFC 2284, defining EAP was published in 1998 and only specified its use within PPP. The IEEE document is very important because it defines mechanisms by which EAP can be implemented in LAN environments and called the process 802.1X. This document provides the definitions of many pieces-parts that are used today.

The revolutionary part of the document is the definition of the EAPOL. EAPOL is concerned with being able to transport EAP and support necessary LAN connection behavior. Again, up to this point in time, EAP was defined only as part of PPP, which is concerned with serial connectivity and not LAN connections. The IEEE document defines the use of EAP over 802 media. The IEEE emphasized 802.3 (Ethernet) and 802.5 (Token Ring) frame formats in the document, but did not preclude the application of EAPOL in other formats. It may be obvious, but should be noted anyway that 802.1X is concerned with single connections that have the characteristics of a Point-to-Point connection. As stated earlier, this means that even though 802.1X is defined in a LAN environment, it must not be a shared environment.

Why is that? Go back to the beginning. 802.1X had its initial foundation in PPP, which has a fundamental premise of one-to-one operation. Shared media, on the other hand, has the assumption of a one-to-many relationship—or even many-to-many. Remember that the premise is that Port-Based Authentication takes place prior to allowing any other communication. This means that in a shared environment the Supplicant would need to be able to communicate only with an Authenticator and would need to exchange only encrypted messages. The intent of Port-Based Authentication is to disallow communication with other devices prior to the authentication occurring. This is difficult in a shared environment because the intent of a shared environment is to provide the type of communication that 802.1X is trying to prohibit. Is not it more realistic to implement 802.1X in an environment that truly and fundamentally operates with the characteristics of Point-to-Point, such as a switched environment, than to require adjustments to the functional workings of a shared environment? Classical shared LANs like Ethernet and Token Ring cannot support the mechanisms necessary in 802.1X. Only switched environments that are essentially Point-to-Point links can support 802.1X.

Yet, wireless is a shared environment. Can it support 802.1X? Yes. But what are the connectivity attributes of wireless? At this time, and being careful to stress this, wireless is a Point-to-Point system. If and when Peer-to-Peer communication becomes prevalent, then 802.1X no longer applies—using its current definition.

With the publication of the IEEE specifications for 802.1X in 2001, all three tracks were established. EAP, RADIUS, and 802.1X had been defined and the fundamental interrelationships documented. At that point, it was very confusing. It seemed that there were a plethora of documents exploding on the scene that were related. And that was true. It also seemed that these documents were loosely related and supported one another. That also was true. As noted earlier, it is interesting to see that the same people authored many of the documents. Keeping this in mind will help clarify issues that might come up. The authors generally did an excellent job of keeping the documents as independent entities while ensuring that they support one another. It would be appropriate to assume that the intent in all of the documents was to provide a consistent approach and that any confusion should be clarified by assuming the intent to be consistency among the documents.

Now back to the IEEE 2001 document defining 802.1X. It contains one additional item of interest. It defines the role of the Authentication Server, the backend in RFC 2284, as a RADIUS server, but does not require it. It also defines the RADIUS attributes that are useful within the 802.1X framework.

The IEEE definitions are consistent with the RFC published two years later that discusses RADIUS attributes, RFC 3580.

This brief discussion of the birth of 802.1X in 2001 also established a link to the RADIUS track. Let us go back to that track and move forward from 2001 to 2003. Multiple RFCs were published in 2003 regarding RADIUS. The two that were most involved with 802.1X are RFCs 3579 and 3580. RFC 3579, RADIUS (Remote Authentication Dial In User Service) Support For Extensible Authentication Protocol (EAP), was published almost simultaneously with RFC 3580—which we have been discussing. RFC 3580 delineates the use of RADIUS attributes within the 802.1X process and RFC 3579 discusses the behavior of RADIUS as it interacts with EAP. Thus, by mid-2003, there were documents that clearly identified RADIUS as the backend of choice and described how to use it within 802.1X.

RFC 3579 does not discuss methods of authentication. It simply identifies a set of uniform mechanisms, protocols if you will, that must be utilized to support the actual methods of authentication. It defines how communication will occur, how lost packets will be handled, how fragmentation will occur, etc. The concept is that documents such as RFC 2716 (EAP-TLS) will continue to describe the logical authentication process while RFC 3579 describes the lower level physical processes that must be supported.

As discussed earlier, RFC 3580 describes the behavior of RADIUS within the 802.1X framework. RFC 3580 is entitled: IEEE 802.1X Remote Authentication Dial In User Service (RADIUS) Usage Guidelines. It is heavily concerned with the use of RADIUS attributes and how those attributes can be used to modify the behavior of the Authenticator when a successful authentication has been accomplished.

By 2003, there were definitions of EAP, 802.1X, methods of authentication such as EAP-TLS, and significant work on how RADIUS fit in as the backend Authentication Server. At this time, there were a robust set of standards and informational documents describing this Port-Based Authentication process. But technology has continued to evolve and malicious individuals have exploited holes in the definitions. This means that the standards have had to evolve as well.

Everything discussed so far is the historical documentation. Assume that the modern world began in 2004. Since that time an entirely new breed of initiatives have been developed to enhance and extend 802.1X. The first of those initiatives was to replace RFC 2284 with a new definition in RFC 3748, EAP. The IEEE also has supplemented the definition of 802.1X with IEEE 802.1X-2004. Both documents were published in 2004. They are much thicker than the originals, and weightier in both the physical and logical sense.

The new releases of RFC 3748 and 802.1X-2004 expand the definitions in the EAP and 802.1X tracks significantly, but do not change the fundamental processes previously established. That is kind of an oxymoron because if they did change the process, then they would no longer be revisions. They would be new standards.

The IEEE document, 802.1X-2004, does not spend much more verbiage describing the basics than the 2001 document does. It does have a number of pages devoted to clarifying functions and also includes several new areas of discussion. The EAPOL state machines are described in detail. A huge portion of the document is devoted to a discussion of how management of ports and the management process occurs. The Management Information Base (MIB) is covered in detail. Where three pages were dedicated to the subject of management in the 2001 document, almost sixty pages (roughly one third of the entire document) are dedicated to the subject in the 2004 version. Work is continuing in this area with 802.1aa—802.1X Maintenance. This document is currently in draft status.

Another significant addition to the 2004 IEEE document is an annex that describes the use of RADIUS. Primarily this focuses on the various attributes available: the definition of content and function during the authentication process. These descriptions are consistent with RFC 3580, in the RADIUS track, published a year earlier. The document also describes the few attributes specifically available for use by 802.1X in the accounting portion of AAA.

The standard also provides significant information concerning 802.1X behavior with regard to various attacks. This information is consistent with that provided in RFC 3748. Specifically, piggybacking, snooping, crosstalk, rogue bridge, bit flipping, and negotiation attacks are discussed and the behavior of 802.1X in each attack is defined.

RFC 3748, Extensible Authentication Protocol (EAP), expands on the original definitions of EAP contained in RFC 2284. Just like IEEE 802.1X-2004, it does not fundamentally alter the behavior of the protocol. Instead, it recapitulates and expands the definitions. One EAP Type—an Expanded NAK—was added to allow for negotiation of EAP-Method.

The first sections of the new RFC are dedicated to a discussion not contained in the previous specification—how EAP functions between Supplicant (now called an EAP Peer) and Authenticator. Four distinct Layers of function are described: Lower Layer, EAP Layer, EAP Peer or EAP Authenticator, and EAP-Method. Even though this is a dry, technical portion of the document, it is very important because it shows how the entire thought process is maturing. This section formalizes exactly how the pieces-parts fit together in a much more structured fashion than was originally proposed. This type of detail is shown in discussions regarding the flow of packets and the responsibilities of the Supplicant and the Authenticator within each flow.

The second major change in the new EAP specification is a discussion of threat mitigation. EAP is either in use or being proposed for use in some shared environments. Wireless is the first shared environment where EAP is truly being implemented. This environment, while exhibiting connection characteristics of Point-to-Point, is still a shared one. This means that a much larger vulnerability exists. Therefore, the new RFC expends significant effort in describing the behavior of EAP in the face of various types of attacks. This is consistent with the aspects of security discussed in IEEE 802.1X-2004.

This is a bit of a side issue, but work is also progressing in detailing the use of 802.1X in wireless with 802.11i. IEEE 802.11i-2004 was published in July 2004 to detail security requirements in wireless. References to 802.1X in this document are significant both in terms of quantity and relevance. Specific EAP-Methods are not detailed, but several types of authentication are. The use of key material also is described in detail. The use and delivery of pairwise and group keys are documented, along with a four-way handshake among Supplicant, Authenticator, and Authentication Server. The entire process defined in the document exists within the 802.1X environment. This document establishes that 802.1X is a fundamental building block within future wireless environments.

The EAP track supported the IEEE wireless initiative with the publication of RFC 4017, Extensible Authentication Protocol (EAP) Method Requirements for Wireless LANs, in March 2005. This document essentially formalizes RFC 3748 for the wireless environment with regard to EAP-Methods. It ties security requirements for wireless environments defined in 802.11i to security definitions for EAP in RFC 3748.

In summary, EAP and 802.1X are continuing to be the port-based method of choice for authentication in both the wired and wireless worlds, and it is apparent that this is the way it will go in the future. There are a rich set of documents that define EAP, RADIUS, and 802.1X. There are a multitude of informal documents, such as this one, that attempt to interpret, explain or evaluate various portions of 802.1X. Reviewing the documentation from a historical perspective clearly shows the evolution of ideas. The first documents are relatively simple and the concepts are clear. As time passes, the detail of those concepts becomes much more refined and complex. In addition to the informal documents, there are a significant set of formal documents that are authoritative on the subject and provide the specifications. Table 1.1 provides a summary of some of those formal documents.

All documents identified in the table above are available on the Internet from one or more sources. As a practical matter, the IETF and the IEEE maintain websites that contain these documents.

1.3 HOW DOES IT WORK?

1.3.1 Chapter Summary

This chapter is going to describe how the 802.1X authentication process functions by discussing the flow of information between Supplicant and Authenticator, and between Authenticator and Authentication Server. All of

Table 1.1   Pertinent Formal Documents

Document	Date of Publication
RFC 1171—Point-to-Point Protocol for the transmission of multi-protocol datagrams over Point-to-Point links	July 1990
RFC 1661—The Point-to-Point Protocol	July 1994
IEEE 802.11-1997	November 1997
RFC 2284—PPP Extensible Authentication Protocol (EAP)	March 1998
RFC 2716—PPP EAP TLS Authentication Protocol	October 1999
RFC 2865—Remote Authentication Dial In User Service (RADIUS)	June 2000
IEEE 802.1X-2001	October 2001
RFC 3579—RADIUS (Remote Authentication Dial In User Service) Support For Extensible Authentication Protocol (EAP)	September 2003
RFC 3580—IEEE 802.1X Remote Authentication Dial In User Service (RADIUS) Usage Guidelines	September 2003
RFC 3748—Extensible Authentication Protocol (EAP)	June 2004
IEEE 802.1D	June 2004
IEEE 802.11i-2004	July 2004
IEEE 802.1X-2004	December 2004
RFC 4017—Extensible Authentication Protocol (EAP) Method Requirements for Wireless LANs	March 2005

the major flows will be discussed and many of the less common flows will be described. Several additional deviant scenarios will be detailed in later sections. A number of successful authentications, as well as failures, are included in this section.

As discussed earlier, the authentication process consists of the interaction among three entities: a Supplicant, an Authenticator, and an Authentication Server. The Port-Based Authentication process is anchored in EAP and EAPOL for communication between Supplicant and Authenticator, in RADIUS for communication between Authenticator and Authentication Server, and finally in EAP-Methods for logical conversations between Supplicant and Authentication Server.

802.1X operates within the IEEE specifications for 802. This body of standards pretty much defines all local and metropolitan networks in existence. Of particular interest to 802.1X is an associated standard, 802.1D—Media Access Control (MAC) Bridges. This standard is fundamental in the development of switches. A switch is as close to a Point-to-Point link as can be implemented in a local network. And EAP, which is fundamental to

802.1X, requires the use of Point-to-Point links. So 802.1D is necessary for 802.1X. This standard defines the use of Spanning-Tree, and 802.1X leverages Spanning-Tree in its initial connections. Because 802.1X is grounded in the basic concepts of LANs, it is functional across a wide variety of environments. It is readily implementable in Ethernet and 802.11(wireless) environments. These are the most common environments in production at the time this book was written.

Under normal conditions the Authenticator will initiate the authentication process when it senses a link going from down to up. If it does get a response to its Request Identity, it will contact a RADIUS server to validate the content of the response. The RADIUS server will tell the Authenticator whether or not the Supplicant should be allowed to connect to the network.

There are really four scenarios that can occur. The one described above, which is the one desired. Then there is a possibility of the Supplicant not participating in 802.1X. Either the device does not house the code or it has not been configured. The Authenticator will get no response to the Request-Identity packets transmitted and usually will place the device in a Guest VLAN.

The next variation, is when there is a Supplicant on the device being plugged into the network, but 802.1X has not been enabled on the port to which it is attaching. In this case, the Supplicant has two choices. It can be passive and wait for an EAPOL Request-Identity from an Authenticator or it can issue an EAPOL-Start. The EAPOL-Start tells the Authenticator to begin the process. In either case, the Supplicant will not get a response. It will eventually quit attempting to authenticate and will connect to the network.

The last alternative is when there is a Supplicant and an Authenticator, but there is no Authentication Server. For some reason the Authenticator cannot converse with RADIUS. In this situation, the early implementations would leave the port in an unauthorized state. This means that the Supplicant was never allowed to connect in any VLAN. In more recent implementations, the Supplicant can be placed in the Guest VLAN.

There are minor variations on these connections, but those four scenarios cover the majority of the situations. The details of these scenarios are discussed in the next section.

1.3.2 The Initial Connection

Consider this situation. A device is plugged into a switch on a Fast Ethernet port but is not powered on. The Link is down. When the device, the Supplicant, is powered up, one of the first things to occur is that the Network Interface Card (NIC) becomes active and both the Supplicant and the switch, the Authenticator, become aware that there is "something" on the other end of the wire. The Physical Layer, Layer 1, of the link becomes active. In an

Ethernet environment, the common term for that situation is that "link has been established."

The port on the switch is really a MAC bridge and functions according to the specifications pertaining to bridges as defined in IEEE 802.1D. According to the definitions of 802.1D, including Spanning-Tree, there are certain activities that must take place before full connectivity is established. The bridge must ensure that the device attempting to connect will not cause a loop and "break" the existing network. Thus, a certain amount of communication to resolve that question takes place across the link prior to other communication being allowed. This is very important to both Spanning-Tree and 802.1X. There is a finite period of time prior to full communication being allowed, and there are activities required to take place in that time prior to the establishment of communication across a new link. Because 802.1X, like Spanning-Tree, does not want communication immediately available to a device that has caused link to be established, it can leverage Spanning-Tree implementations. Since Spanning-Tree is a basic concept, this means that 802.1X can leverage something that is implemented in every network connection. Of course, there are some situations where Spanning-Tree is not implemented—and 802.1X will not be implemented in those either.

Now note the characteristics of the link. It is between two—and only two—devices. This is pretty much the definition of a Point-to-Point link. Is not it reasonable, therefore, to leverage definitions in the protocols defined for that type of link in links that exhibit similar characteristics as well? The basic premise of Point-to-Point connectivity is essential to 802.1X and is present in both a switched wired and a wireless network. Well, it is and it is not. Because there is no peer-to-peer communication really available in wireless, it seems to be a Point-to-Point network. But it is not. All the traffic is available for anyone to read. It is also possible to spoof messages between a client and an access point. The same situation also applies to a switched network because a hub can be inserted between the Supplicant and the Authenticator. Neither type of network can really guarantee a true Point-to-Point environment. This means that a wide variety of attacks are possible and must be mitigated. This is why there is so much interest in EAP-Methods that can be used to secure credential exchanges.

So a device is plugged into a port enabled for 802.1X on a switch. The first thing that happens is for the Supplicant, in some fashion, to cause the port to become active. The physical layer connection is established as shown in Figure 1.3.

When link is established, the 802.1X process is initiated in either or both of the connecting devices. By definition, the Authenticator must initiate a conversation when it senses that the physical link has been established. It asks the supposed Supplicant to identify itself through the use of an EAP Request Identity message. The Authenticator waits for a response. Either a response is received and the process continues or a response is not received

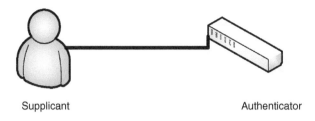

Supplicant   Authenticator

Figure 1.3   Link Is Established.

and the Authenticator continues to wait. There can be a variety of reasons why a response is not received from the Supplicant. The device might not be configured for 802.1X. The NIC on the device might be faulty. Or the port on the Authenticator might be faulty. Or the wire connecting the two might be bad. Et cetera. Meanwhile, the Authenticator placidly awaits a response. It will sit there for a while and then send the request again. Finally, if it gets no response it will shut down the link as shown in Figure 1.4. This is the most simplistic situation and there are alternatives that will be discussed later. Of course, there are a number of configurable parameters that come into play. The number of Request Identity packets to issue, the amount of time to wait between issuing packets, and what to do if no response is received are the most common of these parameters.

What happens if there are both an Authenticator and a Supplicant present when Link is established? This is the optimum outcome in 802.1X. This means that Port-Based Authentication can start to happen. The following sequence of events occurs. The Link comes up. The Authenticator recognizes this and issues an EAP-Request Identity. The Supplicant receives the packet and sends a response. This is shown in Figure 1.5.

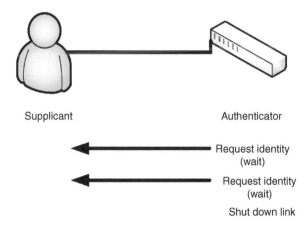

Supplicant   Authenticator

Request identity
(wait)

Request identity
(wait)

Shut down link

Figure 1.4   Link Is Shut Down.

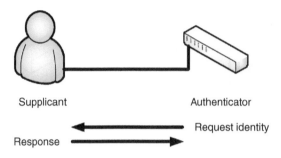

Figure 1.5 Authenticator and Supplicant.

The response from the Supplicant must contain information regarding its identity. This will be encapsulated in the data portion of the EAP frame sent as a response. This packet is normally sent in the clear and can provide information regarding a legitimate user of the network. This information can be very useful to an intruder. There are no passwords included in this initial exchange—which is a good thing. The Authenticator will use the information, supplied by the Supplicant, in its initial contact with the Authentication Server.

If 802.1X is enabled on a port, the Authenticator will always block traffic from a device on an unauthenticated port. However, there is one exception to that rule in the IEEE 2004 specifications for 802.1X. There is a special case that was developed to cover situations where an unauthenticated device needs to transmit alert information. In situations where a port is enabled for 802.1X, the Supplicant can issue special frames, known as ASF-Alert frames, which the Authenticator will forward. These frames are usually SNMP traps and they are intended to supply information about abnormal environmental conditions on the Supplicant. These alert frames must be encapsulated in a specific EAPOL frame and specific conditions must exist on the Authenticator for these frames to be translated from EAPOL and forwarded as SNMP.

In its default state, the Authenticator will never allow traffic to flow into an unauthenticated port unless it is proper 802.1X traffic. Furthermore, it will not allow traffic to flow out of the port while the port is unauthenticated, except for EAPOL Request Identity packets constructed by itself. This is called bi-directional control and it is the default state. The ASF Alert is illustrated in Figure 1.6.

It is possible to configure 802.1X to allow one specific flow from the network to the Supplicant while the port is unauthenticated. This situation is called "Wake-on-LAN" and will be discussed in more detail later in the chapter.

What if there are machines on the network that perform a network bootup? This situation requires that the device, a pre-Supplicant, be able to obtain information from another device on the network in order that the

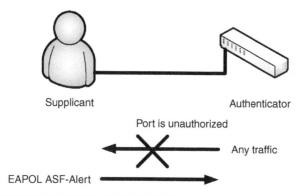

Supplicant   Authenticator

Port is unauthorized

Any traffic

EAPOL ASF-Alert

Figure 1.6   ASF Alert.

pre-Supplicant becomes fully functional. This situation would require that 802.1X allow a pre-Supplicant to obtain an IP address and then contact a device, probably a TFTP server, that would then download an Operating System or a configuration file. 802.1X does not allow this. Traffic is controlled and the control parameter can be modified to allow "Wake-on-LAN" traffic from the network to the device. Only ASF-Alert traffic is allowed from a non-authenticated Supplicant, and even this traffic must be encapsulated in EAPOL. At least that is the current situation.

Recently, Intel was working with Extensible Firmware Interface (EFI) and Pre-boot Execution Environment (PXE) to imbed 802.1X capabilities in their chipset. This initiative has been abandoned. The reason this is important is that PXE relies on DHCP to obtain the address of a TFTP server that will be used to provide information to finish the boot. This TFTP server can be used to provide a very wide range of upgrade information, such as BOIS upgrades, and to install controls that a corporation feels are necessary on equipment that is allowed to attach to the network. Without the imbedded certificate capabilities, the PXE environment does not currently work in the 802.1X environment.

The problem is: How do you prevent unauthorized devices and still allow a PXE process to function? 802.1X requires authentication prior to allowing DHCP. The PXE state does not normally have credentials that can be provided. In the situation with EFI, credentials would have been imbedded in the chipset to allow the PXE environment to participate in 802.1X implemented on a switch and would authenticate the device. The thought was to require the exchange of Public and Private keys during which both the network and the device in a PXE state would be authenticated.

The unidirectional state for "Wake-on-LAN," and the potential require-ment for network bootup, is an exceptional circumstance. It is best to describe the expected situations before continuing to explore the exceptional. There are a number of factors that affect an initial connection. Obviously, the presence or absence of a Supplicant is fundamental, but it is also the easiest to handle. If there is no Supplicant, or at least no recognizable communication from the Supplicant, then the Authenticator will quickly recognize the situation and take action. The default action is to not allow any further communication. However, this action is configurable and one option is to place the device in a Guest VLAN.

What happens if there is a Supplicant present and there is no Authenticator? This actually has two possible variants. The specifications define the communication process as being initiated from the Authenticator to the Supplicant. The Supplicant is the passive partner and the Authenticator is the active partner. This can be likened to people standing in a line waiting to get information. A person will step up to the window and wait to be recognized before speaking. Eventually, the ticket buyer will get tired and wander off if there is no indication that communication can now occur. This scenario is illustrated in Figure 1.7.

The Supplicant will wait for a Request Identity from the Authenticator until it gets tired and goes away. Actually there is a defined period of time it will wait before assuming that no Authenticator is present at the other end of the Link. This is the default condition. But the specs for 802.1X allow for an EAPOL-Start message to be issued by the Supplicant. This is similar to the person waiting in line described above getting to the window and saying, "Excuse me?" This usually will cause the person behind the counter to recognize that communication is desired. In 802.1X, this packet causes an Authenticator to begin, or restart, the authentication process.

The EAPOL-Start is pretty much only a flag that indicates that a Supplicant is on the other end of the link and wishes to initiate the 802.1X authentication process. If there is truly no Authenticator on the other end of the link, then the scenario in Figure 1.8 occurs.

The creation of an active Supplicant is a configurable process. Because the defined default state is for the Supplicant to be passive, it might not be an

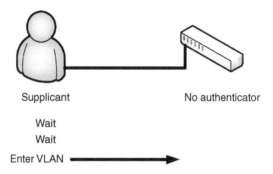

Supplicant   No authenticator

Wait
Wait
Enter VLAN ➔

Figure 1.7 No Authenticator and Passive Supplicant.

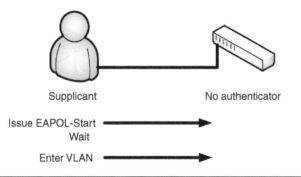

Supplicant   No authenticator

Issue EAPOL-Start ━━━━━━━━▶
Wait

Enter VLAN ━━━━━━━━▶

Figure 1.8   No Authenticator and Active Supplicant.

obvious configuration. In some Microsoft Windows implementations, the parameters are buried in the registry and must be set by manually editing it. This is not usually something that administrators want users to do. Some care needs to be taken before making this a requirement. On the other hand, depending on the design of the network, this just might be something that has to be done. There are situations where the Supplicant must notify the Authenticator that it is available and wishes to communicate. Consider two of them: the data port on an IPT phone and the use of a hub.

In both situations, it is highly likely that the port on the Authenticator has already become active. The physical layer is already up. This means that the Authenticator has already executed the authentication process and the port is in an unknown state. It is up to the Supplicant then to ask the Authenticator to reinitiate the process. This can cause some very interesting things to happen with the use of hubs and will be discussed in more detail in the third chapter of this book. Remember that the usual situation is for the VLAN to be associated with the port on the switch and applied to all connections through a hub. The connection to a hub is not a trunked port, so a single VLAN is applied to all connections. The possible outcomes of different types of devices connecting to a hub, and the sequence in which they connect, create a very unpredictable situation.

Up to this point, all of the discussion presumes that 802.1X is being implemented in a switched environment. What happens in wireless? Well, everything described in all the previous scenarios is valid for wireless as well as wired. The real difference is in how Link is established and recognized. Link in the wired world is the actual, physical, electrical connection between two devices conforming to specifications for a certain type of connection—Ethernet, as an example. In wireless, there is no physical connection—another oxymoron. Link in wireless is called an "association." If you want all the nitty-gritty details on wireless, read a different book. But Figure 1.9 roughly describes the association process.

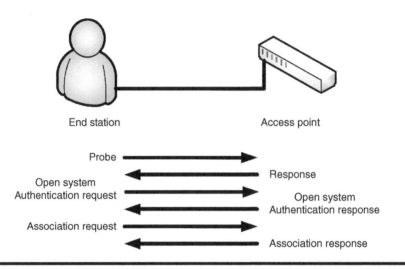

Figure 1.9 Wireless Association.

Communication is required between two devices—an Access Point and an end station occur prior to any other communication being allowed—for an association between the two end points to be established. Once an association has been formed, the 802.1X authentication process can be initiated and flow in the same fashion that was described for wired. It is entirely possible for an Association to be established and the authentication process to fail. In 802.1X, an association should be considered to be absolutely nothing more than the establishment of Link. In this situation, the wireless client will be associated but not authenticated, and no communication with the network will occur.

Now that the Authenticator and the Supplicant have link on a wired network, or an association in a wireless network, and have established their roles through the initial exchange of EAPOL packets, the communication between the Authenticator and the Authentication Server must be established. For all practical purposes, the Authentication Server is an external RADIUS server. The Authentication Server is not a required entity, nor is it required to be RADIUS in any specification, but this is so common that it has become a de facto standard. There are situations, especially in mobile communications, where the Authentication Sever process is partially imbedded in the Authenticator. More on that later.

The connection to the Authentication Server is a three-legged beast from the perspective of the Authenticator. The first leg is to have sufficient information about the Authentication Server to be able to communicate with it. The Authenticator must know two things about the Authentication Server. It must know the network address so that traffic can be directed and it must know the "shared secret." The shared secret is the same character string coded on both devices and is used to authenticate the sender and encrypt portions of messages between the two. This provides some guarantee to each that the other is authentic and communication is allowed between them. The second leg is the use of Authentication, Authorization, and Accounting (AAA) parameters to tell the Authenticator what mechanisms are to be used for the Authentication process. The last leg consists of parameters that tell the Authenticator what it is supposed to do depending on the success or failure of a Supplicant's authentication. The combination of these three legs becomes pertinent after the Authenticator and the Supplicant have established communication with an initial, successful exchange of frames.

To begin working with the Authentication Server, the Authenticator must have received a response to the Request Identity packet sent. This response contains some "identity" information supplied by the Supplicant. Now the Authenticator must find a RADIUS server that is a functional Authentication Server. One or more addresses of servers must be configured in the Authenticator. It will use these addresses to initiate a conversation with the Authentication Server. Likewise, the Authenticator must have been previously identified to the Authentication Server. No communication will be allowed to take place unless the devices can identify each other as a legitimate potential source of packets. This is accomplished through the mutual recognition of IP addresses and of the shared secret.

The Authenticator issues a RADIUS frame to the primary Authentication Server configured. This frame is known as an Access Request. It will contain the credential information supplied by the Supplicant. The Authenticator will attempt to contact all RADIUS servers configured until a response is received. If no response is received from the primary server, it usually will attempt a second time, wait and then proceed to the next one on the list. This can continue for a long time, in real time, and may not ever resolve in a fashion that will allow the Supplicant to enter the network either as a Guest or an Authorized user.

Communication could fail with an Authentication Server for a wide variety of reasons. The NIC on the server might be faulty. The port on the Authenticator connecting the LAN/WAN might be faulty. The LAN/WAN between the two devices might be faulty. Or the shared secret might be misconfigured. Those are some of the possibilities. In any event, the Authenticator will try for a long time to access the defined servers. The process is illustrated in Figure 1.10.

If there is no Authentication Server willing to communicate with the Authenticator, then it has options. Usually, it will continue to attempt to find a valid RADIUS server, leaving the port in an unusable state. This situation is not defined in the specifications, but seems to be the determination that the Supplicant is unauthenticated. Again, the configuration of RADIUS and AAA will have a significant impact on what will happen.

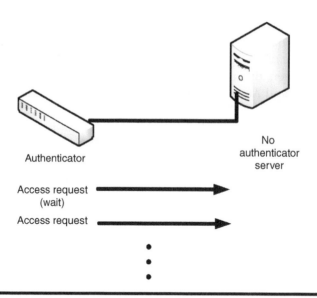

Figure 1.10 No Authentication Server.

If there is an Authentication Server that receives the Access Request from the Authenticator, it will process the request and take one of two actions. Either it will accept the request or reject it. If the Authentication Server can verify that the sender IP address and the shared secret are valid, then it will process the additional information contained in the Access Request. If it cannot validate the Authenticator's IP Address, it will "silently discard" the Access Request and the situation illustrated in Figure 1.10 will occur. However, if the shared secret sent by the Authenticator cannot be validated it will send an Access Reject as shown in Figure 1.11. As described previously, a shared secret password has been configured on both devices. The Authentication Server will always issue an Access Challenge in response to the Access Request from a known Authenticator. The Access Challenge will contain a proposed EAP-Method. Either the Supplicant will accept the proposed method or reject it and usually propose an alternative.

If it receives an Access Reject, the Authenticator is now in a quandary. What to do? It has a Supplicant waiting to be allowed into the network, the Authentication Server will not process the credentials supplied, but the Authenticator has not received a notification of failure. It has not even gotten that far. The Authenticator can try other Authentication Servers, if any have been configured. If there are none, it must assume that the Supplicant is unauthorized and must take the actions configured for that situation. The specifications allow devices participating in 802.1X, Supplicants, which do not pass authentication to be placed into a Guest VLAN. However, the implementation is not consistent and, in some cases, the port may remain in an unauthorized state. Whether or not any of this happens, or happens quickly, is determined by the exact configuration of

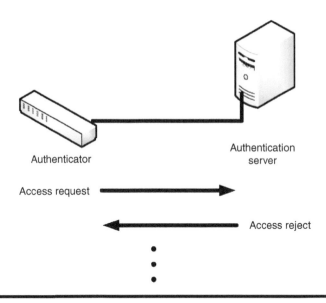

Figure 1.11 Authentication Server Reject.

RADIUS, AAA, and 802.1X functions on the Authenticator. This is a flexible situation and must be designed.

Also, remember the timeline and the range of documents discussed in the previous section. 802.1X and EAP are dynamic, evolving specifications. The earliest versions were brief documents. The later versions still adhere to the original requirements, but detail a much wider range of flexible options. Depending on the age of the equipment or operating system implemented, it is entirely possible to have different outcomes to some situations.

In a pure RADIUS environment, if the Authentication Server can validate the requestor, and the information contained in the Access Request is acceptable to the server, then the server notifies the requestor of that status with an Access Accept message. In most circumstances, that message alone would cause the authentication process to be finished. But in 802.1X the Authentication Server must allow for a further selection of authentication method by negotiating with the Supplicant. Thus, the server will send an Access Challenge back to the Authenticator. The challenge contains information that must be processed by the Supplicant and not by the Authenticator. The Authenticator becomes a man-in-the-middle passing information back and forth. The specifications require that the MD5-Challenge be supported—even though it is not a good choice for an authentication method. This is shown in Figure 1.12.

The specifications for RADIUS, in RFC 2865, define the attributes that can be sent in the Access Challenge. Many of these attributes are not pertinent within the 802.1X authentication process. An accurate list of acceptable attributes is detailed in RFC 3580. A full discussion of the attributes will also

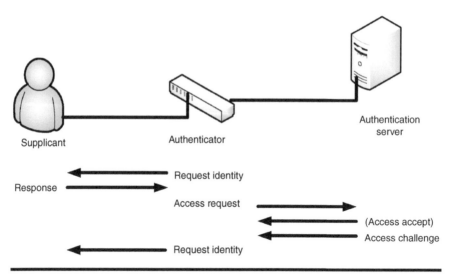

Figure 1.12   MD-5 Challenge Initiated.

be conducted in the Technology chapter of this book that focuses specifically on RADIUS.

Because the type of authentication method, the EAP-Method, is variable, the Access Challenge will propose a method. This will be the preferred method available to the Authentication Server. If this method is acceptable to the Supplicant, it will respond appropriately by echoing the code for the proposed method. If it cannot support the proposed method, it will respond with a NAK and propose an alternative method. EAP has two NAK codes and it is the "Expanded NAK"—Type 254—that is used to carry this information according to the latest specs.

If the Authentication Server or the Supplicant cannot support the new method proposed, it then will propose another method if one is available to it. Should the Supplicant and the Authentication Server not be able to agree upon any method for authentication, then the server will send a Failure. The Authenticator will become aware that a failure has occurred. It will notify the Supplicant of the failure and the port will remain in a condition appropriate for failed authentication. Either it will remain unauthorized or it will be placed into a Guest VLAN. This process is illustrated in Figure 1.13.

The reverse situation also applies. If the Supplicant and the Authentication server can agree on a method, then the process required to support that method will be conducted. If the authentication fails, then the result is similar to that shown in Figure 1.13. If the authentication succeeds, then a success message is sent instead of a failure. Of course, the number of exchanges between the initial Request Identity and the final success or failure is hugely variable. In some methods, key negotiations must take place or certificates must be exchanged before credentials can be sent.

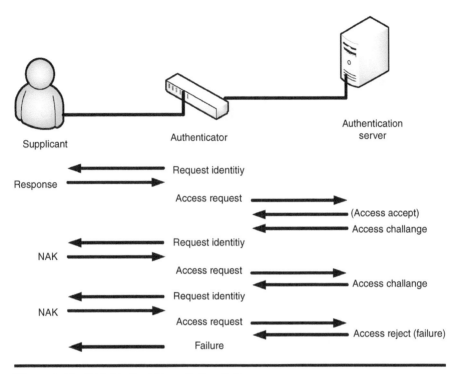

Figure 1.13 EAP-Method Negotiation Failure.

If the credentials provided by the Supplicant are valid and the Authentication Server declares success, then the Authenticator's behavior can be modified dynamically. It is possible to associate a VLAN or an access list to a set of credentials on a RADIUS server. When an authentication is successful, the Authentication Server will send this information to the Authenticator. The Authenticator will apply this information dynamically for the period during which the port is authorized. At the time the port becomes unauthorized, this information is discarded.

Earlier it was stated that the specifications required support for a MD-5 Challenge. The specifications for EAP, originally in RFC 2864 and replaced by RFC 3748, require support for three types of authentication. These are MD-5 Challenge, One Time Password, and Generic Token cards.

For the use of One Time Passwords, the exact process is defined in RFCs 2289 and 2243. The following diagram, Figure 1.14, describes this type of exchange. The initial establishment of 802.1X connectivity takes place between the Supplicant and the Authenticator. Then the Authenticator assumes a passive role forwarding traffic between the Authentication Server and the Supplicant until the server declares success or failure. All of the exchange of credentials is between the Supplicant and the Authentication Server, but must pass through the Authenticator.

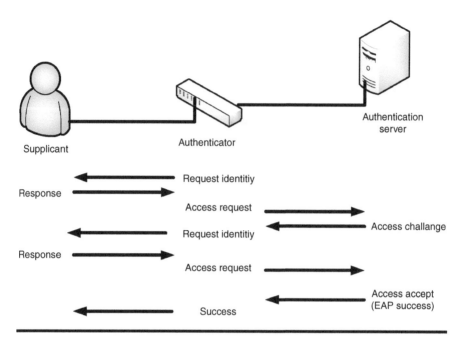

Figure 1.14 One-Time Password Success.

Additional iterations of the Access Challenge/Request Identity/Response/Access Request cycle may be present in the conversation depicted in Figure 1.14. Typically, these additional iterations are caused by the user on the Supplicant not knowing the proper credentials, or mistyping them, thus causing the Authentication Server to reject them. The process for Generic Token Cards is very similar to that for One-Time Passwords. The information contained in the exchange is different, but the actual flow is essentially the same. The use of a Token card will always require that the user enter information rather than use credentials supplied when the Supplicant was booted.

Assuming that the Supplicant is authenticated, it is obvious that a port should not be allowed to be placed in an authorized state forever. While the specifications for EAP do not require reauthentication, nor make recommendations regarding reauthentication, it is a normal function. The frequency of reauthentication is a configurable parameter.

Reauthentication takes place in the background as far as possible. Should user input be required to complete the authentication process, then that input will be solicited. The difference between an initial authentication and a reauthentication is that of port status. During the initial authentication process, the port is placed in an unauthorized state. With reauthentication, the port remains active until a failure is declared by the Authentication Server or the authentication times out. At that time, the port will become

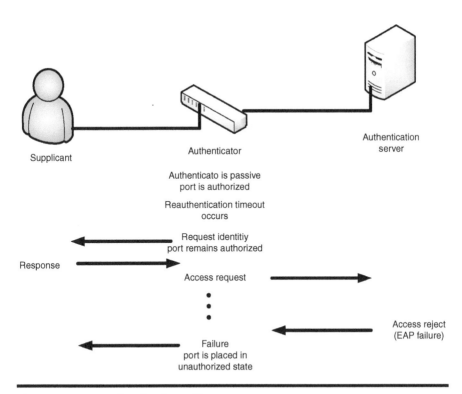

Supplicant

Authenticator

Authentication server

Authenticato is passive
port is authorized

Reauthentication timeout
occurs

Request identitiy
port remains authorized

Response

Access request

Access reject
(EAP failure)

Failure
port is placed in
unauthorized state

Figure 1.15   Reauthentication Failure.

unauthorized. The port then may be placed into a Guest VLAN or all access may be blocked. This situation can cause some confusion to the user because the machine that failed will need to acquire a new IP address from the DHCP server if the port it attached to was placed in a different VLAN. Figure 1.15 illustrates what happens in a reauthentication failure.

Should reauthentication be successful, and this is the desired state, then frequently the user will not be aware of the process that occurred. Traffic will continue to flow without interruption. There will be no requirement to obtain new IP addressing because the port will never be placed in an unauthorized state or a different VLAN. It is possible that the Authentication Server could have received updates that affect the attributes that are passed to the Authenticator. These new attributes then would be passed during the reauthentication process. If this event, however unlikely, happens, then the new attributes would be applied to the port as part of the reauthentication. This could conceivably include a different VLAN or an access list, but, hopefully, this is a rare case.

Thus, 802.1X is implemented to block traffic between the network and the supplicant. This means that a non-authenticated Supplicant cannot converse with anything on the network but the Authenticator. The reverse is true, as well—except for one circumstance. Earlier in this section, it was noted that there are situations where a device that causes the Link to come up might be asleep and the port would eventually become unauthorized. Then this device might require a wake-up call to be supplied from within the LAN to become fully active. This situation is called Wake-On-LAN. There is a real possibility of a device going to sleep and either dropping the link or not being awake during a reauthentication process. In these cases, the port will become unauthorized.

The Wake-On-LAN scenario requires that a device from within the network send a "magic" packet to the sleeper. This magic packet is received by the sleeping device and causes it to awake. Once it is awake, it is intended to be fully functional and participate in normal LAN activities. If 802.1X is blocking traffic from the network, then the magic packet never arrives and the sleeper never awakes.

802.1X is configured to block traffic from the network by default, but can be configured to allow unidirectional traffic from the LAN to the Supplicant. A special case has been established within the implementation of Spanning-Tree on 802.1X enabled ports. This special case allows ports, with Spanning-Tree PortFast enabled, to be placed in a unidirectional state. Traffic from the Supplicant must be 802.1X, EAPOL, until authentication has been successful, but special traffic—the magic packet—is allowed from the network to the Supplicant.

The way this works is that while the Supplicant is sleeping and the Link state is down, Spanning-Tree is placed in a forwarding state. If the magic packet is passed through the port from the network, then the port is placed in a full blocking state until the Supplicant is authenticated. This actually allows a device on the network to wake the sleeper and cause it to perform an authentication. Figure 1.16 illustrates this process.

Up to this point, this presentation has clearly delineated the role of Supplicant and Authenticator as distinct pieces of equipment. The Supplicant has been viewed as a device, usually some form of Personal Computer, that is attempting to link into a network through an Authenticator, usually a switch or a wireless access point. That is the customary implementation. However, the IEEE specifications do not require that to be the case. It is "legal" for a port to actually be both an Authenticator and a Supplicant, or, more properly, to perform both roles. If you actually read the specifications repeatedly, it starts to make sense. Essentially this is a special case where mutual authentication must take place and that authentication relies on each partner making use of an Authentication Server to complete the process. The specification offers as an example a mutual authentication between network devices, specifically "bridges." This situation will probably become more significant when network devices authenticate one another prior to establishing/allowing communication between them. This case is proposed, and is not required, but does make sense. Why should a network device assume that another network device is not a rogue? At any rate, this situation is covered in the specs and is even extended into management functions.

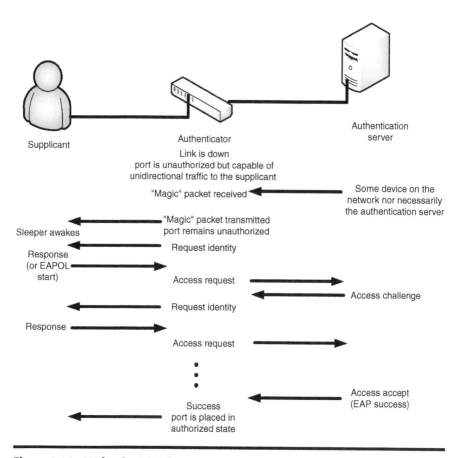

Figure 1.16   Wake-On-LAN Success.

That topic will be covered a little more in a later section discussing management in the Technology chapter.

In general, the Port-Based Authentication process, commonly referred to as 802.1X, consists of three entities: Supplicant, Authenticator and Authentication Server. The authentication process itself is usually a three-stage effort. First, the Authenticator and the Supplicant must establish communication; then the Authenticator and the Authentication Server must establish communication; finally, the Authentication Server and the Supplicant must exchange credentials. The final outcome of these three stages is either a success or a failure. Based on that outcome, the Authenticator then will determine if the Supplicant can be allowed to enter the network, where it will be placed, and what restrictions will be placed upon its ability to communicate within the network.

That is how it works.

2

TECHNICAL DISCUSSION

This chapter of the book will consist of six sections. It will focus on the technical aspect of 802.1X and the related protocols and components involved in implementing it in a network. The preceding chapter provided a level set of what it is, how it came about, what the standards are, and how it works. The relationships between 802.1X, EAP, EAPOL, EAP-Methods, and RADIUS have been defined. This chapter will establish a firm background in the technical aspects of those components.

EAP-Methods is the actual mechanism by which a set of credentials is authenticated. The various methods will not be discussed in great detail. There is a relatively fine distinction between the method in which credentials are authenticated and the process in which that method is employed. This book is about the process rather than the method. The process is consistent no matter what the method is. The first section of this chapter will discuss some of the methods, but will not advocate one in particular.

There are six sections in this chapter that will provide detailed discussion of distinct aspects of the technology. Each can stand alone, to a certain extent, but the sequence here is intended to develop the technology from the ground up.

The first section—EAPOL, EAP, and EAP-Methods—will discuss the individual protocols in detail. It will focus on the encapsulations necessary to construct a packet that can be transported across a network. The various options and codes available within a given protocol are identified. This section builds upon the basic understanding of the flow between a Supplicant and an Authenticator. The flow between the Authenticator and the Authentication Server is discussed, but not in as much detail. An overview of several more popular EAP-Methods is presented at the end of the section.

The next three sections provide supplementary information regarding the control of 802.1X Port-Based Authentication. The first section is dedicated to discussing RADIUS and the particular functions involved that pertain to the Port-Based Authentication process. The second section is about Management and the particular functions described in the various specifications. The third section discusses security aspects for the authentication process, as defined in the specifications. These sections are parallel discussions and their physical sequence is somewhat arbitrary. The content of one is not built upon the one immediately preceding. However, each of these sections assumes a fundamental knowledge of the flow of packets as presented in the sections: How Does It work? and EAPOL, EAP, and EAP-Methods.

The discussion on RADIUS will cover the flows in detail. The RADIUS protocol utilizes the term "attributes" to describe data elements that are available in conversations. The attributes of particular interest in the 802.1X process are detailed as well. This section will provide technical background necessary in the third chapter of the book: Design, Implementation, and Troubleshooting.

The sections on Management and Security follow along the same lines as the chapter on RADIUS. They will discuss the pertinent specifications for the particular subject and go into detail regarding those specifications. Just as with RADIUS, these sections will provide useful technical background for the final chapter of this book.

The fifth section in this chapter is devoted to configuration commands available within the traditional Cisco environment. Although the majority of the section is spent discussing configuring the Authenticator, both the Supplicant and Authentication Server are addressed. Configuration of the Authenticator includes 802.1X, as well as touching on RADIUS and authentication, authorization, and accounting (AAA) commands.

The final section deals specifically with Wireless. Wireless is a special case of an 802 LAN, and requires special treatment. The majority of 802.1X applies to any 802 LAN, but recent specifications—802.11i in particular—have focused attention on 802.1X. This section will focus on specific aspects of key exchanges that are relevant to wireless and will discuss some considerations that 802.1X imposes on mobility. The subject matter in this chapter builds upon that presented in Overview and prepares the reader to enter the final chapter of the book.

2.1 EAPOL, EAP, AND EAP-METHODS

2.1.1 Section Summary

This section is about the architecture of conversations primarily between the Supplicant and the Authenticator. Just like virtually every conversation since the advent of the OSI Seven-Layer Model, the packets in an 802.1X conversation are a series of encapsulations. For illustration purposes, I will use Ethernet as the fundamental transport, but it could be any

802 protocol. The encapsulation follows this progression: Authentication information—usually credentials—is encapsulated in EAP-Methods, then EAP, then EAPOL, and finally in Ethernet—or another 802 protocol.

As stated in Overview, 802.1X leverages MAC bridges—IEEE 802.1D. The reason is that 802.1X must be the first packets issued when Link comes up on a connection. Spanning-Tree is fundamental in the specifications for MAC bridges and 802.1X utilizes addressing reserved for Spanning-Tree.

EAPOL is the protocol that was created by the IEEE to transport EAP over a LAN Environment. Remember: EAP is actually part of the PPP Protocol Suite and makes no provision for transport in an 802 environment. EAPOL is very simple and has defined only five types of packets. The most common is Type 0, which is used to actually transport EAP messages. Two of the packet types can be used by a Supplicant to Start an authentication and to Logoff, thereby ending an authenticated session. The remaining two types are used to transport Key information, usually used in wireless, and for environmental alerts from a nonauthenticated Supplicant.

EAP, like EAPOL, is a very simple protocol utilizing four types of packets. The Authenticator utilizes three of them. The primary type is a Request Identity, and the other two are used to indicate success or failure of the process. The Supplicant only uses one of the possible EAP types to respond to packets sent by the Authenticator. EAP utilizes a lock-step mechanism to ensure that responses from the Supplicant are, in fact, related to an issued request. So the Supplicant must wait for a Request packet to send any information to the Authenticator—and that packet will always be a Response packet.

The packet structure for EAP-Method packets is also simple. The information in these packets comprises the conversation between the Supplicant and the Authenticator. There are a very large number of packet types. The original specifications allowed for 255 by utilizing a one-byte field as the container. This proved to be insufficient and has been expanded by incorporating additional fields identifying the Vendor and some vendor-specific information regarding the method employed for authentication. Four of the original EAP-Method codes are reserved for communication between the Supplicant and the Authentication Server that may or may not contain credentials. This makes for a very simple communication between the two, with the majority of the communication within the protocol relating to specific exchanges of credentials, as required by a particular method.

There is a very large number of EAP-Methods available today. Three types—MD5-Challenge, one-time passwords (OTP), and Generic Token Card—are required by the specifications for EAP. A few of the EAP-Methods have been documented in IETF RFCs, but the majority are proprietary. Some of the more common methods are EAP-TLS, EAP-TTLS, PEAP, and EAP-FAST. This book is primarily concerned with the process of authentication and not the particular method employed, so particular EAP-Methods are discussed only briefly.

2.1.2 The Encapsulations

Thus, 802.1X has three distinct conversations established during an authentication process: Supplicant to Authenticator, Authenticator to Authentication Server, and Supplicant to Authentication Server. Each of these processes utilizes one or more protocols. The port authentication process called 802.1X is actually composed of at least five distinct protocols. These are illustrated below in Figure 2.1.

As stated above, at least five distinct encapsulations are utilized in a full authentication conversation. The reason why the number of encapsulations is not an exact number is that the Authentication Information may actually have multiple encapsulations depending upon the method chosen. The Authentication information is encapsulated in EAP-Methods, which is encapsulated in EAP, which is encapsulated in EAPOL, which, in turn, is encapsulated in an 802 Layer 2 protocol such as Ethernet. Each encapsulation is directed toward supporting a particular function in the Port-Based Authentication architecture. Leaving Authentication information aside, EAP-Methods provides a structure by which the Supplicant and the Authentication Server can exchange information so that EAP is the protocol that transports EAP-Method data from the Supplicant to the Authenticator, and EAPOL encapsulation provides specific LAN functionality that is not present in EAP.

2.1.3 Ethernet and MAC Bridge (802.11D)

802.1X is not a required protocol within Ethernet. By definition, however, if it is implemented, it must own the connection between a Supplicant and an Authenticator. And, this must happen as soon as physical connectivity is established: it must be the first exchange of packets between the Authenticator and the Supplicant. 802.1X is a latecomer to the LAN environment. In a sense, it must usurp the established priority of processing and control the state of a port; yet, it must not "break" anything that is already fundamental to the establishment of Layer 2 connectivity.

The implementation of a brand new Layer 2 protocol could cause significant confusion with the specifications already established for 802-based networks. These established processes for creating a link have existed

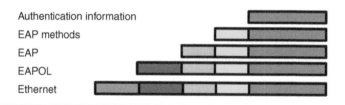

Figure 2.1 802.1X Encapsulation.

for so long that changing them is virtually impossible. This creates a big dilemma. How do you make sure that 802.1X can own the links without causing confusion? The answer is to look at the definition of Ethernet (or another Layer 2 protocol defined to support 802.1X) and determine what can be leveraged. The only real possibility is that of 802.1D—Spanning-Tree.

802.1D is really MAC Bridges, which defines the use of Spanning-Tree, and, as previous chapters have stated, 802.1X is grounded in that functionality. Spanning-Tree is a mechanism fundamental to the implementation of LANs. Before any port on a LAN can be allowed to become fully functional, it must be certified that its activation will not disrupt the flow of existing traffic. Spanning-Tree ensures that the connection of a port will not cause a loop to occur in the infrastructure. So Spanning-Tree implements a process in which a port gradually moves from a blocked to a connected state. Spanning-Tree is a required implementation in Layer 2 protocols such as Ethernet. This means that it can be guaranteed to exist in all infrastructure that utilizes an 802 protocol. 802.1X leverages the requirements of Spanning-Tree to support Port-Based Authentication.

The use of "group addresses" is fundamental to Ethernet, and several of these addresses have been reserved for use in MAC Bridges. A group address is simply a hexadecimal number that is used instead of a broadcast or specific unicast address. In shared media, when this address is used as a destination address, every member of the "group" will receive the frame and act on it. This type of address differs from a broadcast address, as only members of the group will receive the frame. 802.1X has been assigned one address in the Spanning-Tree group address pool. The group of addresses reserved for Spanning-Tree ranges from 01:80:c2:00:00:00 to 01:80:c2:00:00:0f. Several group addresses were unused in Spanning-Tree and one was allocated for use by 802.1X—01:80:c2:00:00:03. This is formally known as the IEEE P802.1X PAE Address. PAE stands for Port Access Entity.

The benefit of using this address as a destination address is that all Network Interface Cards (NICs) will receive this address and attempt to process it. This is because the address is reserved for use in Spanning-Tree and Spanning-Tree is required for all 802 NICs. Processing occurs at Layer 2 before any other function is allowed access to the NIC. Thus, a frame is transmitted with the group destination address. It is received—and then? Well, Ethernet frames contain a field called the Protocol Identifier. The Protocol Identifier tells the NIC where to send the encapsulated data. It can be likened to a hole in the floor that is numbered. If the device is executing the code to support the protocol, then there is a hole in the floor with that number. If the protocol is active on the machine, then the data contained in the frame is conveyed through the hole and processing of the data continues. There are holes at each encapsulation level corresponding to the protocol, type, or code, included as part of the data provided in the packet. This concept applies to all the encapsulations shown earlier.

Preamble (7-bytes)	Start Frame Delimiter (1-byte)	Dest. MAC Address (6-bytes)	Source MAC Address (6-bytes)	Length / Type (2-bytes)	Data (0-n bytes)	Pad (0-p bytes)	Frame Check Sequence (4-bytes)

Destination MAC address:	01:80:c2:00:00:03
Source MAC address:	(device dependant)
Length/Type:	888e

Figure 2.2   802.1X Ethernet Frame.

The protocol number assigned to 802.1X is hexadecimal 888e (0x888e). When this number is present in an Ethernet frame, it means that the data contained is an EAPOL frame. Figure 2.2 illustrates what an 802.1X Ethernet frame will look like.

2.1.4   Request-Identity Packet

By definition, the Authenticator must send an EAPOL frame with an EAP-Request Identity to the Supplicant as soon as Link is established. The Destination Address, the address of the device that caused Link, is not known by the Authenticator when the first packet is sent. It follows logically that the Authenticator must use a Group Address for the first packet directed to the Supplicant. Should the Supplicant respond, then its MAC address would be known to the Authenticator. Yet, the 802.1X specifications require that the Group Address continue to be used as the destination address for both sides of the conversation. This makes it very easy to trace conversations with a packet sniffer because anything with that destination group address is part of an 802.1X conversation and anything without that address is not.

The following packet capture, Figure 2.3, illustrates how the Authenticator attempts to initiate a conversation with a Supplicant. The specifications state that this is the very first packet seen on a connection that has just become active. The source address is that of the Authenticator, the destination address is the group address for 802.1X, and the protocol is EAP.

2.1.5   The First Packet Is Really a Failure

Why is this packet the very first one and it is already a failure? Think about how the devices function as a physical connection is being established. They are independent and unaware of each other. When they become connected they only know that the physical connection is available for use. Each of the devices is working independently of the other at this point and each could attempt to initiate the authentication process. There is a possibility of asymmetric initiation of authentication. The transmission of a Failure as the

```
Frame 1 (60 bytes on wire, 60 bytes captured)
    Arrival Time: May  5, 2005 08:08:49.026466000
    Time delta from previous packet: 0.000000000 seconds
    Time since reference or first frame: 0.000000000 seconds
    Frame Number: 1
    Packet Length: 60 bytes
    Capture Length: 60 bytes
Ethernet II, Src: 00:11:20:a2:8a:03, Dst: 01:80:c2:00:00:03
    Destination: 01:80:c2:00:00:03 (Spanning-Tree-(for-bridges)_03)
    Source: 00:11:20:a2:8a:03 (00:11:20:a2:8a:03)
    Type: 802.1X Authentication (0x888e)
    Trailer: 0000000000000000000000000000000000...
802.1X Authentication
    Version: 1
    Type: EAP Packet (0)
    Length: 4
    Extensible Authentication Protocol
        Code: Failure (4)
        Id: 0
        Length: 4

0000  01 80 c2 00 00 03 00 11 20 a2 8a 03 88 8e 01 00   ........ .......
0010  00 04 04 00 00 04 00 00 00 00 00 00 00 00 00 00   ...............
0020  00 00 00 00 00 00 00 00 00 00 00 00 00 00 00 00   ...............
0030  00 00 00 00 00 00 00 00 00 00 00 00               ...........
```

Figure 2.3 Initial 802.1X Packet.

very first frame from the Authenticator will cause the Supplicant to reset its status. And the specifications for EAP identify that it is the Authenticator's job to actually begin the authentication process with a Request Identity. The extension of EAP into the LAN environment via 802.1X (EAPOL) allows the Supplicant to initiate the conversation, but does not require it. This may seem a little convoluted. So go back to the timeline in the introduction. EAP was defined years before EAPOL. EAPOL leverages EAP and therefore must support the mandatory requirements of EAP. This means that the Authenticator must always attempt to initiate authentication when it detects Link becoming active. However, in a LAN environment, it is desirable to be able to initiate authentication when Link is already up and active.

2.1.6   Extensible Authentication Protocol Over LAN (EAPOL)

Within the data portion of the Ethernet packet there are three additional fields called Version, Type, and Length. These fields are used for EAPOL encapsulation. As a practical matter, EAP is treated as a special case of EAPOL. If the Type is set to 0, then the packet passes through the EAPOL layer without any processing, other than stripping of EAPOL encapsulation, and the remainder is shoved directly up the EAP hole.

The 802.1X specification created the EAPOL encapsulation of the EAP packet as it was initially defined in RFC 2284. This encapsulation was

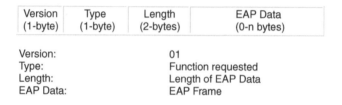

Version (1-byte)	Type (1-byte)	Length (2-bytes)	EAP Data (0-n bytes)

Version: 01
Type: Function requested
Length: Length of EAP Data
EAP Data: EAP Frame

Figure 2.4   EAPOL Frame with Encapsulated EAP Data.

necessary to implement EAP in a LAN environment. EAPOL consists of four fields: Version, Type, Length (Data), and EAP Data. This really is a very simple encapsulation with minimal functionality. Currently, the Version will only be set to 1. The Type identifies the kind of function being requested. The Length is the length of the data, and the EAP Data forms the encapsulated EAP frame, itself. The EAPOL frame is shown in Figure 2.4.

EAP is defined for use in PPP that assumes a serial link. In that situation, Link is either up or down. It comes up when communication is initiated by a user, and goes down when the same user ends communication. This is not always the case in a LAN environment. It is entirely possible for a Supplicant to connect to an intermediate device, such as an IP phone or a hub, and not cause the link to become active—but still require authentication. Thus, for this type of situation, additional EAPOL functionality is required for communications in the LAN environment.

```
Frame 3 (60 bytes on wire, 60 bytes captured)
    Arrival Time: Jun  2, 2005 09:10:05.274354000
    Time delta from previous packet: 3.655141000 seconds
    Time since reference or first frame: 3.655700000 seconds
    Frame Number: 3
    Packet Length: 60 bytes
    Capture Length: 60 bytes
    Protocols inframe: eth:eapol:data
    Ethernet II, Src: 00:0d:56:b7:6f:c2, Dst: 01:80:c2:00:00:03
    Destination: 01:80:c2:00:00:03 (Spanning-tree-(for-bridges)_03)
    Source: 00:0d:56:b7:6f:c2 (169.254.61.241)
    Type: 802.1X Authentication (0x888e)
    Trailer: 00000000000000000000000000000000000000000000000000...
    802.1x Authentication
    Version: 1
    Type: Start (1)
    Length: 0

0000  01 80 c2 00 00 03 00 0d 56 b7 6f c2 88 8e 01 01   ........V.o.....
0010  00 00 00 00 00 00 00 00 00 00 00 00 00 00 00 00   ................
0020  00 00 00 00 00 00 00 00 00 00 00 00 00 00 00 00   ................
0030  00 00 00 00 00 00 00 00 00 00 00 00               ............
```

Figure 2.5   EAPOL-Start Frame.

A capture of an EAPOL frame from the Supplicant to the Authenticator is shown in Figure 2.5. Note that this is actually frame number three. Two packets have been issued prior to this one. They were from the Authenticator and were an EAP failure and an EAP Request Identity. This is consistent with the historical requirement that the Authenticator initiate Port-Based Authentication. This EAPOL frame is from the Supplicant to the Authenticator. It is an EAPOL-Start and is identifiable because the 802.1X Type field, in the 802.1X Authentication portion of the packet, is a hexadecimal 1.

Let us summarize the flow so far. The first packet in this transmission was a Failure. It was issued by the Authenticator very quickly when the physical connection was established. The second packet, again sent by the Authenticator very quickly after the Failure, was intended to initiate the authentication process by requesting the Identity of the connecting device. The EAPOL-Start was sent by the Supplicant. It would seem that this packet was sent in response to the Request. This packet does not seem to be necessary. There are a couple of possible reasons that the Supplicant sent this packet. The first reason is that the Supplicant was configured to be active and this is how it believed it needed to initiate the process. In other words, it was a pretty stupid machine. The other reason is probably more accurate.

The Supplicant was in the process of being booted and had a very large number of tasks to accomplish during that process. It is probable that it missed the first two frames sent by the Authenticator. It took the Supplicant 3.6 seconds to send the EAPOL-Start after the Authenticator had issued its Request-Identity packet. This is a very long time and tends to support the idea that the Supplicant missed those first two packets from the Authenticator. The Authenticator received the EAPOL-Start and promptly responded with another Request for Identity. Here is an interesting point. If the Supplicant is not configured to issue an EAPOL-Start and missed those packets, then both the Supplicant and the Authenticator would enter a wait state. By definition, the Authenticator would reissue a Request-Identity packet after waiting 30 seconds. During that time, it would ignore any packet sent by the Supplicant that was not in response to the Request Identity. That 30 seconds is a very long time.

One other interesting item is seen in the EAPOL-Start Packet. There is no EAP Data encapsulated. That is because there is no information that can be sent in an EAPOL-Start packet. The intent of this packet is to simply notify the Authenticator that there is a Supplicant willing to talk with it and that the authentication process should begin.

In the two packets in the captures shown above, there are two different Type codes in the 802.1X Authentication portion of the packet: 0 and 1. In all, there are five possible EAPOL types as shown below in Table 2.1. Type 0 means that this is an EAP frame and requires no EAPOL processing. EAPOL simply passes it on to the EAP layer. This type is usually seen as a Request

Table 2.1   EAPOL Types

Type	Description
0	EAP Data
1	EAPOL-Start
2	EAPOL-Logoff
3	EAPOL-Key
4	EAPOL-Encapsulated-ASF-Alert

Identity from the Authenticator or as a Response from the Supplicant. Most packets in a conversation will be this type.

Again, Type 1, an EAPOL-Start, is used to tell the Authenticator that it should initiate the authentication process. This is necessary because the Authenticator will normally only do that when the Link state changes. Remember: the normal authentication process is tied to the initial activation of Link on the port. This happens when the port goes from a "down" to an "up" status If the Link is already up, for some reason, then the Authenticator will not initiate the process. A good example of this is in IP Telephony. Usually there is a data port on the backend of an IP phone. Assume that the phone has been plugged into a port that has been 802.1X enabled. When the phone was plugged in, that port became alive and the authentication process was initiated. Because there is no Supplicant, and phones are not currently Supplicants, the data portion of the port would either be disabled or be placed into a Guest VLAN. Now as far as the Authenticator is concerned, all of the required authentication has been performed. It can go to sleep until the Link goes down.

At some time after the phone was activated, a Supplicant was plugged into the back. 802.1X would not necessarily know about that. Certainly it would know that an additional MAC address was active on the data portion of that port, but that will not initiate the authentication process. However, if the Supplicant issues an EAPOL-Start, then the Authenticator will begin the authentication process anew. This situation has some very interesting ramifications that will be explored in later chapters.

The EAPOL Type 2 has a very similar function. It is used to gracefully notify the Authenticator that the Supplicant is leaving and return the port to an unauthorized state. The usefulness of this is apparent in IP Telephony. If the Supplicant feels like notifying the Authenticator that it is leaving, then the Authenticator can do its job of returning the port to an unauthorized state.

Consider the scenario with the phone again. The state of the port on the Authenticator does not change when a Supplicant is removed from the data port on a phone. Again, it is desirable that the Supplicant notify the Authenticator that it is leaving by issuing an EAPOL-Logoff. This does not always happen though. The Supplicant might experience a power failure or some other catastrophic event, like the user unplugging the Ethernet cable, and not issue an EAPOL-Logoff. The Authenticator would not know that the Supplicant was no longer available and would leave the port in an authorized state. It would not be recognized until re-authentication occurred. Re-authentication is disabled by default. This would leave the network in a vulnerable state for a very long time. Some phones have recently been upgraded to sense the Link state of the data port and to issue an EAPOL-Logoff when that state goes from up to down.

EAPOL Type 3 packets are used for the exchange of "key" information between the Authenticator and the Supplicant. The current use of the EAPOL-Key packet is in wireless (802.11). There is an historical implementation of this type that supports RC4, but this has been deprecated in the current 802.1X standard. The EAPOL-Key packet can be issued from either the Supplicant or the Authenticator. The Type 3 packet is used to either obtain or distribute global key information between the Authenticator and the Supplicant. At this time, the definitions regarding the use of Type 3 packets are exclusively in the specifications for 802.11.

The complete process is defined in IEEE-802.11i 2004. There is a very long title that takes up approximately one half of the cover, but what it boils down to is that 802.11i is all about Security Enhancements for Medium Access Control in wireless environments. Briefly the process consists of a four-way handshake. Although the use of encryption is vital to the transport of data in a wireless environment, a complete discussion of the mechanisms utilized are outside the scope of this book. That being said, the 802.11i standards define the four-way handshake in the following manner: first, an Association must be established; second, the normal 802.1X authentication must be successful; third (and fourth), the exchange of Key information must be accomplished between Authenticator and Supplicant. The exchange of Key information may take place one or more times during the lifetime of a connection and may be initiated by either the Supplicant or the Authenticator. Figure 2.6 illustrates the exchange process.

There are situations on some LANs where a device attached to an Authenticator has not completed the authentication process, but may need to communicate with a device on the protected side of the Authenticator. One such situation is the transmission of environmental information. This is similar to the PXE environment discussed in the previous chapter. The last Type defined in EAPOL helps cover this type of situation. It is a Type 4 EAPOL-Encapsulated-ASF-Alert. This type of packet in a non-802.1X environment would normally be issued as an SNMP packet. However, this SNMP packet is blocked when the port is unauthorized in the 802.1X environment.

The Type 4 packet is designed to allow "alerting" to occur without the requirement for authentication. The requirement for the attached device to participate in 802.1X remains, but it is allowed to declare an emergency without requiring authentication through the use of this packet type. The communication process is limited by 802.1X. It would be similar to allowing

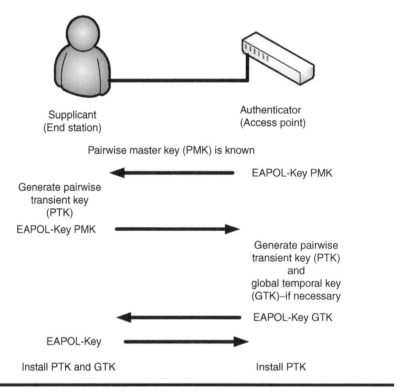

Figure 2.6 EAPOL Key Exchange.

calls to the hospital, police, and fire departments from a pay phone without requiring payment first.

2.1.7 Extensible Authentication Protocol (EAP)

EAP is a simple protocol with a single function. It is used to transport and manage authentication information between the Supplicant and the Authentication Server. This includes negotiation of how authentication will take place, what method will be used, the exchange of credentials defined in the method, and the final declaration of success or failure. Any transfer of configuration information from the Authentication Server to the Authenticator based upon a successful authentication takes place outside of EAP. This sounds like it is doing a lot, but, in fact, it is like a delivery van. It does not know—or really care—what it is carrying.

Let us recap the desired 802.1X flow one more time. The Authenticator will issue a Request-Identity packet. The Supplicant will issue a Response. The Authenticator will remove all encapsulation from the packet, re-encapsulate the EAP message, and forward it to an Authentication Server.

The Authentication Server will process the data and respond. This will continue until the Authentication Server declares either Success or Failure.

Each individual method for authenticating the credentials will specify a further exchange of packets. The specifications require that EAP be able to support MD5, OTP, and the use of Generic Token Cards, but allow for virtually any additional form of authentication. There are no requirements for any specific additional encryption methods, use of certificates, etc. EAP was architected to allow for a plug-in type scenario whereby an authentication module could be installed on both the Supplicant and the Authentication Server without affecting the transport mechanism.

The actual authentication mechanism takes place using EAP-Method Data encapsulated in EAP frames. The number of different types of frames that an Authenticator can send to a Supplicant in the authentication process is very limited. In fact, it can only send three different types of EAP frames. It can request information and indicate success or failure. The Supplicant is even more limited because it can send only EAP Responses.

The EAP protocol does not include any imbedded security for the transmission—no fragmentation mechanisms, etc. Although the protocol does have some imbedded capabilities for ensuring correct ordering of packets, through the use of a "lock step" process, it primarily relies on the simplicity of the wiring that connects the Supplicant and the Authenticator to ensure that the conversation proceeds in an orderly, sequential fashion.

Again, all conversations between the Authenticator and Supplicant are very simple. The Authenticator requests information. The Supplicant responds. The Authenticator will process some EAPOL frames, but it usually just forwards the encapsulated EAP data to the intended Authentication Server. The Authenticator then may be directed by the Authentication Server to obtain additional information. If so, it will send another request to the Supplicant and wait for a response. Eventually, the Authenticator will be told that the authentication process was either successful or not. It then will take appropriate action and echo this status to the Supplicant. As expected, the number and sophistication of available EAP processes are very limited and Table 2.2 defines the EAP Codes.

Table 2.2   EAP Codes

EAP Code	Number
Request	1
Response	2
Success	3
Failure	4

Code (1-byte)	Identifier (1 byte)	Length (2-bytes)	EAP-Data (0-n bytes)

Code:	01-04
Identifier	Lock-step sequence number
Length:	Length of EAP-Data
EAP-Data	Authentication information

Figure 2.7 EAP Frame.

Just as with any interaction, an agreed upon protocol must be established before any communication can take place. This process is twofold: first, the physical medium to be used must be established; and, second, the meaning of the modulation of that medium must be mutually agreed upon. Take human communication as an example. In most cases, the medium is sound, but it does not need to be. Frequently, the medium is sight. If someone attempts to speak with another who does not hear, then communication cannot be established. If two people agree that the medium of communication is sound, then the particular encoding—modulation—of the medium must be mutually understood. Two people talking to one another, one in French and the other in Russian, will not communicate because even though they have agreed upon sound as the medium, they have not agreed upon the modulation of the medium. All of the preceding discussion of Ethernet and EAPOL establishes the medium for authentication as EAP.

An EAP message consists of four fields: the EAP Code, the Identifier, the Length of the EAP-Data, and the EAP-Data itself. The first two fields are the only fields really pertinent to EAP. The first, Code, identifies what kind of EAP packet is being used, and the second is used to ensure correct sequencing. The EAP encapsulation is shown below in Figure 2.7.

2.1.8   EAPOL/EAP Retransmission

By definition, the Authenticator will initiate the authentication process by issuing a Code 1—Request Identity—packet to the Supplicant when Link is established. The Supplicant will respond with a Code 2 Packet. As described in the previous chapter, there are a number of alternative scenarios to this process. One of the more likely is that there is no Supplicant to receive the EAP Request Identity. The specifications for EAP contain a very simple mechanism for retransmission. This consists of timeout and retry parameters.

Remember that, by definition, the Supplicant is passive in this process and only responds to requests from the Authenticator. This is EAP and not EAPOL. Do not get the two confused. They are distinct protocols with distinct functions. The Supplicant may signal the Authenticator that it wishes to begin the authentication process by sending an EAPOL-Start, but then it must wait for a Request-Identity packet from the Authenticator. There are configurable parameters for the amount of time the Authenticator will wait for a response from the Supplicant before retransmitting the request. The number of times it will retransmit the request is also configurable.

2.1.9 Lock-Step Process

Because it is the active partner, it is the responsibility of the Authenticator to ensure that it has received a response to each request sent. It might be possible for the Authenticator to send a request and have the Supplicant actually respond to a different one. This is controlled with a "lock-step" process, which is a primitive method of ensuring reliable transport. A lock-step process is one in which an action made by a "leader" must be followed exactly by a "subordinate." In this case, the lock-step process is an indicator that each participant in the conversation is talking about the same information. Because requests come from the Authenticator and responses come from the Supplicant, the Authenticator always should be the one to indicate new information in this exchange, and the Supplicant only can respond to the current information request.

The Identifier field is used to implement the lock-step. The Authenticator will set the Identifier to a specific value. The Supplicant will echo this value in its response. The Authenticator will change the value of the Identifier for the next request and the Supplicant will echo the new value in its response. The Supplicant will never know if it has not received a request based upon the value of the Identifier, but the Authenticator will always know. In general the contents of the Identifier field will increase in numeric value during the authentication, but are not necessarily required to do so.

In Figure 2.3 where the first packet was a Failure, the Identity field is set to 0. The next packet, the Request Identity, from the Authenticator was set to 1. The Supplicant responds to that packet using a Code of 2 and an Identity of 1. Should the Supplicant actually respond to a prior request, or even to a request never sent by the Authenticator, the authentication in process would be aborted and a new authentication process would be started.

The following diagram, Figure 2.8, illustrates the use of the Identifier in part of a typical 802.1X conversation between a Supplicant and an Authenticator.

In this example, the Authenticator has received a Code 2 response from the Supplicant. It will then attempt to contact the Authentication Server. That attempt will contain the EAP data initially supplied by the Supplicant. If a conversation is successfully established with the Authentication Server, the server will issue a Challenge. This Challenge is forwarded by the Authenticator to the Supplicant as a Request-Identity packet. The Authenticator will have changed the Identifier to a value different than was sent in the first Request-Identity packet.

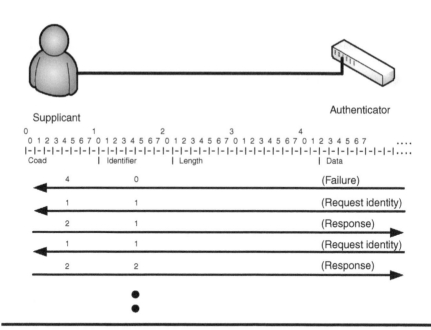

Figure 2.8   Use of the Identifier in EAP.

Now the Authenticator is acting simply as a translator and guardian of the port. During the exchange of credentials between the Supplicant and the Authentication Server, the Authentication accepts packets, re-encapsulates the data being sent, and modifies the Identifier field. In conversations with the Supplicant, it controls the conversation at the transport level and does not concern itself with the actual content of credentials being exchanged in the authentication process.

This continues until the Authentication Server declares either success or failure. At that point in time, the Authenticator will take action. The next section will discuss the interaction between Authenticator and Authentication Server (RADIUS) in more detail. But it should be clear that the process for EAP between Supplicant and Authenticator is extremely simple. EAP does not perform Authentication. The content of the data transported by EAP in EAP-Method Data accomplishes that.

The Authenticator is interested in the contents of the very first packet it sees in the conversation from the Supplicant, the response to it's Request Identity, and the last packet, success or failure, from the Authentication Server. There really is not a lot that happens between the Authenticator and the Supplicant. Communication is established, requests are made, responses are received, and notification of success or failure is conveyed. That is it.

2.1.10   EAP-Method

The data that is encapsulated in an EAP packet is the authentication information exchanged between the Supplicant and the Authentication

Server. The type of authentication data that can be carried in a particular packet is controlled by the EAP Type. As an example, an EAP Type of Response cannot carry an MD5-Challenge. This must be carried in a Request-Identity packet.

Generally stated, the Type used has little impact on the correct functioning of EAP. EAP is the protocol used to transport the EAP-Method. The correct functioning of the method is controlled by the information carried, the EAP-Method Data portion of the encapsulation, and not the EAP-Method protocol itself. However, the EAP-Method Type does have meaning in the number of exchanges between the Supplicant and the Authentication Server. The number of exchanges and, to a certain extent, the direction of the exchanges—request/response pairs—is dependent upon the method implemented. The Supplicant and the Authentication Server process this data according to the algorithm defined for the particular method chosen for authentication.

The EAP-Method information consists of three fields: the EAP-Method Code, EAP-Method Data Length, and the EAP-Method Data. This is illustrated in Figure 2.9.

As with all preceding encapsulations, the EAP-Method Data field is also just an encapsulation of information to be used by the Authentication Server. Again, an agreement on what modulation of the medium, the language, or more properly, the encryption method, must be accomplished. The Type field is used for this purpose.

A huge number of words have been written, and will continue to be written, about the suitability, viability, failure, and inadequacies of the various authentication/encryption methods. This book will not attempt to provide any opinion, or even an in-depth review, regarding the selection of an appropriate method. The next few pages will provide some summary information on the different types. But a discussion of how the basic functioning of the EAP-Method processing occurs must be accomplished prior to a discussion of the kinds of authentication available.

The Authenticator repackages messages from the Supplicant to send to the Authentication Server and also does the reverse. It really does not care what the content is beyond watching for a success or failure. After declaring either success or failure, the Authentication Server, the Radius server, can

EAP-Method Code (1-byte)	Length (2-bytes)	EAP-Method Data (0-n bytes)

Code: 01- 255
Length: Length of EAP-Method Data
EAP-Method Data   Authentication information

Figure 2.9   EAP-Method Frame.

send information back to the Authenticator, the switch in this case, that is used to modify its behavior based on the identity of the Supplicant. Information, such as VLAN number, can be associated with a user in the Radius Server. This information then can be passed to the Authenticator once authentication of that user is successful. This information is more completely discussed in the Radius section.

The Supplicant and the Authentication Server actually negotiate the EAP-Method, the type, to be used in the authentication process. The flow is quite simple. As just indicated, the Supplicant and the Authenticator establish communication, and the Authenticator gathers sufficient information to contact the Authentication Server. At this point, the conversation is very similar to the following example of a conversation between Lyle, a guard, and the boss upstairs.

"I'm Lyle."
"Hey, boss, I've got a guy down here who says his name is Lyle."
"Lyle? Does he speak English?"
"Hey, Lyle, do you speak English?"
"Yes I do."
"Boss, he says: yeah he speaks English."

The Type code corresponds to the discussion of language. If Lyle, as the Supplicant, had not spoken English, he would have issued an extended NAK and proposed an alternative EAP-Method. The boss, as the Authentication Server, would have responded appropriately. At that point, either the authentication process would have failed, and the guard would be notified, or the process would have had additional exchanges before declaring success or failure.

The Type field identifies the "protocol decapsulation" of the data contained in the EAP-Data portion of the packet. The Type can identify a directive/request to the receiving party or it may contain data to be used by the authentication method. The EAP-Method is actually another hole in the floor to shove specific credentials through. The specification for EAP initially identified six types. In the current revision of EAP, RFC 3478, there are eight types that must be supported. The particular specification of EAP functions that are supported is essential information because it affects how processing must occur. In particular this information is used in the determination of how an EAP-Method is selected through the use of the NAK/extended NAK. Table 2.3 shows the current types defined.

When looking at that table, two good questions would be, "Why, are they duplicating Identity and Notification? Are not those contained in the EAP Code field?" The answer is that the EAP Code field is used in conversations between the Supplicant and the Authenticator. This information is not formally passed to the Authentication Server, so the same information must

Table 2.3   EAP Codes

EAP-Method Type	Number
Identity	1
Notification	2
NAK (response only)	3
MD5-Challenge	4
One-Time Password	5
Generic Token Card	6
Expanded NAK	254
Experimental	255

be imbedded in the Type field that is part of the Data field that is passed between the Supplicant and the Authentication Server.

The Identity, Type 1, is used to convey information regarding the credentials of either—or both—the Supplicant and the Authentication Server. This means that the conversation between the Authenticator and the Supplicant will consist of EAP Request Identity and responses, and usually will contain EAP-Method Type 1 exchanges. This is the desired scenario, because the Identity exchanges mean that the process has actually reached the point where authentication information is being exchanged and will lead to either a success or failure.

There are three additional types that can be used before or during the Authentication process. The first of these is Notification: Type 2. A Type 2 is sent by the Authentication Server to the Supplicant and contains information regarding the status of authentication. One example of this type of message is the notification to the user that the password used will expire within a period of time. In some methods, the user will be allowed to change the password. Or it may transmit a warning that the authentication process has failed and will allow the user to reenter credentials. Some Authentication Methods prohibit the use of notification messages to the user.

A Type 3, legacy NAK, is sent by the Supplicant to the Authentication Server when the Supplicant rejects the proposed authentication method. In limited cases, it can be used to propose one or more alternative methods of authentication. The Type 3 is one of the original codes implemented. An exchange with a NAK resulting in a failure to select an authentication method is illustrated in Figure 2.10.

2.1.11   The EAP-Method Expanded NAK

In the current specification, an Expanded NAK, Type 254, is defined that will allow the Supplicant to propose an authentication method. The difference between the Type 3 NAK and the Type 254 Expanded NAK is in the format of

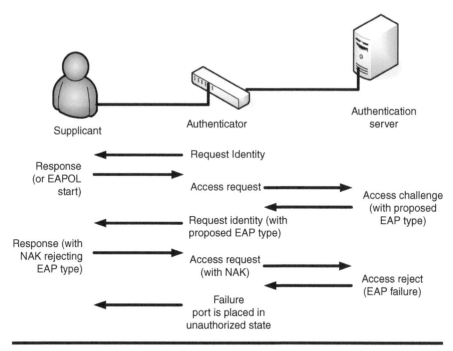

Figure 2.10   Reject EAP-Method (Legacy NAK).

the Data field. The Expanded NAK has a structured table with an undefined number of repeating rows. The table is processed from top to bottom with the first proposed method assigned the first priority as the proposed method of authentication. The row consists of three data elements: a one byte Type field always equal to 254, a one byte Vendor field, and a 4 byte Data field containing the proposed method. If the Vendor field is 0 then the vendor is IETF and the proposed method must be one of the three identified in the RFC: Type 4, 5, or 6. If the Vendor is a different number, then the Data field can be any defined type—including one of the three required types. The use of the Expanded NAK allows for a quicker convergence for the selection of an authentication method. It should be noted that neither of the NAK types can be used to transport error messages. These conversations must take place using a Notification: Type 2.

2.1.12   Additional EAP-Methods

Once the EAP-Method has been negotiated, the use of EAP Codes 1 and 2— Request Identity and response—will carry the authentication conversation between the Supplicant and the Authenticator. The Authenticator and the Authentication Server will exchange Access-Request and Access-Challenge messages until the Server finally issues an Access-Accept or Access-Reject packet. The encapsulated EAP-Method will be used to exchange information between the Supplicant and the Authentication Server.

There are a significant number of EAP-Methods that are "plug-in" modules for the Supplicant and the Authentication Server. Most of these modules are proprietary, and only three are required by the Standards: MD5 Challenge, OTP, and Generic Token Cards.

There are generally two types of authentication implemented. The various methods that exchange credentials generally rely on the use of either certificates or passwords. There are also several methods that simply define a secured tunnel through which a second EAP-Method is carried. Table 2.4 identifies most optional types available at the time this book was written.

A relatively brief discussion of some of the more prominent EAP-Methods is warranted. These methods are called "vendor-specific" and are allocated a "method" number for identification purposes. The EAP-Method Data field has been defined to contain a possible subprotocol. This structure is not required and is not necessarily present in every EAP-Method. But where it is present, the EAP-Method Data field is parsed according to Figure 2.11.

All of the fields, with the exception of the Vendor Code, are entirely defined within the context of the particular vendor's application. No controls are imposed, nor documentation required, for these fields within an EAP-Method. The Vendor Code is the SMI Network Management Private Enterprise Code specified by IANA. If the Vendor Code is zero, then the Vendor Specific Type field is an extension of the EAP-Method type. The original 255 possible EAP-Methods were very limited. The expansion provides a virtually unlimited number of possible methods.

There are a couple of items that should be clarified regarding Vendor Specific Methods. The first is probably so obvious that it could be skipped, but we will go over it anyway. Part of the intent of these types of methods is to secure the exchange of credentials. This means that it should be difficult to interpret any capture of an exchange of packets. The use of a sniffer will be ineffective for troubleshooting the details of most of these exchanges. A sniffer will capture the packet and correctly classify the packet according to the EAP type utilized, but will frequently be unable to process EAP-Method Data specifically as it pertains to Vendor Specific Methods. Thus, for our purposes, it is marginally valuable to actually detail exchanges that occur within a particular method. In most of the discussions, only enough description of the flow to give a very basic understanding will be provided here. Some methods will be fleshed out to illustrate general processes that can occur. Yet, describing a process in a particular Method does not mean that it is exclusive to that method. It means that it was simply convenient to discuss the process at that time in that method. Remember that the following discussions of various methods is not exhaustive by any means—either in the methods available or the functions of individual methods.

The second item that should be clarified—and emphasized—is that many of the methods incorporate a specific protocol that is encapsulated within

Table 2.4   EAP-Method Authentication Types

Type	Description
9	RSA Public Key Authentication
10	DSS Unilateral
11	KEA
12	KEA-VALIDATE
13	EAP-TLS
14	Defender Token (AXENT)
15	Windows 2000 EAP
16	Arcot Systems EAP
17	LEAP
18	EAP-SIM, GSM Subscriber Identity Modules
19	SRP-SHA1 Part 1
20	SRP-SHA1 Part 2
21	EAP-TTLS
22	Remote Access Service
23	EAP-AKA, EAP method for 3rd Generation Authentication and Key Agreement
24	EAP-3Com Wireless
25	PEAP, Protected EAP
26	MS-EAP-Authentication
27	MAKE, Mutual Authentication w/Key Exchange
28	CRYPTOCard
29	EAP-MSCHAP-V2
30	DynamID
31	Rob EAP
32	SecurID EAP
33	MS-Authentication-TLV
34	SentriNET
35	EAP-Actiontec Wireless
36	Cogent Systems Biometrics Authentication EAP
37	AirFortress EAP
38	EAP-HTTP Digest
39	SecureSuite EAP
40	DeviceConnect EAP
41	EAP-SPEKE
42	EAP-MOBAC
43	EAP-FAST, EAP Flexible Authentication via Secure Tunneling
44	ZLXEAP, ZoneLabs EAP
45	EAP-Link

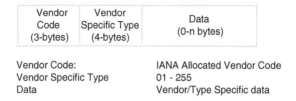

Vendor Code (3-bytes)	Vendor Specific Type (4-bytes)	Data (0-n bytes)

Vendor Code:	IANA Allocated Vendor Code
Vendor Specific Type	01 - 255
Data	Vendor/Type Specific data

Figure 2.11   Vendor Specific EAP-Method Data Frame.

EAP. This means that only the partners in an exchange can interpret the data. However, keep in mind how 802.1X functions. The Authenticator, not one of the partners in the exchange of credentials, is the owner of the port that must be placed in an authenticated status. This can only happen when the Authentication Server, either separate or imbedded in the Authenticator, notifies the Authenticator of a Success. Thus, in many of the EAP-Methods, there are imbedded success and failures within the specific protocol that must be acknowledged prior to an EAP-Success transmission to the Authenticator. This situation is discussed in a couple of the methods later in this section.

Back to the EAP-Methods currently available. At the time of this writing, the Microsoft Windows environment has a huge presence in the PC world. There are several EAP-Methods that are available within the Microsoft Windows 2000 environments. These include EAP-MD5 CHAP, EAP-MSCHAPV2, and PEAP. Windows XP also includes support for EAP-FAST. In most cases, the particular manufacturer of the wireless NIC installed will include drivers or other tools to configure an SSID with specific 802.1X characteristics, including a variety of EAP-Methods.

2.1.12.1   EAP-MD5 CHAP

The acronym, MD5 CHAP, stands for Message Digest 5 Challenge Handshake Authentication Protocol. This EAP-Method relies on the use of Username and Password to complete an authentication. It is Method Type 4 and is a mandatory implementation within EAP.

EAP-MD5 CHAP uses the same handshake protocol as the PPP based CHAP. Typically, this protocol is used to authenticate against an internal database—frequently the NT Domain. The basic flow is what has been described thus far in this book. The identity of the Supplicant is requested by the Authenticator and forwarded to the Authentication Server. The Server responds with a "Challenge." The Supplicant responds and authentication is either successful or not.

Full details of the CHAP protocol are available from a variety of sources, including the IETF.

2.1.12.2 EAP-TLS

Unlike EAP-MD5 CHAP, EAP-TLS is not a required method. It is an optional implementation. The acronym TLS is an abbreviation of Transport Layer Security and is EAP-Method Type 21. This is the one of the few methods that is actually described inside an RFC (RFC 2716). Although this method is not required, it is available for implementation by any vendor.

EAP-TLS is a certificate-based protocol. And though this makes it a strong method, it does complicate the environment. The exchange of messages within the TLS protocol provides mutual authentication, integrity-protected ciphersuite negotiation, and secured private key exchange between the Supplicant and the Authentication Server. The use of smart cards requires EAP-TLS as the EAP-Method.

The biggest downside to this method, and others of this class, is the required cost or administration of certificates. If certificates are not purchased from an authority recognized by the devices on the network, then a private system must be established. In either case, the cost of implementation, in money or expertise, can be significant. The environment that implements certificate-based authentication becomes more complex and requires an increased level of administration. Furthermore, the use of certificates generally authenticates the device on which the certificate resides and not the user. For some organizations, this defeats the purpose of implementing 802.1X.

The use of certificates also increases the number of exchanges required between a Supplicant and an Authentication Server. While this makes a relatively small impact on a given network, it does increase the time required for authentication and could conceivably impact time sensitive applications. Wireless is one example. Due to mobility, it is possible for re-authentication to disrupt an application in progress.

The transaction flow with EAP-TLS is very similar to that of any other EAP-Method. The Authenticator and Supplicant will recognize each other and the Authenticator will assume a pass-through role after establishing a session with the Authentication Server. At this point, the Authentication Server will conduct all conversations with the Supplicant (through the Authenticator) using the EAP-TLS protocol encapsulated in the EAP-Method Data. The first packet sent by the server will be an EAP-TLS-Start. The Supplicant will respond with an EAP-TLS packet containing the TLS version number, a session ID, a random number, and a list of cybersuites supported. This information will be used by the server to ensure the session is correct and to supply additional information to the Supplicant to be used during the authentication process.

At this point, the Supplicant will validate that it is conversing with a legitimate Authentication Server. The server may authenticate the Supplicant, but is not absolutely required to do so. Upon successful authentication, the server will notify the Supplicant using an EAP-TLS Success message and the

Supplicant must acknowledge the message. When the server receives the acknowledgement, it will issue an EAP-Success that will allow the Authenticator to place the port in an authorized state.

2.1.12.3 EAP-MS-CHAPV2

EAP-MS-CHAPV2, developed by Microsoft, is not a required method. It is a password-based, challenge-response, mutual authentication protocol. Responses are encrypted using message digest 4 (MD4) and Data Encryption Standard (DES) algorithms. EAP-Method Type 29 has been assigned to this method. It is a handshake protocol that requires each party, Supplicant and Authentication Server, to authenticate each other. MS-CHAPV2 was originally developed as a PPP authentication protocol to provide better protection for dial-up and virtual private network (VPN) connections. This version of CHAP provides better protection than previous challenge-response protocols. However, it is still susceptible to an offline dictionary attack. If a thief can capture a successful MS-CHAPV2 exchange, he can then guess passwords until the correct one is determined.

EAP-MS-CHAPV2 uses the following process to perform authentication. The Server challenges the Supplicant and the Supplicant challenges the Authenticating Server. If either challenge is not correctly answered, the connection is rejected. Authentication within this method is initiated when the normal 802.1X link is established between the Authenticator and the Supplicant. The Supplicant will issue a Response. As expected, the Authenticator forwards this to the Authentication Server. The Server then issues an encrypted challenge. The Supplicant sends an encrypted response derived from the user credentials.

At this point the authentication is either a success or failure. The Authentication Server may issue a failure for a variety of reasons. Table 2.5 identifies these codes.

If a 648, Password Expired, failure is sent, then the Supplicant can optionally update the password. This process actually requires a new

Table 2.5   EAP-MS-CHAPV2 Failure Codes

Failure Code	Explanation
691	Authentication Failure
646	Restricted Logon Hours
647	Account Disabled
648	Password Expired
649	No Dial-in Permission
709	Error Changing Password

exchange of challenge packets where the Supplicant will send a new password in response to the new challenge.

When a success packet is sent by the Authentication Server, the Supplicant must use information contained in the packet to perform an authentication of the Server. If the authentication fails, then the Supplicant must terminate the process and remain unauthenticated. This is required because the Authentication Server will not issue an EAP-Success packet until the Supplicant has acknowledged that it has authenticated the Server. Without the issuance of an EAP-Success packet, the Authenticator will not place the port in an authorized state.

A full description of the protocol flow and the various codes utilized in a variety of situations has been published and is available from a variety of sources including the IETF.

2.1.12.4   PEAP (Protected EAP)

Just as the name suggests, PEAP protects EAP exchanges. This authentication process occurs in two parts. The first part is used to establish a tunnel between the Supplicant and the Authentication Server, and the second part is the actual authentication of credentials. The first part of PEAP is the establishment of a TLS tunnel. Just as with EAP-TLS, PEAP can utilize a certificate to establish the tunnel, but is not required to do so. Once the tunnel is established, another EAP-Method is used for authentication of user credentials.

The PEAP flow is also very similar to that of all the other 802.1X methods. The Authenticator issues a Request-Identity, and the Supplicant responds. The Authenticator forwards to the Authentication Server; the server responds with a challenge specifying a Start PEAP. At that point the establishment of a TLS tunnel begins.

PEAP Leverages TLS to create a secured tunnel that is used then to transport credentials. An entirely different EAP-Method is encapsulated within the TLS tunnel. One of the more popular methods is EAP-MS-CHAPV2. Because the credentials exchanged in the authentication process are tunneled, there is no possibility of snooping. This eliminates one of the vulnerabilities of MS-CHAPV2—that of an offline dictionary attack.

One point that must be considered for a PEAP implementation is that the authentication effort is doubled. First, the establishment of the TLS tunnel must occur. This requires exchanges between the Supplicant and the Authentication Server. Then authentication utilizing another EAP-Method must be conducted through the tunnel. This increases the complexity of authentication as well as the duration and volume of traffic required. This method would seem to be a poor choice for mobile users in a wireless environment. However, it is possible for the RADIUS server to cache the TLS session created as the first part of the authentication process after the second part has been successful. This allows the RADIUS server to issue an EAP-Success immediately when a reconnect is attempted.

2.1.12.5   EAP-TTLSV1 (EAP Tunneled TLS Version 1)

EAP-TTLS is a proprietary method owned by Funk Software. However, Funk has issued Internet-Draft documents that provide significant information on how the method works. The most recent was published in February of 2005.

The method's name implies that it is an enhanced version of TLS. That is a simplistic but basically accurate description of the protocol. EAP-TTLSV1 extends TLS through the use of TLS/IA (Inner Authentication). The major difference between TLS and TTLS is that TTLS does not require the use of certificates in the establishment of a tunnel. PEAP is very similar to EAP-TTLS, except that PEAP currently exists only in a Windows environment.

2.1.12.6   EAP-FAST(EAP Flexible Authentication via Secure Tunneling)

EAP-FAST is a Cisco proprietary method and, like EAP-TTLS, an Internet-Draft has been written to document the workings of the protocol. It was published in April of 2005. The major extension of EAP-FAST is in tunnel creation. EAP-FAST relies on the use of preshared keys to construct a tunnel through the use of "symmetric cryptography." This tunnel is then used by another EAP-Method for credential exchange. From an operational perspective, the major advantage to this method is that it does not require the use of certificates.

2.1.12.7   LEAP (Lightweight EAP)

LEAP is a Cisco proprietary method utilized primarily in wireless environments. The protocol, like EAP-MD5 and EAP-TLS, leaves the identity in the clear. However, LEAP does provide for mutual authentication between the Supplicant and the Authentication Server. This protocol is being phased out in favor of PEAP and EAP-FAST.

2.1.12.8   EAP-SPEKE

EAP-SPEKE is a proprietary method that utilizes a patented algorithm for the development of keys. The method relies on very strong encryption to protect passwords and eliminate the need for certificates.

That summarizes some of the available EAP-Methods. Now the disclaimer: there is no intent to promote any given method because of inclusion or exclusion in the previous discussion. Implementation of any particular method should be the result of the organization planning the implementation and the design effort that evaluates the particular characteristics of the existing infrastructure.

The selection of a particular EAP-Method will depend upon what the intended environment looks like. A large number of factors will come into play when determining which method is the best for the particular situation. Considerations of existing hardware/software implementations are large. But the impact of some "soft" factors will be equally important. Such factors include the complexity of support required, and the general sophistication of users in understanding what is being done and how to work with it on their equipment.

Now, a quick summary. The implementation of 802.1X is really the cascading of at least five encapsulations that ultimately results in an exchange of credentials between a Supplicant and an Authentication Server. In general, each encapsulation and the functionality required to support the process is fairly simple. However, when taken as a whole, it is robust and develops a framework for applying security to a huge number of connections to a network.

2.2   RADIUS

2.2.1   Section Summary

Radius is the "backend server"—Authentication Server—in virtually all 802.1X implementations. RADIUS is covered in specifications from the IETF and has been around for much longer than 802.1X. Two RFCs from the IETF—2865 and 3579—extend the specifications into 802.1X. One additional RFC, 3780, identifies particular elements, known as attributes, that are useful with 802.1X. These RFCs cover both Authentication and Accounting functions. RADIUS functions cover three aspects of security: AAA.

The specifications for EAP do not make RADIUS a required component, but it is a de facto one. Potentially, any RADIUS server will perform the functions required. It will almost certainly be able to handle the mandatory EAP-Methods. However, if a newer EAP-Method is chosen, or, in some cases, a proprietary method, then a newer or proprietary server capable of supporting the method must be implemented. This means that particular attention must be paid to the EAP-Method chosen and its support on a RADIUS server already implemented on the network. As stated, a proprietary method may require both a specific Supplicant and a specific RADIUS server from a particular vendor.

RADIUS operates on the Client-Server model where the network access device passes authentication information on behalf of a client to the server. Security is preserved in this model through the use of a shared secret password coded on both the access device and the RADIUS server. The server will perform the necessary authentication of a Supplicant—and inform the access device of the result—only when the access device has provided valid credentials to RADIUS. This basic functionality performs as described within the 802.1X environment.

Configuration necessary to ensure validity of identity to the Authenticator and the Authentication Server—RADIUS—is simple, but must be accurate. Each partner must know two pieces of information. First, the "other" end must be known to each device. This is accomplished by identifying the partner's IP address. Second, a password must be coded on each device. This is known as a shared secret. A more detailed discussion about configuring these items will be conducted in a later section on Configuration.

The Authenticator and the Authentication Server, RADIUS, converse using the RADIUS protocol. The protocol utilizes a lock-step process, similar to that used in EAPOL, to synchronize the conversation between the Authenticator and the Authentication Server. The RADIUS packets are primarily composed of attributes. Each attribute is a specific data element that is either utilized by the Authenticator or is passed on to the Supplicant. More than one hundred attributes have been allocated, but only a small fraction of these are pertinent in an 802.1X-based conversation.

Encapsulated in the packet exchanges between the Authenticator and the Authentication Server is the EAP-Method Data. This element is used to exchange authentication information between the Supplicant and the Authentication Server. The data is encrypted in the exchange between the Authenticator and the RADIUS server. The shared secret is part of the key necessary to decrypt the EAP-Method Data.

If an authentication is a success, then the RADIUS server can be configured to provide information to the Authenticator that will be used to dynamically modify either or both the VLAN to be assigned and an access list. This information is contained in two specific attributes that are passed to the Authenticator outside of an EAP-Method exchange.

2.2.2 RADIUS Packet Architecture, Protocol, and Flow

The RADIUS protocol used to carry the conversation between the Authenticator and the Authentication Server is very similar in layout to EAP. Like EAP, RADIUS identifies the function to be performed via an element called Code and uses a lock-step synchronization process through the use of an element called an Identifier. Figure 2.12 illustrates the RADIUS packet layout.

Code performs much the same functionality with RADIUS that type performs with EAP. There are six values for this element that are pertinent to 802.1X. Four of the values are used by the server for transmissions to the Authenticator, and two are used by the Authenticator to communicate with the server. The Authenticator will issue a request to the Authentication Server either as an Access-Request or as an Accounting-Request. The Authentication Server has several options available. It can respond to an

Code (1-byte)	Identifier (1-byte)	Length (2 bytes)	Authenticator (16 bytes)	Attributes (0-n bytes)

Code:	Message Type
Identifier:	Lock-step code to match requests to replies
Length:	Message length including header
Authenticator:	"Random unpredictable number" used to validate Information exchanges
Attributes:	Authentication information (EAP-Method)

Figure 2.12 RADIUS Protocol.

Accounting-Request, either declare a Success or Failure with an Access-Accept or Access-Reject, or it can request additional information with an Access-Challenge. The most common conversations will consist of Access-Requests from the Authenticator, followed by Access-Challenges by the RADIUS server, and a final Access-Accept or Access-Failure from the RADIUS server. The six values for Code that are pertinent to 802.1X authentication are shown below in Table 2.6.

The RADIUS server will have a "dual" conversation. It will conduct a conversation with the Authenticator using the RADIUS protocol, and an EAP-Method conversation with the Supplicant. The flow within any particular method will appear to be essentially the same as that in any other method. However, the credentials or other authentication information contained will vary depending on the particular method.

Remember that the Authenticator physically converses with the Authentication Server while the Supplicant logically converses with the Authentication Server. Figure 2.13 recaps this flow.

Although the actual authentication process depends upon the specific EAP-Method utilized, the basic flow is as described above. The EAP-Methods have been discussed previously and the EAP flow has been detailed. That leaves only two topics regarding RADIUS to be covered: What attributes are available for use, and how can the behavior of the Authenticator be modified.

Table 2.6 RADIUS Codes

Code	Description
1	Access-Request
2	Access-Accept
3	Access-Reject
4	Accounting-Request
5	Accounting-Response
11	Access-Challenge

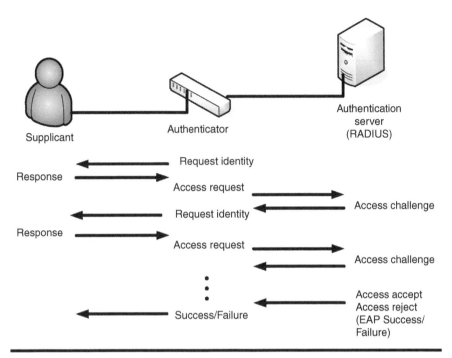

Figure 2.13   General RADIUS Flow.

2.2.3   Radius Attributes

RFCs 2865, 2866, 2867, and 2868 describe RADIUS and all of the attributes. RFCs 2865 and 2868 describe functional attributes. RFCs 2866 and 2867 describe accounting attributes. RADIUS is not exclusively utilized in 802.1X—EAP more properly—and not all attributes are pertinent. RFC 3580 recaps the attributes and identifies their usability within the 802.1X authentication process. RFCs 2867 and 2868 extend the radius "base" definitions to include support for Tunnel Protocol Support. It is this extension that is most pertinent for 802.1X. Table 2.7 summarizes the RADIUS attributes, which RFC documents a particular attribute, and whether or not the attribute has particular usefulness with the 802.1X authentication process.

In addition to the attributes shown, there are more than one hundred vendor attributes in use. The table shows how robust the RADIUS implementation really is. Only a very small fraction of the attributes defined are specifically pertinent within 802.1X, and the majority of those are defined in RFCs 2867 and 2868. Those two RFCs define RADIUS for Tunnel Protocol Support. The most common application for tunnels is in VPN. However, when looking at EAP-Methods, the EAP-Method currently ratified in an RFC and commonly implemented is EAP-TLS, which defines the use of a tunnel for the credential exchange between Supplicant and Authenticator.

Table 2.7   RADIUS Attributes

Attribute	Description	RFC	Specific 802.1X Requirements?
1	User-Name	2865	Yes
2	User-Password	2865	No
3	CHAP-Password	2865	No
4	NAS-IP-Address	2865	Yes
5	NAS-Port	2865	Yes
6	Service-Type	2865	Yes
7	Framed-Protocol	2865	No
8	Framed-IP Address	2865	No
9	Framed-IP-Netmask	2865	No
10	Framed-Routing	2865	No
11	Filter-ID	2865	Yes
12	Framed-MTU	2865	Yes
13	Framed-Compression	2865	No
14	Login-IP-Host	2865	No
15	Login-Service	2865	No
16	Login-TCP-Port	2865	No
17	Change-Password		No
18	Reply-Message	2865	No
19	Callback-Number	2865	No
20	Callback-ID	2865	No
21	Password-Expiration		No
22	Framed-Route	2865	No
23	Framed-IPX-Network	2865	No
24	State	2865	No
25	Class	2865	No
26	Vendor-Specific	2865	Yes
27	Session-Timeout	2865	Yes
28	Idle-Timeout	2865	No
29	Termination-Action	2865	Yes
30	Called-Station-ID	2865	Yes
31	Calling-Station-ID	2865	Yes
32	NAS-Identifier	2865	Yes
33	Proxy-State	2865	No
34	Login-LAT-Service	2865	No
35	Login-LAT-Node	2865	No
36	Login-LAT-Group	2865	No
37	Framed-AppleTalk-Link	2865	No
38	Framed-AppleTalk-Network	2865	No
39	Framed-AppleTalk-Zone	2865	No

(continued)

Table 2.7   Continued

Attribute	Description	RFC	Specific 802.1X Requirements?
40	Acct-Status-Type	2866	No
41	Acct-Delay-Time	2866	No
42	Acct-Input-Octets	2866	No
43	Acct-Output-Octets	2866	No
44	Acct-Session-ID	2866	No
45	Acct-Authentic	2866	No
46	Acct-Session-Time	2866	No
47	Acct-Input-Packets	2866	No
48	Acct-Output-Packets	2866	No
49	Acct-Terminate-Cause	2866	No
50	Acct-Multi-Session-ID	2866	No
51	Acct-Link-Count	2866	No
55	Event-Timestamp		No
60	CHAP-Challenge	2865	No
61	NAS-Port-Type	2865	Yes
62	Port-Limit	2865	No
63	Login-LAT-Port	2865	No
64	Tunnel-Type	2868	Yes
65	Tunnel-Medium-Type	2868	Yes
66	Tunnel-Client-Endpoint	2868	Yes
67	Tunnel-Server-Endpoint	2868	Yes
68	Acct-Tunnel-Connection	2867	No
69	Tunnel-Password	2868	Yes
70	ARAP-Password	2869	No
71	ARAP-Features	2869	No
72	ARAP-Zone-Access	2869	No
73	ARAP-Security	2869	No
74	ARAP-Security-Data	2869	No
75	Password-Retry	2869	No
76	Prompt	2869	No
77	Connect-Info	2869	No
78	Configuration-Token	2869	No
79	EAP-Message	2869	Yes
80	Message-Authenticator	2869	Yes
81	Tunnel-Private-Group-ID	2868	Yes
82	Tunnel-Assignment-ID	2868	No
83	Tunnel-Preference	2868	No
84	ARAP-Challenge-Response	2869	No
85	Acct-Interim-Interval	2869	No

(continued)

Table 2.7   Continued

Attribute	Description	RFC	Specific 802.1X Requirements?
86	Acct-Tunnel-Packets-Lost	2867	No
87	NAS-Port-ID	2869	Yes
88	Framed-Pool	2869	No
90	Tunnel-Client-Auth-ID	2868	No
91	Tunnel-ServerAuth-ID	2868	No
95	NAS-IPv5-Address	3162	Yes
96	Framed-Interface-ID	3162	No
97	Framed-IPv5-Prefix	3162	No
98	Login-IPv5-Host	3162	No
99	Framed-IPv5-Route	3162	No
100	Framed-IPv5-Pool	3162	No

Please note that while many attributes listed are not flagged as having specific 802.1X requirements, it does not mean that these attributes cannot be utilized within an 802.1X authentication conversation. It simply means that the function and use of these attributes is not modified because of 802.1X. Again, RFC 3580 documents the use of specific RADIUS attributes within an 802.1X environment. The following pages will supply a minimum amount of information regarding the attributes of specific interest during the Authentication process.

Radius Attribute 1—User Name. The User Name is fundamental to many RADIUS applications and not just 802.1X. Within 802.1X, the Supplicant may return the MAC address rather than the customary text for User Name. This is done when the Authenticator initiates a conversation with the RADIUS server prior to soliciting the Supplicant's identity. The Authenticator assumes that the Supplicant is capable of conducting an EAP-Method conversation and initiates the exchange of credentials prior to the Authentication Server requesting credentials from the Supplicant.

Radius Attribute 4—NAS IP Address. This is the IP address of the Authenticator and is an IP version 4 address. If IP version 6 is used, then Attribute 95—NAS-IPv5—Address will contain the correct address.

Radius Attribute 5—NAS Port. This is the port on the Authenticator to which the Supplicant wishes to attach. If this is an 802.11 connection, then the association ID is used as the port.

Radius Attribute 6—Service Type. This attribute indicates what function is being requested by the Authenticator. Within 802.1X, three functions are judged to be the most common Service-Types. These are: Framed, Authenticate Only, and Call Check. Framed indicates that appropriate 802 framing should be used; Authenticate Only indicates that no Authorization exchanges need occur; and Call Check requests acceptance or rejection of the attempted connection based upon the MAC address of the Authenticator or the Supplicant.

Radius Attribute 11—Filter ID. It is possible to associate a specific "filter," or access-list, to each individual Supplicant. This attribute identifies that filter to the Authenticator. This filter must exist on the Authenticator prior to the authentication. No values for an access list are contained in this attribute, only a "name" of an existing filter.

Radius Attribute 12—Framed MTU. This attribute is used, potentially, by a wide variety of applications, but the actual value varies with an 802.1X implementation. The MTU specified is the total packet size available for an EAP packet, minus four bytes. This is the overhead of the required EAP fields: 802.1X Version, Type, and Length.

Radius Attribute 26—Vendor Specific. This attribute may be used to hold specific information required in some EAP-Methods. This will entirely depend upon the fashion in which the vendor has implemented the proprietary method. This attribute requires the inclusion of information regarding the particular vendor intended to utilize the attribute. The information includes the Vendor ID, the type of function included as data, and the vendor-specific data itself. This information will be discussed very briefly in the section on configuration when discussing the application of per-user access lists. The access list is stored in this attribute. This attribute differs from Attribute 11 in that specific filters are defined within it. The filter is dynamically applied and does not have to exist prior to authentication.

Radius Attribute 27—Session Timeout. This attribute can be used in three different ways. First, if it is sent as part of the challenge, then it is used to determine the number of seconds the Authenticator will wait when not receiving a response from the Supplicant before retrying. Second, if this attribute is sent as part of the Access-Accept (EAP-Success) along with a Termination-Action attribute, it specifies the lifetime of the session before re-authentication is initiated. Third, if this attribute is sent as part of the Access-Accept (EAP-Success) without a Termination-Action attribute, it specifies the lifetime of the session and no re-authentication is attempted upon expiration.

Radius Attribute 28—Idle Timeout. This attribute is pertinent in wireless implementations only. It specifies the number of seconds a session will remain "alive" without contact from the Supplicant.

Radius Attribute 29—Termination Action. This attribute has either a value of 0 or 1. A "0" indicates that the session should be terminated after timeout without any re-authentication attempt. A "1" indicates that re-authentication should be initiated upon session timeout.

Radius Attribute 30—Called Station ID. This attribute holds the MAC address of the Authenticator. It is stored in the following format: 00-00-00-00-00-00 with dashes included. If the Authenticator is a wireless access point, the SSID is concatenated (if known) and is stored in the following format: 00-00-00-00-00-00:SSID.

Radius Attribute 31—Calling Station ID. The address of the Supplicant is stored in this attribute. The format is the same as shown in Called Station ID.

Radius Attribute 32—NAS Identifier. This attribute contains a string that identifies the Authenticator—usually the hostname of the device.

Radius Attribute 61—NAS Port Type. Only Ethernet, Wireless, Token Ring, and FDDI are valid within 802.1X. The values for those LAN types are 15, 19, 20, and 21 respectively.

The following six attributes are defined to support tunnel mechanisms. Attribute 64 is the one that is most pertinent to 802.1X. There are three attributes: 65, 66, and 67 that identify addresses of the Supplicant, the Authenticator, and the Authentication Server. These attributes seem to be a replication of earlier attributes, but each plays a role in the Tunnel process, and the content of previous attributes may not have contained the exact information required by this process.

Two additional attributes, 81 and 82, relating to the tunnel functions are discussed later.

Radius Attribute 64—Tunnel Type. For quite a while it has been said that the VLAN in which a Supplicant is placed can be determined by the RADIUS server. This attribute works in conjunction with two other attributes to set the VLAN for an authenticated user. If Tunnel-Type is set to VLAN and Tunnel-Medium-Type is set to 802, then the contents of attribute 81, Tunnel-Private-Group-ID, identify the VLAN in which to place the authenticated Supplicant. The following is an example of the input to the Cisco RADIUS server that accomplishes this:

Tunnel-Type=VLAN
Tunnel-Medium-Type=802
Tunnel-Private-Group-ID=20

The actual value stored on the RADIUS server is numeric. Tunnel-Type= VLAN is stored as the number 13. Of course there are a number of other values that can be used within the Tunnel-Type. Table 2.8 identifies the available types.

Radius Attribute 65—Tunnel-Medium-Type. Only 802 is valid in 802.1X.

Radius Attribute 66—Tunnel-Client-Endpoint. This is the address of the Supplicant.

Radius Attribute 67—Tunne-Server-Endpoint. This is the address of the Authentication Server.

Radius Attribute 68—Acct-Tunnel-Connection. This is an Accounting attribute specific to the Tunneling Protocol.

Radius Attribute 69—Tunnel-Password. This field contains a password, or seed value, used in establishing a connection with a remote server.

After having discussed a fairly large number of attributes, the next two are the ones that actually are involved in the exchange of credential information. They are arguably the most important attributes.

Table 2.8   Tunnel-Type Codes

Tunnel Code	Description
1	Point-to-Point Tunneling Protocol
2	Layer 2 Forwarding
3	Layer 2 Tunneling Protocol
4	Ascend Tunnel Management Protocol
5	Virtual Tunneling Protocol
6	IP Authentication Header in the Tunnel-Mode
7	IP-in-IP Encapsulation
8	Minimal IP-in-IP Encapsulation
9	IP Encapsulating Security Payload in the Tunnel-Mode
10	Generic Route Encapsulation
11	Bay Dial Virtual Services
12	IP-in-IP Tunneling
13	VLAN

Radius Attribute 79—EAP Message. This is the most important attribute in an 802.1X authentication. EAP packets are encapsulated within this attribute. All other attributes are peripheral to this one. The RADIUS server will utilize a particular EAP-Method to decapsulate and process credential information contained within this attribute. The Authenticator will not process the contents of this attribute, but, rather, will reincapsulate and ship it to the Supplicant. The Supplicant then will use the particular EAP-Method to interpret the contents. Within EAP, this attribute will always be encrypted using a combination of the shared secret and the contents of attribute 80. Whenever an Attribute 79 is an element in a packet, it must be encrypted and an attribute 80 must also be present.

Radius Attribute 80—Message Authenticator. This attribute is a key used by Authenticator or and Authentication Server to ensure the validity of the sender and content of the packet. Message-Authenticator is an HMAC-MD5 [RFC2104] hash of the entire Access-Request packet. It utilizes the shared secret as the key. The specific algorithm is available in RFC 3579.

Radius Attribute 81—Tunnel Private Group ID. Within 802.1X, the value contained is that of a VLANID. The VLANID can be a string value between 1 and 4094.

Radius Attribute 82—Tunnel Assignment ID. This is the address of the Supplicant.

Radius Attribute 87—NAS Port ID. This attribute identifies the port on the Authenticator used to authenticate the Supplicant. This attribute is similar to NAS-Port. NAS-Port is 4 bytes and is a numeric value, whereas this attribute is a string.

Most of the accounting attributes do not have special meaning within 802.1X and the definitions provided in RFC 2865 are sufficient. There are three attributes that are exceptions though: Acct-Terminate-Cause, Acct-Multi-Session-ID, and Acct-Link-Count are useful in troubleshooting to determine what has happened or is happening on an 802.1X session.

Radius Attribute 49—Acct-Terminate-Cause. This attribute contains information on why a session was terminated. Although there are many reasons why a Supplicant might have a session terminated, there are really only two that are specific to 802.1X. The first is the receipt of an EAPOL-Logoff. In this situation, the contents of this attribute will indicate that a User Request causes the session to be terminated. The second is a Re-authentication Failure.

Radius Attribute 50—Acct-Multi-Session-ID. One of the uses of this attribute is to indicate the use of aggregated ports, which, at this time, 802.1X does not permit. However, mobility in a wireless environment potentially can provide this indication if there is a graceful handoff between access points. The recommended structure of the session ID is the concatenation of three elements: Original access point MAC Address, Supplicant MAC Address, and a Timestamp. This would result in a session ID that looks something like: 00-11-B2-23-19-C0-00-1A-C5-14-23-DF-AA-21-23-C0-71-B0-44-C8.

Radius Attribute 51—Acct-Link-Count. This attribute, when used within 802.1X, will contain the number of access points traversed within a particular session.

2.2.4 Dynamic Modification of the Authenticator

The modification of the behavior of the Authenticator, based upon the authentication of a particular Supplicant, is a very important option within 802.1X. RADIUS allows this as shown in the discussion above. The manipulation of one or more attributes will allow the specific application access-lists, definition of session time parameters—including re-authentication—and definition of the VLANID in which to place the Supplicant.

An access-list, a filter, can be applied to a Supplicant through the use of attribute 11. This filter must have been defined previously on the Authenticator. An access-list can be supplied by the RADIUS server through the use of attribute 26. The access-list is fully dynamic in the sense that it is unknown by the Authenticator until authentication is successful and the contents of the attribute are forwarded to the Authenticator.

The combination of attributes 27 and 29, Session Timeout, and Termination Action can be used to determine whether re-authentication will take place, the time between re-authentication, or the total amount of time the session is allowed to exist. If Termination Action is a 0, then re-authentication will not be attempted, and the value contained in Session Timeout is the number of seconds that the session is allowed to remain active. If Termination action is a 1, then re-authentication will occur based upon Session Timeout. The value of that attribute then will be the number of seconds between re-authentications.

Session Timeout can be used in one other way. If it is sent as part of a challenge from the RADIUS server, then the value is the number of seconds for the Authenticator to wait for a response from the Supplicant before executing a retransmission of a request.

The combination of three other attributes will allow the RADIUS server to notify the Authenticator which VLANID is to be used for the authenticated Supplicant. This requires the RADIUS server to be defined as an IETF device, and attributes defined in RFC 2868 regarding the use of Tunnel Protocols are used. The Tunnel-Type, Tunnel-Medium-Type, and the Tunnel-Private-Group-ID must be set in the following manner:

Tunnel-Type = VLAN
Tunnel-Medium-Type = 802
Tunnel-Private-Group-ID = VLANID

The VLANID is a string that identifies the particular VLAN to be used. It should be noted that the specifications require the Tunnel-Private-Group-ID to be a string representing a numeric value, but not all Authenticators, or even RADIUS servers, adhere to the requirement and implement the attribute as an integer. Within Cisco, the VLANID is input as a numeric value, such as 20.

RADIUS functioning as the Authentication Server is vital to a successful implementation of 802.1X. A solid understanding of the attributes is very useful when designing a Port-Based Authentication implementation.

2.3 MANAGEMENT

2.3.1 Section Summary

As of 2004, with the publication of IEEE-802.1X 2004, Management was defined for 802.1X. A completed definition of management information base (MIB) elements was included along with all other considerations for 802.1X. In fact, a large portion of the document is devoted to those definitions. The MIB is pertinent to what we call the Authenticator. Management is divided into five different functions: Configuration, Fault, Performance, Security, and Accounting. The managed objects are then further categorized as pertinent to: Authenticator, Supplicant, or System. The System elements are global and apply to the entire device. Authenticator and Supplicant elements apply to the individual port. The specifications in 2004 require that a port be able to perform both Authenticator functions and Supplicant functions.

The 802.1X MIB is called the IEEE8021-PAE-MIB. The acronym PAE stands for Port Access Entity. As noted, a port can have multiple characteristics and PAE seems to be a neutral term that does not carry the same baggage as Authenticator and Supplicant. Some of the functions of 802.1X are optional and, as such, are not covered by the IEEE MIB. Vendors implementing some optional features, or wishing to enhance reporting, have implemented supplementary MIBs. Cisco is one of those vendors.

The MIB defined in IEEE 802.1X-2004 encompasses three states that can exist on the infrastructure device. The global state, as it pertains to 802.1X functionality and performance, is covered by System MIB elements. The function usually associated with a port—that of being the Authenticator— is covered by Authenticator elements. Finally, the port may actually perform Supplicant functions, and these functions are covered by Supplicant elements.

It should be noted that the MIB only encompasses an infrastructure device. Usually, this is the device housing the Authenticator. It is not really feasible to apply MIB requirements to an end device connecting to a network. This causes the Supplicant and the Authentication Server to be excluded, although the Authentication Server may have a RADIUS MIB. Neither is really a part of the "network" from a network management viewpoint, and each can be implemented on a wide variety of equipment.

A second item to note is that EAP-Methods is not included in the MIB. It is not possible to include any discussion of EAP-Methods in the MIB because the Authenticator is not involved in the selection or manipulation of information regarding EAP-Methods. The Authenticator simply facilitates the exchange of that information between Supplicant and Authentication Server. The content of the exchange is dictated by the EAP-Method utilized. The Authenticator is concerned with two items only: the establishment of connectivity with a Supplicant, and the ultimate success or failure of the authentication as indicated by the Authentication Server. The MIB covers both of those items.

2.3.2 Authenticator, Supplicant, and System

The MIB for 802.1X is divided into three parts: Authenticator, Supplicant, and System. The Authenticator and Supplicant parts are concerned with specific characteristics of an individual port. System is concerned with the entire device that houses one or more ports.

It is very easy to think of a device, a switch, or a wireless access point as being an Authenticator. But that is an oversimplification. In order for the device to participate in 802.1X, all the ports, or the "system," must be enabled for 802.1X; but after that is done, each port status can be manipulated. This will be shown in the discussion of management elements for the Authenticator and Supplicant.

The port on the network device, the Authenticator, can house both Supplicant and Authenticator functions, so any reference to Supplicant signifies that type of function being performed by the port on the network device, and not an end station attaching to the network.

2.3.3 The MIBs

Because it is defined in the specifications, the IEEE MIB encompassed by IEEE 802.1X-2004 is the minimum that must be supported by any vendor. These specifications cover the functions performed by the network infrastructure. This device may be a switch or a wireless access point.

The 802.1X MIB functions in conjunction with MIBs covering other functions performed on the infrastructure device. 802.1X is specifically concerned with connectivity between the Supplicant and the Authenticator—ultimately, the authorization of a port. 802.1X connectivity with an Authentication Server, RADIUS, relies on previously defined mechanisms: AAA and RADIUS definitions. MIB information regarding these mechanisms is not dependent on any implementation of 802.1X, but does support the implementation of 802.1X. MIB information for them is not included in this discussion, but must be considered when implementing a network management solution.

The 802.1X MIB is called the IEEE8021-PAE-MIB and it supports only the mandatory functions in IEEE-802.1X-2004. Optional functions implemented by any vendor must be supported by a vendor specific MIB. Cisco has extended the 802.1X MIB with Cisco-PAE-MIB. This MIB will be included in the discussion of 802.1X Management. The Cisco MIB elements can be identified easily because they all will begin with a "c." An example is "cpaePortMode." As a point of clarification, any reference to a MIB can be assumed to be the IEEE MIB. The Cisco MIB will be identified explicitly.

As identified in an earlier section, the modification of the MIB can significantly alter the behavior of the particular device. In the case of 802.1X, all of the elements defined to be modifiable are configurable parameters and are exclusively related to functions for which the Authenticator is responsible. The elements discussed here will also be considered in the discussion of configuration.

The management elements for the System are described below in Table 2.9.

The SystemAuthControl element indicates whether an 802.1X has been enabled for the device. The elements: Port Number, Protocol Version, and PAE Capabilities are kept for each port on the device. The Port Number is a

Table 2.9 System MIB

| Description | Configuration | | Initialize |
	Read	Set	
SystemAuthControl	X	X	
Port Number	X		X
Protocol version	X		
PAE Capabilities	X		

numeric identifier assigned by the system and is initialized when ports become available for use by the system—usually during bootup. The Protocol Version identifies particular EAPOL capabilities available in different versions. At the time of this writing, only Version 1 is available. The last element, PAE Capabilities, identifies how the port will function—as an Authenticator, as a Supplicant, as both, or neither.

The 802.1X MIB is fairly simple and straightforward in that it has relatively few variables. It is interesting to note, and should be expected, that the majority of the variables are directly controllable through explicit configuration parameters. Elements shown in the tables for the Authenticator and Supplicant are directly related to specific ports.

The Authenticator elements are described in Table 2.10. This table indicates which attributes are "read-only," which can be set through configuration or direct access to the MIB, which pertain to Authenticator functions, which relate to Supplicant functions, and which are available specifically for diagnostic functions. The variables marked in the Statistics column are read-only and most will be available through the use of "show" commands on Cisco appliances.

Several of the elements in the MIB indicate "backend" as part of their name. There are two state machines being executed when a device is an Authenticator. They are the Authenticator PAE and the backend state machines. This is because the Authenticator is conducting two discrete conversations. One is with the Supplicant, which is conducted with the device attempting to authenticate, and the other is with the backend, which is conducted with the Authentication Server. The status of these state machines is shown in Table 2.11.

Most of the values in the table are self-explanatory. There are two in the Authenticator PAE machine that are not: Force_Auth and Force Unauth. Briefly, the specifications require that every port should be able to be placed into one of three states. The port can be explicitly Authorized, Unauthorized, or not forced in either direction. The state is explicitly identified in the element, AuthControlledPortControl, with the values of ForceAuthorized, ForceUnauthorized, and Auto.

As discussed in an earlier section, it is possible to "nudge" a Supplicant awake. This process utilizes a "magic packet" which the Supplicant recognizes as a request for it to become active. This process only works if that packet is allowed through the Authenticator while the port is in an Unauthorized state. Two elements define the direction in which traffic is controlled—meaning, it is allowed. These elements are AdminControlledDirections and OperControlledDirections. If the direction is set to "Both" then no traffic is allowed in either direction. If the value is "In" then traffic from the Supplicant is controlled and certain traffic to the Supplicant is allowed. Additional details regarding this function are included in the section on Configuration.

Table 2.10 Authenticator Management Elements

| Description | Configuration | | Statistics | | Diagnostics |
	Read	Set	Authen-ticator	Session	
Port Number	X	X	X	X	X
Authenticator PAE State	X				
Backend Authentication State	X				
AdminControlledDirections	X	X			
OperControlledDirections	X				
AuthControlledPortControl	X	X			
AuthControlledPortStatus	X				
quietPeriod	X	X			
serverTimeout	X	X			
reAuthPeriod	X	X			
KeyTransmissionEnabled	X	X			
suppTimeout		X			
reAuthEnabled		X			
EAPOL frames received			X		
EAPOL frames transmitted			X		
EAPOL Start frames received			X		
EAPOL Logoff frames received			X		
EAP Resp/ID frames received			X		
EAP Response frames received			X		
EAP Initial Request frames transmitted			X		
EAP Request frames transmitted			X		
Invalid EAPOL frames received			X		
EAP length error frames received			X		
Last EAPOL frame version			X		
Last EAPOL frame source			X		
authEntersConnecting					X
authEAPLogoffsWhileConnecting					X
authEntersAuthenticating					X
authAuthSuccessWhileAuthenticating					X
authAuthTimeoutsWhileAuthenticating					X
authAuthFailWhileAuthenticating					X

(continued)

Table 2.10   Continued

Description	Configuration Read	Configuration Set	Statistics Authenticator	Statistics Session	Diagnostics
authAuthEapStartsWhi-leAuthenticating					X
authAuthEapLogoffWhi-leAuthenticating					X
authAuthReauthsWhileAuthenticated					X
authAuthEapStartsWhi-leAuthenticated					X
authAuthEapLogoffWhi-leAuthenticated					X
backendResponses					X
backendAccessChallenges					X
backendOtherRequestsToSupplicant					X
backendAuthSuccesses					X
backendAuthFails					X
Session Octets received				X	
Session Octets transmitted				X	
Session Frames received				X	
Session Frames transmitted				X	
Session Identifier				X	
Session Authentication Method				X	
Session Time				X	
Session-Terminate-Cause				X	

Table 2.11   Authenticator State Machine Values

Value	Authenticator PAE	Backend
1	Initialize	Request
2	Disconnected	Response
3	Connecting	Success
4	Authenticating	Fail
5	Authenticated	Timeout
6	Aborting	Idle
7	Held	Initialize
8	Force_Auth	Ignore
9	Force_Unauth	
10	Restart	

One other variable that should be discussed is KeyTransmissionEnabled. This element enables the transmission of key information between the Authenticator and the Supplicant once authentication has been completed. Usually, the key information is used then to encrypt subsequent transmissions. Currently, this is used only in wireless environments. This particular field relates specifically to EAPOL frame Type 3—EAPOL-Key.

The elements that can be set are consistent with configuration capabilities that will be discussed in a subsequent section. There are a significant number of Statistical and Diagnostic elements. The names of these values are relatively self-explanatory in terms of content.

Back in the first section of this chapter, it was identified that a particular port could be both a Supplicant and an Authenticator. Why? One use for this is in a potential situation where two network devices, that presumably would be Authenticators, must mutually authenticate each other. This situation would allow a switch connected to a trunk to require that the other switch at the end of the trunk be authenticated prior to the establishment of any communication. This would require each switch to act as an Authenticator

Table 2.12 Supplicant Elements

Description	Configuration		Statistics
	Read	Set	
Port Number	X	X	X
Supplicant PAE State	X		
HeldPeriod	X	X	
AuthPeriod	X	X	
StartPeriod	X	X	
MaxStart	X	X	
SuppControlledPortStatus	X		
Backend Supplicant Status	X		
Supplicant Access Control With Authenticator	X	X	
EAPOL frames received			X
EAPOL frames transmitted			X
EAPOL Logoff frames transmitted			X
EAP Resp/Id frames transmitted			X
EAP Response frames transmitted			X
EAP Req/Id frames received			X
EAP Request frames received			X
Invalid EAPOL frames received			X
EAP length error frames received			X
Last EAPOL frame version			X
Last EAPOL frame source			X

and a Supplicant because of the bi-directional nature of the authentication. Thus, a MIB needs to exist that provides elements to be used in that type of process. The Supplicant MIB is described below in Table 2.12.

As with the Authenticator, there are elements that identify the state of the Supplicant. Those elements are the Supplicant PAE State and the Backend Authentication State. The possible Supplicant values for the state machines are shown below in Table 2.13.

One element in the MIB associated with the Supplicant is not intuitively obvious: Supplicant Access Control With Authenticator. This particular variable is used to modify the behavior of the Supplicant/Authenticator regarding a second authentication (bi-directional) when the first authentication was a mutual authentication (uni-directional). Essentially, this is what has been published to explain the rationale. To be honest, even after having it explained, it is less than clear.

The IEEE MIB was originally developed to support IEEE-802.1X 2001 definitions. The actual definitions appear in the IEEE-802.1X 2004 document and encompass the required functions defined therein. There are several optional functions identified in the specifications, and, if implemented, they must be covered in MIBs specific to that implementation. Cisco has opted to implement some of the optional functions and has issued a MIB to cover them. Table 2.14 identifies elements in the Cisco MIB. Again, these elements are supplementary to the IEEE MIB.

The significant entries in the Cisco extension relate to how many hosts may be authenticated on a given port and what happens to unauthenticated Supplicants. Both of these items are allowed by the current specifications, but are not required. The Cisco MIB extension is quite new and is not available in all IOS releases or on all models of equipment. A great deal of care must be exercised when planning to use these functions. That situation will be discussed in more detail in a subsequent section on Configuration.

Table 2.13   Supplicant State Machine Values

Value	Supplicant PAE	Backend
1	Disconnected	Initialize
2	Logoff	Idle
3	Connecting	Request
4	Authenticating	Response
5	Authenticated	Receive
6	Unused	Fail
7	Held	Success
8	Restart	Timeout
9	S_Force_Auth	
10	S_Force_Unauth	

Table 2.14 Cisco MIB Elements

Element	Configurable
CpaeMultipleHost	Yes
CpaePortMode	Yes
CpaeGuestVlanId	Yes
CpaeInGuestVlan	No
cpaeShutdownTimeoutEnabled	Yes
cpaeGuestVlanNumber	Yes
cpaeRadiusAccountingEnabled	Yes
CpaeUserGroupTable	No
CpaeUserGroupEntry	No
CpaeUserGroupName	No
cpaeUserGroupUserIndex	No
cpaeUserGroupUserName	No
cpaeUserGroupUserAddrType	No
cpaeUserGroupUserAddr	No
cpaeUserGroupUserInterface	No
cpaeUserGroupUserVlan	No

The specific elements that are of significant interest in the Cisco MIB are discussed below.

cpaeMultipleHost—This element indicates whether or not more than one Supplicant is allowed to connect to a specific port. This element does not indicate how many hosts may connect.

cpaePortMode—This element is the one that identifies how a port will allow a number of hosts to connect to a single port. There are three possible values: single host, multi-host, and multi-host with multiple authentications. Single host mode is what the name implies—only one mac-address is allowed on the port. Multi-host allows more than one host on the port. The port assumes the VLAN of the last Supplicant with a successful authentication. Multi-host with multiple authentications interacts with port security features to restrict host connectivity.

cpaeGuestVlanId—This element identifies the VLANID associated with a port that has a Guest VLAN configured. The configuration of the Guest VLAN for IOS and CATOS is discussed in a later section.

cpaeInGuestVlan—This element indicates whether or not the port is in Guest VLAN mode. If the device housing the port allows multiple authentications, or multiple Guest VLANs, then this element has no meaning.

That is a relatively brief discussion of specific management available in 802.1X. The only third party MIB presented is the Cisco-PAE-MIB. If other vendor equipment is implemented, then a MIB specific to that implementation should be available and have similar elements.

An explanation of every element is imbedded in the actual MIB itself. In some cases the explanation is of limited help, but it is there. In most cases the Network Management application implemented will provide a better discussion of the use of a particular element. Ultimately, there may be several MIBs that are required to fully "manage" the implementation of 802.1X. Certainly the IEEE MIB is essential along with standard MIBs for AAA and RADIUS. There also may be several proprietary MIBs for vendor implementations of EAP-Method and optional 802.1X functions.

2.4 SECURITY CONCERNS

2.4.1 Chapter Summary

It is ironic that something intended to provide Port-Based Authentication and restrict access to authenticated devices is, in itself, a source of security concerns. But 802.1X does have issues with security. There are at least three places that it can be attacked: the Supplicant, the Authenticator, and the Authentication Server. Accordingly, there are three conversations to be concerned with: the Supplicant/Authenticator, the Authenticator/Authentication Server, and the Supplicant/Authentication Server.

The assumption for port-based authentication within EAP is that the physical link between the Supplicant and the Authenticator is secured. For all practical purposes, 802.1X is implemented as Ethernet and Wireless LANs. As discussed previously, neither switched Ethernet nor Wireless is truly a point-to-point system. Wireless is a totally shared environment, and it is fairly easy to insert a shared hub between a Supplicant and an Authenticator in a switched Ethernet environment. This situation allows traffic between Supplicant and Authenticator to be susceptible to capture and inspection.

Traffic capture—snooping—is only one of the susceptibilities in an 802.1X implementation. Frequently an attack is intended only to disrupt the connection rather than capture traffic. The lock-step process implemented is a simple method that provides continuity in a conversation. But its simplicity also makes it vulnerable to various Denial Of Service attacks. Depending upon where these attacks occur in the course of an authentication, they might also influence the selection of an EAP-Method. In this case, the intention is to increase the probability that a weak encryption method will be selected—thus making it easier to gain access to authentication credentials.

Implementation of a Port-Based Authentication system such as 802.1X does not construct a complete security environment. At the very least, physical security is an essential supplement. Both of the situations discussed above require that an attacker be able to have access to an 802.1X conversation. Just as 802.1X reduces the likelihood of an unauthorized user being able to successfully connect to a network, stringent physical security virtually can ensure that a "clean" authentication occurs between a Supplicant and an Authenticator.

2.4.2 Types of Attacks Identified in the Specifications

RFC 3748 is the most current specification for EAP and it specifically identifies several types of attacks that might be mounted. These include:

- Snooping traffic to obtain user identities. Remember that the initial response to a Request Identity is sent in the clear. This could provide a valid Username to an attacker.
- EAP packets themselves could be spoofed in an attempt to gain additional information regarding the network and or specific user.
- Replaying Success or Failure packets can be used to perform a denial of service attack. Also, modifying the Identifier field, or simply replaying packets out of sequence, could disrupt the Authentication process.
- Snooping the authentication of a user could provide information that would be susceptible to an offline dictionary attack. Also, if the EAP-Method implemented utilizes weak keys it might be possible to derive the key.
- A man-in-the-middle attack could be used to convince a user to attach to an untrusted network.
- Because EAP-Method is negotiable, it is possible to influence the selection of a weaker method than is optimal.

The specifications for 802.1X, itself, found in IEEE 802.1X-2004, do not identify security risks in the same way as the specifications for EAP. One section of the specifications identifies certain risks involved with MIB access. The concern is that there is no real guarantee that SNMPV1 can provide sufficient security for access to sensitive MIB elements.

2.4.3 EAPOL Vulnerability

EAPOL is an unsecured protocol in and of itself. In a wireless environment, a variety of encryption methods can be implemented that will provide a degree of protection for EAPOL exchanges. This is not the case in a wired environment. There are several issues with unencrypted connections, wired or wireless, where an EAPOL exchange occurs.

The specifications for 802.1X detail the use of an EAPOL-Start frame. This frame causes the Authenticator to initiate the authentication process. However, this frame is not protected. Nor can the issuer be realistically authenticated at the time it is received. Therefore this frame could be spoofed. The content of the Start frame is fairly innocuous, but it causes the process to be initiated or reinitiated. The issuance of a large number of these frames could disrupt legitimate traffic, resulting in a type of Denial of Service.

The same type of scenario exists for EAPOL-Logoff frames. This frame causes the Authenticator to place the port in an unauthenticated state. The EAPOL-Logoff is directed toward the group address of the Authenticator and should contain the legitimate MAC address of the Supplicant. The Authenticator should verify that the MAC address is one that is legitimately authenticated on the network. But remember the use of the Ethernet Group Address in 802.1X. Under "normal" circumstances, the group address in a packet invokes the 802.1X process. Simply flooding a link with packets using that address will require that the packet be given to 802.1X for some form of processing. The packet subsequently may be discarded, but it will impact available resources on the device. It is also possible for the intruder then to disrupt legitimate traffic through the issuance of EAPOL-Logoff frames. Even checking the MAC address is minimally effective because it is fairly easy for an intruder with access to the link, wired or wireless, to spoof a MAC address.

In a wireless environment, it is possible for an intruder to issue frames indicating failure of the link or send disassociate frames to the Supplicant. This mechanism is used by some wireless products to disrupt connections to a rogue access point. This would have similar results to those described for EAPOL-Start and EAPOL-Logoff. The intent would be the disruption of service for one or more users, rather than the theft of information. Of course, if an intruder has access to a link and has the capability of forcing a user to re-authenticate, he then would have access potentially to frames issued during the authentication process. Depending upon the encryption and the EAP-Method employed, the attacker actually might be able to obtain credentials to enter the network.

It is interesting to note that Cisco IP phones can now spoof the EAPOL-Start and EAPOL-Logoff frames on behalf of devices attached to them. The phone monitors the status of the link port used by the Supplicant, then sends an EAPOL-Start or Logoff frame to the Authenticator. This is necessary because the Authenticator cannot ascertain the status of this port as it is "hidden" behind the phone. Phones that cannot do this leave the port on the Authenticator in a vulnerable state. The use of hubs creates a similar risk. Both of these scenarios are explored in much greater detail in the next section of the book.

As discussed earlier, 802.1X can be susceptible to Denial Of Service attacks at the link level. There does not seem to be any way around this given the current definitions. There are some configuration mechanisms that will help mitigate those types of attacks. 802.1X is usually implemented to allow a single MAC address on a port by default. Should a second address be recognized, then all traffic from that address is discarded. Not allowing more than a single MAC on a port is a good design decision, as well. It helps reduce the potential for successful attacks on the Supplicant/Authenticator Link.

One concern about the connection between the Supplicant and the Authenticator is that there is no guarantee of the authenticity of the partners. None of the protocols actually provide a mechanism by which identity can be validated and maintained during the authentication process. If there were some form of identity validation, many of the security issues enumerated would be resolved. But that is somewhat of an oxymoron. How can you pre-establish identity for an authentication process when that is the intended purpose of the process in the first place?

2.4.4   RADIUS Vulnerability

The link between Supplicant and Authenticator is susceptible to certain attacks. The same holds true to a more limited extent for the link between the Authenticator and the backend Authentication Server. This link is less susceptible because the backend is a Radius server. The Radius server and the Authenticator share a secret password and perform mutual authentication of each other. Snooping conversations, therefore, have limited use.

The exchange between the Authentication Server and the Authenticator provides multiple levels of security. As noted, the first level is the required mutual authentication of the partners. In the previous section on RADIUS, the encryption of EAP-Data using the shared secret provides the second level. The third level is the encryption method implemented in the EAP-Method itself. The combination of these three layers makes the decryption of captured packets difficult.

The specifications for EAP do not require the use of a backend Authentication Server. Furthermore, the specifications only require a mandatory implementation of three EAP-Methods. It is possible to implement these methods on an Authenticator and avoid the use of an Authentication Server entirely. This has been extended to other methods as well and is implemented to provide a fast roaming process for wireless. The caching of credentials allows the access point to avoid the lengthy process of a full re-authentication when physical movement causes a new association to occur. The actual implementation of wireless affects how easily this may or may not be accomplished. A centralized system of control over multiple access points makes caching and fast roaming potentially a little easier. This subject will be covered in more detail later when discussing wireless.

The topology of not using a backend strengthens the authentication process by ensuring that the Authenticator is fully aware of the authentication status. The use of EAP-TLS in this scenario would cause the Supplicant and the combined Authenticator and Authentication Server to authenticate each other.

The Authenticator/Authentication Server connection is more difficult to protect because it is not necessarily a single piece of wire and therefore it is not necessarily a Link-Layer connection. This allows for a wider variety of attacks. However, the connectivity required by RADIUS does provide a degree of protection. And, as discussed above, it is possible to eliminate the Authentication Server in some circumstances.

Initial arguments against the incorporation of the backend into the Authenticator were mainly performance and cost-based. It requires additional processing capability for the Authenticator to perform the authentication function, rather than to act simply as a pass-through device. Potentially, a significant amount of storage or processing is required in this situation. Thus, the backend Authentication Server is a reality even if it is not required. As indicated, this creates its own set of security issues. Additionally, there are some significant design issues that must be taken into account. Some of these issues will be addressed in the third chapter of this book: Design, Implementation, and Troubleshooting.

There are specific issues regarding RADIUS that should be enumerated. Several of the vulnerabilities are the same as those between the Supplicant and Authenticator. Many of the issues that exist in protecting a conversation between those entities exist in the conversation between Authenticator and RADIUS. Denial of Service and replay attacks are obvious possibilities. A man-in-the-middle attack is mitigated somewhat by the required mutual authentication of server and Authenticator and the encryption of EAP Data.

Because the Authenticator sits between the Supplicant and the Authentication Server, there is a built-in man-in-the-middle. EAP requires that the RADIUS Message Authenticator attribute be used to authenticate all messages between the Supplicant and the Authentication Server. This attribute was briefly mentioned in the section on RADIUS. The content of this message is an MD5 hash of the entire message, with the shared secret being the key. The use of this attribute ensures that messages between the Authentication Server and the Authenticator have not been hijacked.

2.4.5 EAP-Method Vulnerability

Contrary to the heading, this section is not going to discuss vulnerabilities of particular methods in detail. Instead, I will discuss vulnerabilities surrounding EAP-Methods as a generic topic.

In an earlier section, the situation of the Authenticator not having complete knowledge about the Supplicant/Authentication Server conversation was shown to cause problems. That situation also exists in reverse to a certain extent. Neither the Supplicant nor the Authentication Server can have an absolute guarantee that the information received is actually from the other. The role the Authenticator plays as an insulator between the two also creates certain vulnerabilities. An attacker that can successfully spoof being an Authenticator can create a connection that will further his motives.

Assuming the Authenticator is legitimate, this leaves the Supplicant/ Authentication Server connection. This is a logical connection based upon the two physical connections through the Authenticator. The weakness of this connection really involves the EAP-Method chosen for the connection. Some Methods are so trusting that the credential exchanges are sent as clear text or are reversibly encrypted. EAP-MD5, which is a mandatory method, is the primary example of this. Exchanging credentials in clear text makes it simple for an intruder to be able to capture the exchange and assume a legitimate identity.

There are several certificate-based or "tunneling" Methods that are intended to protect credential exchanges. Each has its own set of weaknesses and vulnerabilities. The actual selection of a Method has as much to do with the impact on the organization as it does with the level of security provided. The current specifications for EAP in RFC 3748 require that proposed EAP-Methods identify security claims so that a potential implementer can make a clear evaluation of impact.

The following is a summary of the security claim discussion now required:

- A definition of the mechanism(s) used for authentication;
- A specific statement of the claimed security based upon the mechanism implemented;
- If keys are implemented,
  □ An estimate of the strength of the key;
  □ A reference to the key hierarchy specification, and;
- A definition of possible vulnerabilities for which protection is not claimed.

The specifications for EAP include a discussion of several types of vulnerabilities and what must—and should—be done regarding each type of attack. The first type discussed is the "man-in-the-middle" attack. Of specific concern is tunneling EAP within another protocol that does not include peer authentication. This enables a rogue Authenticator to send tunneled EAP messages to the Authentication Server. In this scenario, the rogue Authenticator could actually obtain the key. This would allow it to establish an awareness of the authentication process and subsequent exchanges after the port has been put into an authenticated state. Thus, while tunnels are a legitimate way to ensure privacy, the way they might be utilized within some EAP-Methods does allow for this type of vulnerability.

This leads to the second vulnerability—that of packet content modification. If the header of EAP packets is unprotected, an attacker could modify any of the data elements: Code, Identity, or Length. Usually, this would result in a form of DOS attack. The specifications recommend mutual authentication and key derivation, integrity, and replay protection within a strong cyphersuite to mitigate this type of attack. Moreover, the specifications recommend that the header be protected—and not just the EAP-Method data. It is also desirable to extend the protection defined for the EAP-Method to those EAP packets not strictly covered by the method: Identity, Notification, and NAK.

Dictionary Attacks are a common concern because it is possible to capture the exchanges in an authentication. These are of particular concern to EAP-Methods that do not utilize tunnels or certificates, such as EAP-MD5 and MS-CHAPV1. Newer methods usually provide a stronger protection against this type of attack.

As stated earlier, in some methods, such as EAP-MD5, the Supplicant does not authenticate the Authenticator. This exposes the Supplicant to a rogue Authenticator posing as a legitimate device. Obviously, this opens up the possibility that a man-in-the-middle might influence exchanges between a Supplicant and an Authenticator. Again, it should be emphasized that EAP does not require authentication between Supplicant and Authenticator.

Another item that has already been discussed, but is included specifically in RFC 3748, is Negotiation attacks. This is where the Authenticator and the Supplicant are convinced to negotiate a less secure EAP-Method than the one they would mutually prefer. The specifications recommend that the Supplicant not be given the choice of negotiation and allow one—and only one—EAP-Method to be selected. In cases where the Supplicant needs to connect utilizing a different method in different situations, the specifications recommend the use of multiple identities with only one method associated with each identity.

If an EAP-Method utilizes keys, the specifications require that a minimum of 64 octets be used in the derivation of the key. It is required in a situation where the EAP-Method utilizes keys, that it must implement mutual authentication between the Supplicant and the Authentication Server.

In summary, EAP/802.1X has vulnerabilities. The various EAP-Methods have vulnerabilities. Most of the vulnerabilities can be mitigated through judicious design, and some vulnerabilities can be mitigated through prudent implementation such as physical control of wiring and Authenticators. Some of the issues that 802.1X was intended to resolve still remain, but have become much more difficult for an intruder to exploit. All in all, 802.1X is a significant improvement in the realm of securing the environment.

2.5   CONFIGURING 802.1X

2.5.1   Section Summary

All three of the participating 802.1X entities require configuration and they must be configured in a fashion that allows them to function as a whole system. If any one of the three is misconfigured, then the expected results will not happen.

The primary component that is configured in the 802.1X Port-Based Authentication process is the Authenticator. It must be configured for the desired functionality to be implemented for conversations with both a Supplicant and the Authentication Server. Because the actual exchange of credentials is between the Supplicant and the Authentication Server, no configuration of the EAP-Method implemented is available on the Authenticator. The configuration of 802.1X is supported by the MIB implemented. The MIBs were discussed in detail in the previous section on Management. As was noted in that chapter, there are three functions that are configurable on the Authenticator: the system wide functions, and the Authenticator and Supplicant functionality on specific ports.

The Authenticator must also be configured to converse with a RADIUS server functioning as the Authentication Server. This requires the configuration of an IP address for at least one RADIUS server and the configuration of the shared secret password. This is accomplished through the configuration of RADIUS and AAA parameters.

Configuration of the RADIUS server must similarly include the address of the Authenticator and the shared secret. This is necessary for the two devices to establish a connection. There are a large number of additional parameters in RADIUS that are available for use in an authentication. The particular EAP-Method chosen will make use of these parameters as necessary. As discussed in Radius, there are RADIUS parameters that support the dynamic assignment of VLANs or access lists to a port housing an authenticated Supplicant.

Configuration of the Supplicant really consists of a maximum of four items. The first is enabling 802.1X to be functional on the device. The second is specifying whether or not the Supplicant is active or passive—specifically, whether or not the Supplicant will issue an EAPOL-Start and, potentially, an EAPOL-Logoff. The third item is the configuration of wireless drivers in some situations. The last item that must be configured is the particular EAP-Method to be used for authentication. The configuration of the EAP-Method must be synchronized to the configuration of the user on RADIUS. The first three items that are configurable on the Supplicant are independent of configurations on the Authenticator or RADIUS.

2.5.2 Authenticator Configuration

The specific configuration examples provided in this chapter are Cisco-centric. Where reasonable, both IOS and CATOS commands are explored. Both wired and wireless situations are included, and both Aironet and Airespace are considered for wireless.

2.5.2.1 802.1X Parameters

Configuring the Authenticator for 802.1X is straightforward because the actual number of parameters is pretty small. It is important to understand that there are variations in capabilities based upon the age of the operating system. There have been two releases of the specifications for 802.1X—in 2001 and 2004. The basic capabilities remain the same, but functionality has been expanded in the later release. This means that most operating system releases available at the time of this writing only provide the minimum functionality described in the earlier release. Some of the variations will be discussed, but a comparison of operating systems is not the intent here. Care must be exercised in selecting a particular operating system when the functionality identified in the 2004 release is desired.

Earlier, it was mentioned that 802.1X must be enabled for an entire System in addition to enabling it on a port. A global configuration parameter is available in IOS, both for Aironet and switches, which causes this to occur. 802.1X is enabled in Airespace by default.

dot1x system-auth-control

In earlier versions, this is the only 802.1X command available in the global configuration. If this line is present in a configuration, then 802.1X is enabled for the device. If it is not present, then 802.1X is not enabled. This parameter sets the MIB element SystemAuthControl.

This same command is available in CATOS:

set dot1x system-auth-control enable.

In more recent operating systems, it is possible to allow a device with a Supplicant that cannot be authenticated to be placed into a Guest VLAN. This capability becomes more useful as 802.1X becomes more prevalent. Historically, Supplicants that could not be authenticated were not allowed to enter the network. This meant that "guests" that had 802.1X enabled were in a very awkward situation. Either 802.1X needed to be disabled on their machine, or they needed to be included as a valid member on the Authentication Server. Neither of the alternatives are attractive. The global command in IOS to allow a nonauthenticated Supplicant to be placed into a Guest VLAN is:

dot1x guest-vlan supplicant.

Once 802.1X is enabled globally, it must be enabled explicitly on each port that will utilize it. There are three states in which a port can be placed. It can be forced into an Authorized state or an Unauthorized state, or it can be placed in an Auto state. The forced authorized state is the normal state when a port has not been enabled for 802.1X. The Auto state requires that a Supplicant perform authentication. The forced states do not cause the 802.1X authorization process to be invoked. Enabling a port to be Auto is accomplished in IOS by configuring an interface with the following command:

dot1x port-control auto.

The same function is performed in CAT-OS with the following command:

set port dot1x <mod/port> port-control auto.

It is interesting that frequently in IOS a port is automatically placed in a state where trunking is desirable. A port that participates in 802.1X cannot participate in trunking. The following is an example of an IOS configuration with the port in a desirable mode:

Interface FastEthernet0/16
switchport access vlan 100
switchport mode dynamic desirable
no ip address.

The following error will occur if a port is left in a desirable mode when 802.1X is applied:

Test8021X(config-if)#dot1x port-control auto.
Command rejected: Dynamic mode enabled on one or more ports.
Dot1x is supported only on Ethernet interfaces configured in Access, Routed, or private-vlan Host Mode.

The port needs to be explicitly identified as an access port by using the following command: switchport mode access.
Identifying the VLAN in which the port is to reside while in an authorized state is not exclusively an 802.1X command, it is usual within 802.1X as well. It is possible not to identify the VLAN explicitly within the port configuration and to rely solely on RADIUS to supply the VLAN appropriate for an authorized user. Note that in some very early versions of IOS, pre 12.1(14) EA1, the VLAN was required to be explicitly identified in the manner shown below. The commands below are the customary methods of setting the authorized VLAN in IOS and CATOS respectively:

switchport access vlan <vlanid>
set vlan <vlanid> <mod/port>

The default state for a port enabled to participate in 802.1X allows a single MAC address to be active on the port. This is modifiable through the use of the following commands in IOS and CATOS respectively:

dot1x host-mode multi-host

set port dot1x <mod/port> multiple-host enable

This command allows more than one MAC address to be active on an 802.1X enabled port. Control of the number of MAC addresses, or even the address itself, must be accomplished through configuration of port security.

Nonetheless, the port will be associated with only one VLAN no matter how many MAC addresses are using it. The port will be placed in the VLAN associated with the last MAC address to have gone through the authentication process. Thus, it could be a Guest VLAN or a dynamic VLAN from the Authentication Server, or the configured access VLAN, or even no VLAN at all. This is not a configuration option to be used lightly.

In CATOS, there is an associated configuration command that will require that each MAC address go through the Authentication process if the multiple-host mode is enabled:

set port dot1x <mod/port> multiple-authentication enable

Although each host is authenticated, only one VLAN is associated with the port and it happens to be the one that was the last valid authentication.

The Guest VLAN is configurable on a port by port basis. This must be a VLAN that is defined on the Authenticator, and any access control must be associated with the VLAN because it cannot be applied dynamically. Only upon a successful authentication can a VLAN or access list be applied dynamically. The commands used to configure this option are shown below for IOS and CATOS:

dot1x guest-vlan <vlanid>
set port dot1x <mod/port> guest-vlan <vlanid>

In the Cisco wireless environments of Aironet and Airespace, no capability for assignment of a Guest VLAN exists. Access to a Guest VLAN is accomplished through the configuration of a separate SSID.

In some recent versions of IOS, there is an interface-based command that allows the use of Wake-on-LAN (WoL) functionality. The WoL relies on a magic packet from inside the network that is allowed to traverse a nonauthorized port toward the Supplicant to awaken it. The Supplicant then must participate in the authentication process to cause the port to be authorized and allow traffic to flow back into the network. The port is placed in what is called a unidirectional state, meaning that all traffic is blocked from the Supplicant, but the magic packet can flow from the network. This capability is useless in a wireless environment. The command is shown for both IOS and CATOS:

dot1x controlled-direction in
set port dot1x <mod/port> port-control-direction in

Note that in some cases controlling the direction of the port conflicts with the establishment of a Guest VLAN. They can be mutually exclusive configurations.

Essentially this command causes Spanning-Tree to be placed in a forwarding state. When a magic packet is received, the port begins to control traffic in both directions for five minutes. If no EAPOL traffic is received, the port is returned to a unidirectional state awaiting either another magic packet or for the Supplicant to awaken and begin the authentication process.

Several times it has been indicated that a particular packet will be reissued. This is the case when attempting to contact the Supplicant and the Authentication Server. The number of attempts to make is configurable. In IOS, this is configurable on a perport basis and in CATOS it is a global parameter. This parameter controls the number of retries to make in any situation. The same parameter applies to the number of retries when contacting either the Supplicant or the Authentication Server:

```
dot1x max-req <number>
set dot1x max-req <number>
```

A retry is intrinsically tied to a timer that signals that a reissue of a particular packet is required. In 802.1X there are various timers that are configurable. These relate to both Authentication Server and Supplicant responses. When one of the timers expires, the Authenticator will reissue the packet it had originally sent in an attempt to contact the other entity. The Supplicant timeout defaults to 30 seconds, so after 30 seconds without a response, the Authenticator will attempt to contact the Supplicant. This will occur up to the number coded for max-req. Increasing the number of retries or the length of time between retries can have a significant impact on the perception of timeliness by a user. As an example, assume that max-req is set to four and the Supplicant timeout is set to 45 seconds. When a guest attempts to connect and the computer does not have a Supplicant coded, it will take 180 seconds before the port is authorized into a Guest VLAN. This is three minutes of real time that a person is sitting in front of a computer without any perceivable activity. And that is a very long time.

Unlike the number of attempts to retry making contact, the timers used are allocated to both the Supplicant and the Authentication Server. The configuration commands for these timers are shown for both IOS and CATOS:

```
dot1x timeout server-timeout <seconds>
dot1x timeout supp-timeout <seconds>
set dot1x server-timeout <seconds>
set dot1x supp-timeout <seconds>
```

Another interface timer that is available in IOS on a port basis, but only globally in CATOS, is the quiet period. This timer identifies the length of time to wait before initiating another authentication attempt following an unsuccessful one. The quiet period comes into play when the port has not been placed in an authenticated state and all attempts have resulted in a failed authentication. The failure could be due to lack of a Supplicant, the inability to access an Authentication Server, or a failure in exchange of credentials. The reason does not matter; only the fact that the port is active, but has not been successfully authenticated. The command to set the quiet period is:

    dot1x timeout quiet-period <seconds>
    set dot1x quiet-period <seconds>

The final item that is configurable is Re-authentication. There are several parameters that can be set relating to this process. The first is whether or not re-authentication will take place. By default, it does not occur. The configuration commands to enable it for IOS and CATOS are:

    dot1x re-authentication
    set port dot1x <mod/port> re-authentication enable

A timer is also configurable that identifies when re-authentication should take place. The actual command is:

    dot1x timeout reauth-period <seconds>
    set dot1x reauth-period <seconds>

Just as with other timers and retry parameters like those for Supplicant and Server timeouts, the coding of re-authentication parameters must be carefully considered. The re-authentication is a two-edged sword so to speak. On the one hand, it is not desirable to leave the port available in an authenticated state, which is what might happen if some versions of IPT are implemented. On the other hand, too frequent re-authentication can have deleterious effects on the network—or even the Authentication Server.

There is a parameter available in CATOS that is not configurable in IOS. It is possible to identify the amount of time that an authorized session is allowed to be active. This parameter is configurable on a RADIUS server and is given to the Authenticator upon successful authentication. Upon expiration of this timer, the port is placed in an unauthorized state. The timeout capability is implemented in both IOS and CATOS, but only in CATOS is the parameter configurable on the Authenticator. As stated above, it is downloadable on a per-user-basis from RADIUS. The command is:

    set port dot1x <mod/port> shutdown-timeout enable

Table 2.15   IOS Commands for 802.1X

Command	Parameter	Parameter	Parameter	Default Value
		Global		
dot1x	system-auth-control			disabled
	guest-vlan-supplicant			disabled
		Interface		
dot1x	default			
	guest-vlan	vlan-number		none
	host-mode	single-host		enabled
		multi-host		disabled
	max-req	number between 1 and 10		2
	port-control	auto		disabled
		force-authorized		disabled
		force-unauthorized		enabled
	re-authentication			disabled
	timeout	quite-period	seconds (1–65535)	60
		reauth-period	seconds (1–65535)	3600
		server-timeout	seconds (1–65535)	30
		supp-timeout	seconds (1–65535)	30
		tx-timeout	seconds (1–65535)	30
	control-direction	in		disabled
		both		enabled

These are the essential commands available to configure 802.1X in a Cisco LAN environment. Similar commands are available from different manufacturers. Table 2.15 and Table 2.16 provide a summary of configuration commands and parameters available in IOS and CATOS.

Many of the parameters identified for IOS are available in Aironet configurations where the access point has been enabled for IOS. In some cases, parameters just do not apply, such as Guest VLAN parameters, and are not available. Most timeouts can be configured in a wired and wireless environment. Of course, there are a number of configuration parameters in a wireless environment that are not found in a wired one. Some of these parameters are peripherally related to 802.1X and will be discussed in the sections focusing on wireless.

Table 2.16   CATOS Commands for 802.1X

Command	Parameter	Parameter	Default Value
	Global		
dot1x	system-auth-control	*enable|disable*	disabled
	quite-period	*seconds (1–65535)*	60
	reauth-period	*seconds (1–65535)*	3600
	server-timeout	*seconds (1–65535)*	30
	supp-timeout	*seconds (1–65535)*	30
	tx-timeout	*seconds (1–65535)*	30
	shutdown-timeout	*seconds (0–65535)*	0
	Interface		
port dot1x <mod/port>	guest-vlan	*vlan number*	
	multiple-authentication	*enable|disable*	disabled
	multiple-host	*enable|disable*	disabled
	port-control	*enable|disable*	disabled
	re-authentication	*enable|disable*	disabled
	initialize		
	re-authenticate		

2.5.2.2   Additional Authenticator Configuration—AAA and RADIUS

In previous sections, it has been noted that the total authentication process involves three sub-processes: 802.1X, Radius, and AAA. Thus, configuration of both RADIUS and AAA is required. This book is not going to go into detailed discussion regarding all of the available parameters for either process, but will identify the minimum required to support 802.1X.

There is one AAA statement that is absolutely necessary. The command can be used in conjunction with additional AAA statements, but is absolutely required for 802.1X. The command is shown below for IOS. There are no explicit commands for AAA in CATOS:

    aaa authentication dot1x default group radius

If the design for authentication calls for parameters to be passed back from RADIUS, then one additional command is necessary. It is shown below for IOS:

    aaa authorization network default group radius

The configuration requirements for RADIUS are very small. Only three elements must be identified: the address of the Authentication Server, what

TCP/IP port will be used for authentication, and what is the shared secret. The commands for IOS and CATOS are shown below.

IOS:
radius-server host 10.254.10.70 auth-port 1645 acct-port 1646
radius-server key <text>
CATOS:
set radius server 1.1.1.1 auth-port 1645 acct-port 1646
set radius key <text>

2.5.2.3 Displaying 802.1X Information

Being able to review the status of 802.1X is as important as being able to configure it. There are a variety of show commands available. These commands are both global and interface-specific. The most general one is available on both IOS and CATOS. This command displays the basics of 802.1X functioning on the Authenticator. The command is the same in both IOS and CATOS: show dot1x.

This is a global command and what is displayed is information about globally set elements. The output is different in IOS and CATOS. Just as there were elements set on a perinterface basis in IOS that were different than those in CATOS, there are elements shown in CATOS with this command that are not displayed in IOS. The following is the output from the show command in CATOS:

PAE Capability	Authenticator Only
Protocol Version	1
system-auth-control	enabled
max-req	2
quiet-period	60 seconds
re-authperiod	3600 seconds
server-timeout	30 seconds
shutdown-timeout	0 seconds
supp-timeout	30 seconds
tx-period	30 seconds

Notice the PAE Capability. This reflects the earlier discussion in Management regarding the device's ability to be an Authenticator, a Supplicant, or both. In this case it is performing the functions of an Authenticator only. Virtually nothing that is output from the show command in CATOS is output from the same command in IOS. This is the output from the show command executed in IOS.

Sysauthcontrol	= Enabled
Dot1x Protocol Version	= 1
Dot1x Oper Controlled Directions	= Both
Dot1x Admin Controlled Directions	= Both

This version of IOS is based on the earlier specifications. It is recognizable because IOS based on the 2004 specifications includes one additional line. This line specifies how a Supplicant with invalid credentials will be handled:

Supplicant Allowed In Guest Vlan = Enabled

When displaying information regarding a port that is participating in 802.1X, much of what was displayed globally for CATOS is displayed for IOS. Minimal information regarding the status of 802.1X is also displayed in both cases. The command to display general information about 802.1X for a particular port is shown below for IOS and CATOS:

show dot1x interface <interface>
show port dot1x <mod/port>

The output from those commands is displayed below first for IOS and then for CATOS:

IOS

Supplicant MAC	<Not Applicable>
AuthSM State	= N/A
BendSM State	= N/A
PortStatus	= N/A
MaxReq	= 6

HostMode	= Single
Port Control	= Auto
QuietPeriod	= 60 Seconds
Re-authentication	= Disabled
ReAuthPeriod	= 3600 Seconds
ServerTimeout	= 30 Seconds
SuppTimeout	= 30 Seconds
TxPeriod	= 30 Seconds
Guest-Vlan	= 10

CATOS:

Port	Auth-State	BEnd-State	Port-Control	Port-Status
5/48	-	-	force-authorized	-

Port	Port-Mode	Re-authentication	Shutdown-timeout
5/48	SingleAuth	disabled	disabled

So far only the commands to display the status and capability of a system or a particular port have been discussed. There is one additional class of information that is accessible and that is the statistical/performance characteristics. It is interesting that when displaying statistics for a port both CATOS and IOS display the same information. The commands for IOS and CATOS respectively are:

show dot1x statistics interface <interface>
show port dot1x statistics <mod/port>

The output from those commands is shown below. Most of the information relates to the number of frames seen and the quality of those frames. Refer back to the chapter on Management and note that MIB elements labeled as "Statistics" are displayable with these show commands. One piece of information that could be very important in some troubleshooting is the MAC address of the last transmission. Again, note that the format of the displayed information is different in IOS and CATOS, but the content is the same.

IOS:

PortStatistics Parameters for Dot1x

TxReqId   = 0 TxReq   = 0 TxTotal   = 0

RxStart   = 0 RxLogoff = 0 RxRespId = 0   RxResp = 0

RxInvalid = 0 RxLenErr = 0 RxTotal   = 0

RxVersion = 0 LastRxSrcMac 0000.0000.0000

Port	Tx_Req/Id	Tx_Req	Tx_Total	Rx_Start	Rx_Logoff	Rx_Resp/Id	Rx_Resp
5/48	0	0	0	0	0	0	0

Port	Rx_Invalid	Rx_Len_Err	Rx_Total	Last_Rx_Frm_Ver
5/48	0	0	0	0

Last_Rx_Frm_Src_Mac

00-00-00-00-00-00

There are additional show commands and additional parameters that can be coded beyond what has just been discussed. But, in a practical sense, they will not be used frequently. What has been covered is what will be used in the majority of implementations and situations. Table 2.17 summarizes the show commands.

2.5.3 Debugging 802.1X

Hopefully the following commands are not going to be needed very often. But there are occasions when the actual processes occurring in a given

Table 2.17   IOS and CATOS Show Commands

Command	Parameter	Parameter	Parameter
		IOS	
dot1x			
	all		
	interface	interface number	
	statistics	interface	interface number
		CATOS	
dot1x			
Port	dot1x		<mod>|<mod/port>|cr
	dot1x	guest-vlan	none|VLAN|<mod/port>|cr
		statistics	<mod>|<mod/port>|cr

authentication session must be reviewed. In those cases, the capability to "debug" is very useful. The basic debug command for 802.1X is:

debug dot1x.

The command is not complete as written and must be modified. The following are the possible modifiers. They should be self-explanatory; however, the description included in IOS is also displayed.

all	All Dot1x debugging messages turned on
errors	Error codes
events	Events
packets	Packets
registry	Registries
state machine	State machine

Just as with configuring 802.1X, it may be necessary to debug RADIUS and AAA as well. There are more options in debugging those processes than are shown below, but the following can provide supporting information regarding the backend, inside workings of an authentication event.

debug radius
debug aaa authentication

It is obvious that various capabilities for configuring 802.1X and displaying its function on a device are available depending on both the platform and version of the operating system. Careful consideration of both should be made during the design phase prior to implementation of 802.1X.

2.5.4 Supplicant Configuration

Supplicant configurations are totally dependent upon the vendor, and frequently the vendor is chosen because of the EAP-Method that is to be implemented. However, the Windows 2000 and XP environments are fairly common and can provide a reference for the configuration of other Supplicants. Thus, a brief discussion of configuring a Windows Supplicant is warranted.

The first thing that must be accomplished in a Windows environment is for the Service that supports 802.1X to be made an active process. This service is not intuitive when looking at available services. In Windows 2000 it is: Wireless Configuration. In Windows XP it is: Wireless Zero Configuration.

Even though the service name implies that it is a Wireless service, it actually applies to all network interfaces. Starting this service effectively enables the configuration of Authentication parameters on an interface. If there is not a "tab" entitled Authentication available on an interface, it is likely that the service has not been started.

Diverging from the Windows configuration briefly, there are some wireless drivers that will allow the configuration of 802.1X directly. When these drivers are implemented in a Windows environment, some care must be taken to ensure that the configuration of the adapter within Windows does not include an 802.1X configuration. This can cause an invalid setup on the Supplicant.

Back to configuring adapters within Windows. Selection of the Authentication tab opens a window that allows 802.1X to be enabled on the interface. Once it is enabled, several additional options are available. The mandatory item is the selection of a particular EAP-Method. In Windows 2000, there are three possible methods: MD5 Challenge, "Smart Card or other Certificate," or Protected EAP (PEAP). MD5 Challenge and Smart Card are mandatory methods.

Two additional selections are available for any of the three methods. The first allows for the authentication of the machine. Within the Windows environment, it is possible to include the machine as a member of the domain. If this has been accomplished, then the machine itself can be authenticated.

In Windows XP there are additional options that are selectable when authentication as a computer is selected. Authentication with computer credentials only can be selected, or two options involving both computer and user credentials are available. Essentially these are involved when user credentials are to be used in the authentication process. It is possible to require that both the machine and the user be authenticated. This requires that both the Supplicant and the Authentication Server be configured specifically to accomplish this.

The second option on the initial Authentication tab is to allow the authentication as a guest when no credentials are available. This option works in conjunction with the Authenticator to enable a Supplicant that does not have valid credentials to be allowed entry to a Guest VLAN, instead of remaining in a nonauthenticated state.

If MD5 is chosen as the EAP-Method, there are no additional parameters that can be selected. If Smart Card or other Certificate is chosen, then additional configuration regarding the use of the card or a certificate installed on the machine is available. If PEAP is chosen, then the option of validating the server certificate is presented.

While it appears that there is an option to select a particular Authentication Method, the only available option is to use MS-CHAPV2. There are two additional options. The first is to enable the fast reconnect capability and the second is to use credentials supplied at login or to prompt for credentials.

Fast reconnect allows the use of cached credentials and is used in wireless to enable roaming. This must be set on both the Supplicant and the Authentication Server to function properly. This element is primarily used with PEAP.

A registry setting must be added or modified for Windows 2000 to issue EAPOL frames. If this value is not set, then Windows will react to EAP messages from an Authenticator, but will be entirely passive in the initiation of the Authentication process. It will not issue an EAPOL-Start. There are situations where a Supplicant must initiate the Identity exchange with an Authenticator. One of them is when a data port on an IPT phone is used. The port on the switch is already active. This means that the 802.1X authentication process will not be initiated. Specifically, the Authenticator will not send a Request-Identity frame unless stimulated to do so with an EAPOL-Start. Recent versions of firmware on some IPT phones sense the state of the attached data port and will issue EAPOL frames on behalf of the client based upon that state. But this is not yet common. The registry setting required in Windows 2000 to do this is.

```
HKLM\Software\Microsoft\EAPOL\Parameters\General\Global\
    SupplicantMode REG_DWORD 3
```

The registry setting is not required in Windows XP. Instead, there is an element that can be selected to enable the EAPOL-Start when configuring 802.1X for an interface.

2.5.5 Authentication Server

As with the Supplicant, there are a wide variety of RADIUS servers available to act as Authentication Servers. In some cases, it is necessary to utilize a specific server if a proprietary EAP-Method has been selected for implementation. Any RADIUS server that supports EAP processing must support the mandatory EAP-Methods itemized in the specifications. For the purposes of this book, a very brief discussion of the Cisco RADIUS server will be made. Hopefully, this will provide some insight to the configuration of other server implementations as well. An entire section was devoted earlier to the way RADIUS functions within 802.1X; therefore, this section will briefly describe the basic configuration processes that are useful.

Once the Cisco RADIUS server has been installed on a computer and is functional, the first thing that must be done is to identify the devices that will be communicating with it. This is accomplished by configuring the Network Device. It is in this particular section that the device name, the IP address, and the shared secret are identified. These items correspond with the RADIUS configuration required on the Authenticator. Once the configuration is consistent between the Authentication Server and the Authenticator, communication can take place.

For all practical purposes, only one additional item is required and that is to identify the type of communication that will take place between the network device and the RADIUS Server. The type of server that should be selected is Radius (IETF).

The selection of this type is necessary if additional functions on the server are intended to be implemented. Specifically, if the intent is to dynamically modify the VLAN assignment, then the required RADIUS attributes are only available within this type. Three attributes must be configured on the RADIUS server for this function. They are found in Group Settings. The attributes and the coding are:

64 Tunnel-Type—VLAN
65 Tunnel-Medium-Type—802
Tunnel-Private-Group-ID—<VLANID>

The "aaa authorization network" statement must be present on the Authenticator for this process to work. Also the VLAN returned to the Authenticator must have previously been defined and be recognized as a valid VLAN. If either of these conditions is not met, then an error message is returned and the port remains unauthorized.

It is possible to return an access list upon successful authentication, as well as returning a specific VLAN. Just as with the VLAN, the access list is viable only during the period in which the authentication is valid. When the port reverts to an unauthorized status, both the VLAN and the access list are removed.

The access list is coded on the RADIUS server as a text in the Extended access list format. They are stored as Vendor Specific Attributes (VSA). These attributes are coded as inacl#<n> for ingress and outacl#<n> for egress. It is possible to refer to a precoded standard access list that exists outside of the authentication on the Authenticator. Obviously, a significant amount of design effort must be spent—and ongoing management effort anticipated—when planning the use of user specific functions such as access lists and VLANs.

The IETF attribute 26 is used to store the peruser access list. The Authenticator running IOS must be configured to accept the VSA through the use of the statement shown below. Note: additional modifiers are available, but are not required.

```
radius-server vsa send
```

The coding of attribute 26 is based upon the use of the Cisco attribute/-value pair as defined by the IETF. A brief discussion of attribute 26 was conducted in the previous section on RADIUS. Information included in attribute 26 is the identification of the vendor through the use of an ID, the intended use of the data stored in the attribute, and the data itself. The Cisco Vendor ID is 9, the data format is AV pair, which is a 1, and then the data itself. Shown below is an example of the type of coding that can be applied via attribute 26.

```
cisco-avpair = "ip:inacl#1 = permit ip 10.45.123.0 255.0.0.0 20.20.0.0
     255.255.0.0"
cisco-avpair = "ip:inacl#2 = deny ip 10.0.0.0 255..0.0.0 any"
```

This discussion of configuring the RADIUS server is not comprehensive, but should give a basic understanding. Notable by its absence is a discussion of the actual data used to authenticate the Supplicant. This information is variable and depends on the actual EAP-Method chosen for that purpose. For a Cisco RADIUS server, the EAP-Method is chosen during the configuration of the Database to be used for authentication. Frequently, in a Windows environment, an external Windows Database, relying on domain credentials, will be chosen. This particular option allows for a variety of MS-CHAP selections as well as options for PEAP, EAP-FAST, and EAP-TLS. Coding of these attributes is necessary for the implementation of 802.1X, but the selection of specific options is a design decision that is considered to be peripheral to the intent of this section.

Thus, configuration of 802.1X requires configuration of each of the three entities that exist in the authentication process. Each has a fairly robust implementation both within and outside of Cisco. And the configuration of each affects and is affected by the other participants. Careful design must be conducted prior to implementation in order that all the parts work together well.

2.6 WIRELESS

2.6.1 Chapter Summary

Wireless is simply another 802 LAN implementation and, as such, is defined to be suitable for an 802.1X implementation. There is one consideration and that is that 802.1X is defined to be implemented on Point-to-Point links or switched networks within the 802 LAN suite. Wireless is not really a switched network, but does emulate that characteristic because most implementations do not allow peer-to-peer communication. Wireless clients connect to access points and not to one another. If those circumstances change, the implementation of 802.1X in the environment would be in jeopardy.

Wireless utilizes an 802 protocol and is therefore capable of participating in 802.1X. The physical specifications for wireless are contained in a variety of 802.11 documents. These specifications primarily focus on the physical characteristics of the communication between a wireless client and a base station—an access point. For example, the standard for 802.11b, published by the IEEE in 1999, is devoted entirely to the Medium Access Control (MAC) and Physical Layer (PHY). These types of standards are consistent with publications for all 802 LANs. But because wireless is a shared environment, it has issues that are not as visible as in other 802 LANs. The primary issue is that all traffic is broadcast—and is easily captured by a third party. Because the traffic from any station is so easily monitored, there has been great and justified concern over the usefulness of wireless for anything but the most innocuous traffic. This has been addressed through the definition of additional specifications for the encryption of traffic between an access point and a wireless client.

Wired Equivalent Privacy (WEP) was defined as an option in the initial implementations of 802.11. This protocol was the first real attempt to provide a mechanism to encrypt wireless traffic. It is not the best method and has several vulnerabilities, but it still exists as of the writing of this book. There are a significant number of additional encryption mechanisms that have been deployed. None of these mechanisms relies on 802.1X. They stand alone as encryption tools only. It really was not until recently, in the specifications for 802.11i, that authentication has been identified as a specific requirement in wireless security.

One of the largest advantages in wireless is that of mobility. The capability of an individual to move from one location to another while maintaining network connectivity is extremely advantageous. But this poses an issue in 802.1X. A client that moves from one access point to another must be re-authenticated, and there is no guarantee that the connection was not usurped—depending upon the topology of the network and the particular EAP-Method implemented.

Several EAP-Methods can perform a fast re-authentication. The capability to accomplish a fast re-authentication is also dependent upon the wireless implementation as well as the EAP-Method. The initial authentication must be performed as defined in the specifications for the method. This process follows all of the 802.1X flows illustrated thus far and involves the Supplicant, the Authenticator, and the Authentication Server. However, unlike wired Authenticators, the wireless Authentication system can maintain sufficient information regarding the Supplicant and the successful authentication to quickly perform the re-authentication without involving the Authentication Server or performing the entire process. This requires a wireless system that shares information across access points. Individual access points, each operating independently, cannot perform this type of re-authentication.

2.6.2 Wireless Topology

Several sections ago a brief explanation of how wireless participates in 802.1X was given, but a short recap will help. The main difference between wireless and wired is the establishment of a link. In wireless, link is established when an Association occurs. At that point the customary processing for 802.1X can begin. Figure 2.14 recaps the wireless association and initial exchange in 802.1X in a wireless environment.

So why is wireless such a hot topic? Put simply: Wireless offers a huge potential at the same time it opens a huge risk. Wireless combines flexibility and mobility with inexpensive implementation. The cost of installing a wired environment to provide the same type of coverage can be many times more expensive than implementing wireless coverage. Combine that with the

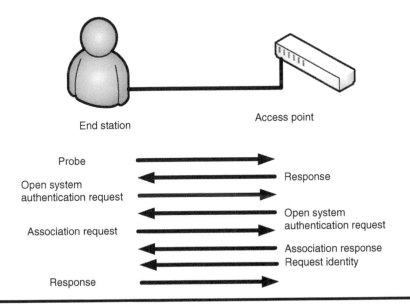

Figure 2.14 Typical Wireless Connection.

capability of supporting traditional computers, personal assistants, and phones in such a way that movement is not restricted and wireless really becomes attractive. However, wireless takes the actual state of the local computing environment, in terms of networking, back to the stone age. Well, maybe not that far; but it takes it back to the beginnings of local networking. This is because wireless is a totally shared environment with no inherent control over connectivity. Wireless is like putting a hub out on the street and erecting a big sign that says "Connect Here!" The problem is how to reap the benefits while reducing the risk to an acceptable level.

2.6.3 Data Encryption and Authentication

Thus, the biggest issues in wireless have been: first, how to encrypt the conversation so that it is extremely difficult to snoop on what is being transmitted; and, second, how to ensure that only authentic users are able to access resources. There is a misconception that these two issues are the same. That may be an overstatement. Perhaps, it is simply that the vulnerability of wireless, and all the publicity regarding the failure of some measures to ensure confidentiality, namely the use of Wired Equivalency Protection (WEP), have overshadowed authentication. Authentication is a separate issue from the continuing problem of data encryption.

Let us leave encryption alone for a bit and concentrate on authentication. As the first paragraph of this section states: because wireless is an 802 protocol, it is inherently capable of supporting 802.1X for authentication of attempted connections. The implementation of 802.1X in a wireless environment is virtually the same as in a wired environment. There are a small number of variations, but the basic roles of Supplicant, Authenticator and Authentication Server are implementable in wireless. One of the significant differences is how the physical connection is established and recognized by the Authenticator and Supplicant. In a wired environment, this is a change in the electrical state of a physical port. In a wireless environment, this is defined as when an "association" has been established between two devices.

As shown in Figure 2.14, once an association has been formed between a wireless access point and a client, then 802.1X functions in the same way in both the wireless and wired world. The same type of packets flow between Authenticator and Supplicant, between Authenticator and Authentication Server, and between Supplicant and Authentication Server. What has already been discussed in the previous sections continues to hold true here.

Therefore, once an association has been formed between the Authenticator and the Supplicant, the authentication process can be initiated. Separately—and distinct from that process—various methods of encrypting data can be applied. Historically, that was through the use of WEP. There are newer methods and each has strengths and weaknesses. The key to remember is that an EAP-Method and a wireless encryption method are separate and distinct. The selection of an EAP-Method does not need to influence the selection of an encryption process and vice versa.

2.6.4 Mobility

Why devote an entire section to a discussion of an environment that does not pose a significant change to the way in which 802.1X operates? Because even though the basic functions of 802.1X are the same in each environment, there are implications for mobility and flexibility that must be considered.

Mobility in a wired world is limited to the length of the cable connecting the user to the network. Mobility is not a real consideration. That is not the case in a wireless world. Whether the intent was there in any given wireless implementation or not, the simple fact is that without a tether people will wander about. This creates two problems. The first is the physical issue of retaining connectivity while switching from one access point to another. This issue has been addressed fairly well. The second concern is a bit more problematic: retaining the logical connectivity above that of physical connectivity.

This is especially true in the area of ensuring that a connection moving between access points is authentic. If 802.1X is applied to the environment, then each access point is required to authenticate a new connection. It really does not matter, within the context of 802.1X, that the user is moving an existing connection.

Think about how most of the discussion of the process has been presented so far. There is a fairly significant conversation that can take place. The establishment of tunnels between Supplicant and Authentication Server, together with the negotiation of EAP-Method—not to mention the actual authentication of credentials—can be a significant event requiring a large number of exchanges between the Supplicant and the Authenticator. Depending on the location of the Supplicant and the Authentication Server within a network, the transaction times can become very long. The latency involved in this process may not be really noticeable in human terms, but can be significant in computer terms. A bottleneck can form and connectivity to applications can be lost. In effect, the primary advantage of a wireless environment can be lost.

However, this can be mitigated to a certain extent. Remember the flow of 802.1X and especially the original specifications. First, it is necessary that the Supplicant have credentials validated by a backend process. In most of the current implementations of 802.1X, the backend process is a RADIUS server known as the Authentication Server. It is not required that the backend process be separate and distinct from the Authenticator. In fact, in the discussion on security earlier in the book, it was noted that a combination of the two is desirable from the standpoint of mutual authentication of those two entities.

2.6.5   Cached Credentials and Re-Authentication

Some wireless implementations allow for credential information to be cached at a location "close" to the Supplicant. In these scenarios, the required process to be compliant with 802.1X specifications occurs when the Authenticator can access this information and reduce the number of exchanges required. Since the information is "closer," then the potential latency involved in accessing the information is reduced. Effectively, what has happened here is that the Authentication Server—the backend—has been integrated into the Authenticator. That is probably an over simplification, but it is effectively what has taken place.

The next real issue with mobility is continuity in the identification of a user to devices resident on the network. More simply said: it is the maintenance of the connection between the mobile partner and the application being accessed. The connection to an application must move from access point to access point as the user moves. In the vast majority of connections, this is the IP address. The preservation of existing connections to applications while moving from one access point to another is an essential attribute of wireless.

Although this is not strictly an 802.1X concern, the maintenance of application connectivity does share the same requirements as authentication. When taken together, the necessary maintenance of authentication and application connectivity in a speedy manner argues for some form of centralized control. Yet, that centralized control must be perceived as being local to the access points and the user. A good implementation of a wireless system must be able to recognize when a client is moving and to ensure maintenance of previously established characteristics, such as authentication and network addressing, across multiple access points.

2.6.6   802.1X Key Exchange

Earlier, the problem of privacy was mentioned as a major concern in wireless. The specifications for 802.1X include a consideration of the situation. In the 2004 specifications, a particular EAP Type was defined to facilitate the exchange of key information. This is EAPOL Type 3 and it was discussed very briefly in the section on EAP, EAPOL, and Ethernet.

Packets can be exchanged between the Authenticator and the Supplicant with the intent of coordinating the establishment of key information. Either participant, Supplicant, or Authenticator can initiate a conversation based upon Type 3. As stated earlier, the definition regarding the use of this type of packet is defined in wireless specifications. It should be noted that RFC 3850 discusses this packet type and indicates that it is likely to be "deprecated" in favor of stronger methods.

The complete process is defined in IEEE-802.11i 2004. It consists of a four-way handshake. Although the use of encryption is vital to the transport of data in a wireless environment, a complete discussion of the mechanisms utilized are outside the scope of this book. That being said, the 802.11i standards define the four-way handshake in the following manner. First, an Association must be established. Second, the normal 802.1X authentication must be successful. Third (and fourth), the exchange of key information must be accomplished between Authenticator and Supplicant. The exchange of key information may take place one or more times during the lifetime of a connection and may be initiated by either the Supplicant or the Authenticator. Figure 2.15 illustrates the exchange process.

As a side note regarding the acceptance of 802.1X as an ongoing standard, 802.11i requires the use of 802.1X as a fundamental process. The wireless standard spends a minimum amount of verbiage discussing this requirement and focuses on the use of keys. 802.11i enumerates the use of TKIP and CCMP.

Temporal Key Integrity Protocol (TKIP) was developed to address weaknesses in the original WEP implementation. Essentially, TKIP implements a code called Michael that is used to ensure the authenticity of the source for each message. Counter-Mode/CBC-MAC Protocol (CCMP) also authenticates packets. Confidentiality is ensured through the use of AES in counter-mode. Authentication is provided through the use of Cipher Block

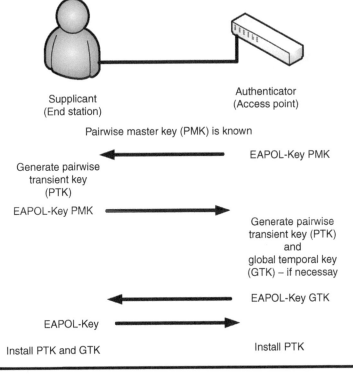

Figure 2.15 EAPOL-Key Exchange.

Chaining Message Authentication Code (CBC-MAC). TKIP is intended for use by legacy equipment and CCMP is intended for new developments. Neither is required for 802.IX—and essentially stand outside of it.

Figure 2.15 illustrates the flow of packets in an EAPOL-Key exchange.

2.6.7   Impact of EAP-Method Selection

Because the 802.11i specifications require the use of 802.1X as a foundation, more drivers for wireless are including support directly. As noted in the previous chapter on configuration, this may cause some conflicts with configuration of wireless in a Windows environment. Care must be exercised when implementing the various products to ensure interoperability.

The choice of EAP-Method is significant in the implementation of wireless. The individual characteristics of a given method significantly impact the confidentiality of information being transmitted through the air. Additionally, the selection of an operating system on the Supplicant will affect the available choices of an EAP-Method.

Within a Windows environment there are different methods available depending on the implementation of Windows 2000 or XP. In 2000, the methods required by the specifications—MD5 and Smart Card—are supplemented with PEAP. In XP, MD5 is not a recommended method because it can have a very weak encryption and be susceptible to dictionary attacks. As a result, it no longer offers the method and, in that sense, is noncompliant with the existing specifications for 802.1X. Instead, EAP-TLS is strongly promoted in the operating system.

The steps that take place in an EAP-TLS exchange, including the EAPOL-Key exchange, are:

1. The Supplicant forms an association with the access point—the Authenticator.
2. The Authenticator issues a Request Identity. The Supplicant may issue an EAP-Start.
3. The Supplicant issues a response.
4. The Authenticator constructs a new packet and forwards the EAP Data to the Authentication Server.
5. The Authentication Server issues an Access-Challenge with a Start-TLS.
6. The Authenticator reformats the frame into an EAPOL frame and forwards to the Supplicant.
7. The Supplicant issues an EAP-Response with EAP-Data containing a TLS Client Hello.
8. The Authenticator reformats the packet into a RADIUS Access-Request packet and forwards to the Authentication Server.
9. The Authentication Server responds with its certificate in an Access-Challenge packet to the Authenticator.

10. The Authenticator reformats the packet and forwards to the Supplicant as an EAP Request-Identity packet.
11. The Supplicant issues an EAP-Response with a TLS Certificate.
12. The Authenticator reformats the packet and forwards to the Authentication Server.
13. The Authentication Server responds with the cipher suite and indicates that TLS is now complete.
14. The Authenticator reformats the packet and forwards to the Supplicant.
15. The Supplicant acknowledges the success with an EAP Response.
16. The Authenticator reformats the packet and forwards to the Authentication Server.
17. The server recognizes the acknowledgement and issues an Access-Accept with an imbedded EAP-Success. This message contains keys for subsequent use by the Authenticator and Supplicant.
18. The Authenticator receives the EAP-Success and authorizes the connection.
19. The Authenticator issues an EAPOL frame containing an EAP-Success to the Supplicant.
20. The Authenticator now issues an EAPOL-Key frame containing the Multicast/Global Key to the Supplicant.

This can be a lengthy process in computer terms and has the possibility of disrupting an application flow, if required, when moving from one wireless access point to another. It is possible in some scenarios to store cache the successful authentication and quickly reinstate the encrypted session on a new access point.

Thus, even though 802.1X functions the same in a wired and a wireless environment, there are serious implications that must be considered for wireless. First is the simple fact that it appears that, based on 802.11i, 802.1X will continue to play an important role in wireless. Second is that the choice of an EAP-Method to be implemented is critical in terms of mobility and confidentiality. Third is that the placement of the Authentication Server in near proximity to the Authenticator is necessary in order that latency be kept to a minimum.

3

DESIGN, IMPLEMENTATION, AND TROUBLESHOOTING

So far we have gone through two chapters of the book that have discussed what Port-Based Authentication grounded in 802.1X is, why it should be implemented, the history of the specifications, and technical discussion of the various elements involved in the authentication process. Everything presented thus far has been directed toward developing a sound footing in the technical functionality. This last chapter will be devoted to presenting a practical view of authentication.

Two sections will be devoted to Design. The initial section in this chapter is devoted to developing an understanding of the approach necessary to be able to go from "I think I want to implement 802.1X." to actually accomplishing it. This is presented as a design overview and describes a process composed of five stages: Requirements, Definition/Information Gathering, Concept, Architecture, and Design.

The design process is grounded in developing and documenting a set of requirements, as well as documenting the existing environment. It is obvious that knowing what you want to accomplish is a prerequisite to accomplishing it. The Requirements/Information Gathering has a dual output. The first documents the environment and the second concretely documents the goals and objectives to be achieved. The next stage is the development of a Concept that takes the goals and objectives and largely illustrates the characteristics of an implementation. The particular functionality desired is described in this section, along with general statements regarding advantages as well as issues or concerns. The fourth stage, Architecture, applies the Concept to the existing environment and documents the flow and interaction of the various participants. The way in which all the desired functionality will be applied and the consequences of the implementation are described in detail. The final stage is called the Design.

It would be easy to say that the prior stages are superfluous; however, that is simplistic. Each of the stages builds upon the information developed in the preceding stage. So Design is grounded in Architecture. The scheduling of changes, the documentation of modifications to configurations, implementation plans for new devices, etc. are all developed in detail. At the end of the design process, everything necessary to begin the implementation of Port-Based Authentication has been accomplished.

The reason that this chapter begins with a discussion of this process and then goes into several sections discussing implementation and troubleshooting is that it is necessary to understand how a design is accomplished together with actual information about various implemented functions. The final section in this chapter will identify specific considerations for going into a Port-Based Authentication Design effort.

There are eight sections between the two devoted to Design. These sections are devoted to describing, in excruciating detail on occasion, what happens in various situations. These sections discuss what happens when it works correctly, what happens when it does not, where it is viable, and where alternative mechanisms must be employed. "It" is 802.1X Port-Based Authentication.

The way in which these eight sections are organized follows the same structure implemented thus far in the preceding sections. A variety of output from available tools will be used to document what is happening during the authentication process. These tools will include the use of "debug" and "show" commands on Cisco infrastructure devices and packet sniffers.

The second section is entitled A Very Simple Network. The simplest authentication is documented. The anticipated behavior is documented and described. The next seven sections evolve the network in a variety of ways and begin to explore situations that are common. The intent is to provide a variety of examples from true situations that will help both design and troubleshooting efforts around 802.1X.

Three sections cover the most common situations in an 802.1X implementation. Section two documents what happens in a very simple environment when everything works. Section three builds upon that by describing situations where it does not work right. The fourth section is devoted to developing what happens when visitors connect to your network and what happens when your users connect to a foreign network.

The next section begins the discussion of how to cope with devices that do not have the capability to function as a Supplicant. There are serious concerns about how those devices are protected and how the network is protected when they are implemented. Some of these devices are printers and servers. Either no Supplicant is available for these devices or it is very awkward to implement.

It seems that no matter how a network is implemented, a situation will arise where there is not enough connectivity. Frequently, users will undertake a resolution of the issue without working with the proper authorities.

I will not get into a discussion of whether or not the user is justified, but will discuss how the implementation of 802.1X prohibits this by default. And then I will discuss the implications of changing the defaults, followed by a discussion of how unplanned expansion of the network is explored.

One of the major applications being implemented that is also integrated with the network infrastructure is IP Telephony (IPT). This has significant implications because a Cisco IP phone operates in specific ways on the network and provides a connection to an Authenticator without providing the functionality of the Authenticator. It is an awkward device in an 802.1X implementation, but there are mechanisms available that make it more compatible. This is explored in the sixth section of this chapter.

Wireless, as expected from the emphasis so far in the book, has a significant impact on 802.1X as well as the general characteristics of the network at a local site. There are two possible implementations of wireless within the Cisco suite of products. They are Aironet and Airespace, and just as their names are different, the functionality inherent in each is different. Aironet is primarily a peer-type implementation that allows each access point to be an independent entity with a centralized overlay. Airespace is a centralized architecture with virtually no independent functionality allowed to access points. The impact and consideration of implementing either has significant impact on both 802.1X and the network in general.

The last section discussing the technology expands the network into a large scale WAN. Placement of various devices, in particular Authentication Servers, is evaluated. The implications of functioning over a network of this scale are presented.

And, finally, the last section of the chapter and the book discusses various considerations that must be included in a design effort. These considerations are based on information presented in the technical chapter of the book, as well as the sections of this chapter detailing the effects of actual situations. Thus, after reading from this introduction through the last section, you will be ready to go start designing your implementation of 802.1X.

3.1 DESIGN

3.1.1 Section Summary

The design of a network is a formal process. It consists of distinct phases encompassing specific work efforts. These efforts are also distinct and build upon one another. The output of each phase must be certified and complete because it provides the foundation for the subsequent phase. Building a design is very similar to building a house. Incomplete work in one phase jeopardizes the stability of the remaining work. To properly determine whether or not 802.1X is a fit for a given network, and how it actually should be implemented, the phases in the design process should be followed.

Those phases are: Requirements Definition, Concept, Architecture, Design, and Implementation. The five phases of a design effort are sequential in nature. Each will build upon the information developed in the previous phases. Requirements Definition documents the current environment and delineates the need for changes to that environment. This information is used to develop a Concept of what the new environment will look like. The vision of the new environment is then Architected. The Architecture really describes how the new environment will function. Following Architecture, the Design phase is initiated. This phase documents exactly what will be done and when it will be done. Implementation is the final phase. It is debatable whether or not this phase is a part of Design or a part of Operations—or even if it is distinct from both. For the purposes of this book, and to support subsequent sections, it will be considered to be a phase in Design. Complete and faithful execution of the phases in sequence is essential.

A design moves through time in the sequence described above. It is not an amorphous thing. A design really focuses on the interactions of various aspects of a network. There are a limited number of these aspects—nine to be specific—and they can be grouped into three collections. Each collection is a "plane" on a cube. The planes are Technology, Access, and Application. The plane of Technology includes the aspects of Transport, Management, and Security. The plane of Access is composed of the aspects of Consumer, Provider, and Support. The plane of Application consists of Significance, Type/Quality of Service, and Operational Characteristics. Each aspect must be evaluated as an independent entity, in association with the other aspects within the plane, and then finally across the other aspects on the other two planes. Each of these reviews and considerations must occur within each of the phases of a design effort.

In the next sections, the exploration of a practical implementation of 802.1X in various environments will evaluate impact, risks, and concerns. The intent is not only to provide insight on how an implementation really functions, but also to begin to point out how that functionality requires a significant design effort prior to an implementation. The implementation will start with a small network and evolve toward a larger and more complex environment. By beginning with a very simple implementation and gradually adding layers of complexity, the breadth of design considerations will become obvious. The first network to be evaluated will be very simple—a single switch—and the final network will be a robust large scale WAN over multiple sites.

After this practical background has been explored, Design will be revisited.

Some of the specific discoveries will be explored in "cubic" terms. The specific functional performance of 802.1X will be evaluated within a single plane and also in terms of interaction of the planes. Hopefully, a treatment of this nature will provide some insight for the unique individual network implementation that is our own network.

802.1X, like virtually every other network function, both affects and is affected by the topology implemented. While 802.1X is a "security" function, it is integrated into the network infrastructure. This integration tends to minimize the real considerations required in a design because it seems to be so very simple. But there are significant considerations regarding design of physical infrastructure and the logical implementation of 802.1X residing on that infrastructure.

3.1.2 The Network Design Cube

A network is not simply a collection of switches and routers hooked together that are intended to allow one device to communicate with another. A network is really a very complex combination of Technology, Application, and Access. A network can be described as a three-dimensional set of planes with each being one of the dimensions. Each plane can be decomposed into three further aspects. The plane of Technology is really composed of Transport, Security, and Management. The plane of Access consists of Consumer, Provider, and Support. The final plane—Application—is composed of Significance, Type/Quality of Service, and Operational Characteristics. Each aspect is significant within its own plane as well as the other two planes. Each aspect intersects with every other aspect in those planes. Figure 3.1 illustrates the various planes and aspects of a network.

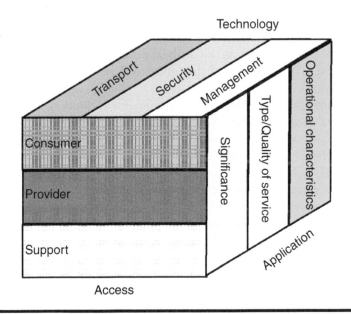

Figure 3.1   Design Considerations.

The three planes: Technology, Applications, and Access can intuitively be seen to have interactions. It is a little harder to envision all of the interactions the various aspects have with one another.

In looking at this cube, 802.1X fits some of the aspects very well. It is pretty obvious that it fits into the aspect of Security in the plane of Technology and probably addresses the entire plane of Access. What might not be as clear are some of the impacts of Management or Type/-Quality of Service. Nor is it painfully obvious how 802.1X fits into the aspect of Provider Access.

This cube is evaluated repeatedly through a formal design process. The process consists of five phases: Requirements Definition, Concept, Architecture, Design, and Implementation. First, the goals and existing environment are documented in the Requirements Definition. This information is used to construct a vision of a new network in the Concept phase. The Concept is fleshed out by describing how it will function in the Architecture phase. Exactly what will be done to the network is developed in the Design phase. Finally, Implementation causes the existing network to become the new network.

3.1.3 Requirements Definition

Let us begin with Requirements Definition. There must be a reason why something is done in a network. Simply implementing interesting capabilities or implementing something because it is the hot topic is not a sufficient reason. A real need must be identified. Certainly, in the case of 802.1X, prudence could be a good reason. But face it, if there is not something worth protecting on the network then increasing the complexity makes little sense. A Requirements Definition is not a trivial process. It needs to be thorough and detailed. The outcome of this effort will be the foundation for the remaining phases.

There are really two parts to a Requirements Definition. The first is the definition of goals and objectives and the second is information gathering. Investigate and describe the current environment in detail. This effort should be comprehensive and complete. While the number of words spent in describing the task here are few, the importance is huge. If the environment is not sufficiently documented, then a real risk of failure exists. As an example, if a clear inventory of all devices that will be expected to implement 802.1X is not made, then there is a real possibility that there will be some that cannot support the function. Also, if there is a blend of vendors, then there may be a specific functionality that cannot be performed across the board. Knowing what will be used to implement 802.1X is absolutely necessary. This obviously includes information regarding what credential information is currently used and available, where it is located, etc. Documentation and comprehension of the complete environment is essential.

In addition to documenting the infrastructure, the definition of why the effort is being undertaken must be detailed. The desired end state—in terms of goals and objectives—must be explicitly described. However, Requirements Definition is not simply the documentation of goals and infrastructure. There are some less obvious areas that must be explored as well.

This means that the cube should be considered carefully and the interactions between the aspects of a plane—and with aspects on other planes—must be considered. As an example: What is the interaction between Security and Type/Quality of Service and what information should be gathered? One possibility—and just one—is the current implementation of Type/Quality of Service parameters affecting a timely conversation between Authenticator and Authentication Server. Thus, the location of each current configuration of all devices in the path must be available for review when considering possibilities of authentication failure due to down links or poor response times.

There are other significant classes of information that will affect the design and implementation of 802.1X besides a definition of the existing infrastructure. One of the more obvious is a timeline. The future must be considered as well as the current state.

What is the direction the network is currently planned to go? Is it expanding? Contracting? When is equipment scheduled to be replaced? What vendors are being used? Will that change? What new applications are going to be developed? Which ones are going to be decommissioned? Gathering that type information is important. The consideration of existing planning is essential in any design.

How does this information affect the implementation of a Port-Based Authentication scheme? On the surface it would seem that this information is peripheral to a design of 802.1X, if not totally irrelevant. Consider the implications of two points. First, what is the dynamic nature of this environment? Is it growing or shrinking? An environment that is shrinking probably will not want to invest the time or dollars required to implement the level of stringent authentication implied by 802.1X. Similarly, an expanding environment has implications regarding the design and placement of equipment, in particular Authentication Servers. Remember that latency and reachability for those servers will affect the performance of a local port. Understanding what the direction is for Application development and the associated security required could affect the structure of Guest VLANs, selection of an EAP-Method, etc. Thus, gathering a complete view of the current state of affairs and the future direction is very important.

It may not seem important, but an overall evaluation of the organization is also necessary. A clear understanding of the organization utilizing the environment must be developed. A definition of the organization, its mode of operations, and the capabilities of its various parts that will use and be affected by any change is as important as knowing the topology of the existing network. The sophistication of the entire organization impacts a successful implementation of any automation. This applies to applications as well as network infrastructure—including 802.1X. There are a number of questions that must be asked and likely answers derived. Is it likely that the end user will understand what is occurring in a given situation at a technical level, and can that user be relied on to be able to modify behavior, configuration of the Supplicant or credentials, and obtain acceptable results in case of unexpected events? Is it reasonable to believe that the support organization can provide assistance effectively? Is it reasonable to assume that the organization empowered to maintain the 802.1X implementation is sufficiently staffed and has a toolset available to be able to ensure ongoing continuity? These are just a few examples of the type of investigation into the organization that must be conducted.

There is a dynamic at play that must be considered carefully. That is: Complexity versus Consciousness. This dynamic must be balanced, or the risk of failure—implosion—is great. The network cannot be more complex than the capability of the organization to use and support it. Nor can it be significantly less complex. If the users are frustrated because the network does not effectively meet their needs—because it is either too complex or not complex enough—then the ultimate risk of failure is great.

When is a network not complex enough? When the network and the applications supported do not provide necessary information in the time-frames required, then the implementation is not complex enough. A situation where a network is too complex is when the capability of supporting organizations—such as the Help Desk and the Network Management team—are insufficiently staffed or trained to readily resolve issues that arise. Another example of a network that is too complex is when a budget is not available to implement supporting technology or personnel. On the other hand, a network is not complex enough when users are more sophisticated than the infrastructure and become frustrated. The first phase of a design effort must document the complexity and consciousness through an inventory of requirements and capabilities. The items discussed above are examples and not a complete definition of a Requirements analysis.

At end of the Requirements Definition phase there should be huge piles of paper that inventory and describe the current state and the existing plans for the future state. The piles of paper should not just be directed at the physical or logical network but should extend into the organization as well. The end state that is desired must be clearly described as a set of goals and objectives.

Then there should be a very simple document that summarizes all of that information into a set of needs—Requirements. This document will not say that 802.1X should be implemented. It might say there is a need that certain information should be made available to certain authorized people—information that is valuable and must be a protected resource. And as we are talking about implementing 802.1X, it would be helpful if the Requirements indicated a need for securing the network.

3.1.4 Concept

After the Requirements Definition phase has been completed, the next step is to develop a Concept of how those Requirements will be addressed. This is the vision or "I have a dream" phase. This phase does not identify products. It identifies how functions should be implemented within the environment that was just documented—and how goals are to be realized.

Take the following situation as an example. In the Requirements Definition phase, an objective of securing all access to the corporate network was established. In the Concept phase, it could be established that 802.1X would be implemented on ports where users are expected to connect and applied universally in the wireless environment. It could be explained further that this is especially desirable because wireless is expected to become more prevalent, due to budgetary benefits, in the 40 new sites to be opened over the next year. This is even more desirable because 802.11i is a new standard in wireless and requires 802.1X. It is anticipated that the standard Windows 2000 Supplicant will be utilized because that is the operating system utilized on all corporate computers. Etc.

The Concept merges three components, the goals/objectives/requirements that were identified, the environment that was identified, and the technical competence of the designer to produce a view of an end state. This may sound like it is more of an art than a science, but it is mostly diligence and hard work.

Consider as an example the plane of Technology. 802.1X fits nicely within the aspect of Security within that plane. Look at each plane and evaluate 802.1X within that context. Ask the following questions: What are the effects of implementing 802.1X and specific 802.1X options in each particular aspect? What information regarding corporate policy on security has been discovered? What is the state of current security implementations toward that policy? Furthermore, what organizational components are in place to support the policy? What infrastructure solutions, software, or hardware are in place to support the policy? What functions and features of 802.1X could be implemented in the environment? This is all very important. Define what functions and features of 802.1X will be implemented and how they relate to the information developed in the previous phase.

Now consider the aspect of Transport in the plane of Technology— which boils down to the state of the infrastructure. What vendors have been implemented with what software? Is 802.1X available as a function on the infrastructure implemented? If so, what functions are available in the current state? Is it possible to upgrade? What is the scale of a potential upgrade? What other functions might be adversely affected by an upgrade? What plans exist for upgrades? Is an appropriate RADIUS server available to act as an Authentication Server? Are there several? Where are they located? Can more severs be acquired? What is the state of the budget?

Once 802.1X has been evaluated in terms of each aspect of each plane, then the interactions of the aspects must be considered. How does the information developed for the aspect of Security interact with the aspect of Management? All of the questions and answers developed must be bounced against one another. Sometimes additional questions will arise that must be answered, but eventually a picture will begin to form as to how 802.1X can—and should—be implemented in the particular environment. Sometimes the answer will be that it cannot—or should not—be implemented.

The output of this phase will consist of a definition of the general implementation of 802.1X, the particular functions/options to be implemented, and a description of where 802.1X might not be implemented. A justification, along with references to the material derived in the Requirements definition, should be included. General statements regarding the placement of Authentication Servers will be included. The EAP-Method or Methods will be selected and justified. Any changes or upgrades to the infrastructure should be enumerated. Tools, desired or required, for control and management of the infrastructure should be identified. The output should also include a discussion of impact to the organization, while discussing processes and procedures that must be implemented. Frequently this portion of the Conceptual Design is ignored and its absence causes problems in later stages. High-level diagrams are usually constructed to illustrate items covered in the Concept. Diagrams describing general flows and infrastructure are useful in later stages of the Design process.

Note that a good job must be done in the Requirements Definition phase to provide sufficient and accurate information for analysis in the Concept phase. This necessity of doing a complete job of addressing each phase prior to moving to the next will exist throughout the process.

3.1.5 Architecture

After Concept comes Architecture. This phase builds on the diagrams and "dreams" just constructed. The anticipated operational characteristics are described in detail, information flows are documented, and potential pitfalls are flagged in this phase.

The documentation of the expected functionality of the implementation of 802.1X is constructed. What is expected when a device connects to a port that is enabled for 802.1X? What are the flows of the 802.1X conversations as applied to the conceptual network? Where are Authentication Servers placed? What is expected to happen in various situations? Describe how required connectivity will be maintained in the event of various failures. This may wind up ultimately being a manual management process. The merger of automation and manual support should be described in detail so that a complete implementation is architected.

Effectively, what must be accomplished is to address each item discussed in the Concept at one lower level. Where one paragraph may have sufficed to describe the issue in the Concept, several pages may be required to encompass necessary detail in the Architecture phase.

Fully define what access each type of user will be allowed and how it will be implemented in the network. Define how guests will be allowed on the network, what they will be allowed to access, how they will be controlled, and what is the information flow that is to be implemented for them. This definition similarly must be constructed for the various types of authenticated users.

Document all anticipated, or even all possible, scenarios that could happen during an authentication. Just as in Concept, ensure that how a particular situation can occur, what the infrastructure does in that situation, what the various tools are expected to do, and what manual processes are invoked are fully documented. The Architecture phase employs a holistic approach to ensure that the intended implementation is completely accountable.

Describe how devices that are not 802.1X capable will be handled. How will access to and from these devices be controlled? What are the devices? How will ad hoc connections be handled? What are the implications for the security requirements developed earlier?

The existing network topology and the new topology defined in the Concept are evaluated here and a Gap Analysis is developed. As an example, if IOS upgrades are required on several devices, then this is documented. If additional servers are required to support a diversified implementation of Authentication Servers, this is documented. If upgrades to personal computer operating systems are required, that too is documented.

One situation that is frequently overlooked in a Gap Analysis is the modification to the way work is performed and managed. The method in which 802.1X will be implemented on personal computers will entail a significant effort and must be described. In addition, how network management will support the implementation must be identified in detail. The organizational components required to support the implementation of 802.1X are as significant as the technological issues. Ignoring them is virtually certain to lead to a failed implementation.

Up to this point in the design process, very little has been done with the appliances or software; but it may be desirable to develop a test lab to provide a high degree of confidence that the performance of 802.1X is actually what has been anticipated. The validation of flows is important. Also, the documentation of actual experiences of the users under certain conditions is highly desirable. The ability to test management procedures and processes is significant.

The Architecture phase expands the Concept just as the Concept phase expanded the Requirements Definition. Everything that was identified in the Concept is extended toward a Design by defining what will be implemented, what the expected results will be, and how those results will be handled by various processes and procedures.

3.1.6 Design

Once the Architecture has been finalized, the Design phase can be initiated. This phase takes the various flows described in the Architecture phase and develops the state that will exist after implementation has been completed. Individual appliances must be identified and modifications to hardware, software, and configurations must be defined.

As an example, this might include the definition of the placement of Authentication Servers in the network. The port on which each server will be placed must be defined. The IP addressing necessary and the coding of parameters on the specific server must be constructed. Routing definitions that might require modification to be able to reach the particular server must be constructed. If a secondary or external database is required, then the method for accessing the database must be configured. Each and every device and port that will be affected must have this type of documentation developed for it.

The implementation of new devices must be planned and detailed. Any upgrades to switches and access points must be documented, along with the process necessary to perform the upgrade. Any impact arising from that upgrade to other functionality, either existing or planned, that will require some form of activity must be detailed. The migration of users must be detailed in terms of technical process as well as training.

Any new management processes, especially in user or network support, must be constructed. These would range from troubleshooting to recovery. The documentation of the process and the plan for merging each into the existing management tolls and functions must be constructed.

Finally, a strategy for Implementation must be developed: A sequence of events that details exactly how all of this will be implemented. Which piece will be implemented where, in what sequence, when, and how it will be validated must be documented. Everything from the implementation of Supplicants to the activation of Authenticators to the sequence in which sites will be modified must be planned as part of the Design phase.

3.1.7 Implementation

The Implementation phase is a combination of constructing the logistics necessary to execute the plan developed in the Design phase and the actual execution of the plan. The logistics include construction of purchase orders, scheduling delivery to specific locations, staging and testing of new hardware or software, identification of personnel needed to execute the plan, training in new or modified procedures, implementation or modification of management tools, etc. Once the logistics have been finalized, it is a simple matter to execute the plan. Actually, that is not quite true, but all of the work accomplished to this point makes it much easier and provides a high degree of confidence in success.

Strict development and execution of a Design effort will certainly make life easier. The next several sections will illustrate issues surrounding an implementation of 802.1X from a practical perspective. The very last section in the book will revisit Design and take into account the technical and practical details described in this book.

3.2 A VERY SIMPLE NETWORK

3.2.1 Section Summary

Let us take some time to look at the implementation of 802.1X and how it really functions. The best way to do this is to develop a topology and explore it thoroughly. A very simple network consists of a switch, a RADIUS Server, and a router. With these three components, an 802.1X environment can be constructed. The RADIUS Server is the Authentication Server. The switch is the Authenticator and the router allows connectivity to external resources.

If everything works right, then the scenarios presented in the last section of Overview—How Does it Work—occur and can be reviewed in network traces and switch debugs. All of that output is illustrated in this section. The various actions and activities that occur on the Authenticator and the network are documented. The basic functions that occur in virtually every scenario are extrapolations of a successful authentication on a very simple network.

The debugs and traces describe the EAPOL exchanges between the Authenticator and the Supplicant that initiate an Authentication. Then the exchanges between the Authenticator and the Authentication Server, together with the corresponding exchanges between Authenticator and Supplicant, show how the Authenticator is simply a middle-man and does not play a significant role in the exchange of credentials. Finally, the declaration of success by the Authentication Server and the notification of that state to the Supplicant is shown.

The final segment of this section documents what truly happens when a Supplicant logs off. This process describes how the Authenticator changes state and moves the port into an unauthorized state. It is interesting to note that the port does not really become unauthorized, but instead moves to a Guest VLAN. The reason for this is that the link state of the port does not go down. This means that the port must revert to a state that will allow a non-Supplicant to connect to the network. The assignment of the port to the Guest VLAN accomplishes this.

3.2.2 The Topology and Configuration

There are many production networks that essentially resemble this topology. The switch might be small, such as the one used in this example, or much larger housing hundreds of ports. The fundamental concept of the very simple network is that a single device has been implemented as the infrastructure and will house all components of the network.

Scenarios presented in subsequent sections will not have nearly as much detail presented as part of the discussion about them. Instead, the detail presented here will be leveraged to provide background. The progression of discussions in this chapter will reflect an increasingly complex environment. However, the general topology of an 802.1X implementation involves only three components, so many of the scenarios that are apt to occur will occur in a very simple network as well as a very complex one. This section will cover many of the most common situations that will be encountered in an implementation.

In this example, a network consisting of a single switch, in this case a Catalyst 3550, has been implemented. The necessary ingredients for 802.1X are in place—an Authentication Server (RADIUS server) and an Authenticator (3350). FastEthernet port FA0/1 has the RADIUS server connected and FastEthernet 0/2 has a router connected for Internet access. Certainly, it will not only be workstations that connect to the remaining ports, but in this chapter these other devices will not be considered. All in all, as illustrated in Figure 3.2, this is truly a very simple network.

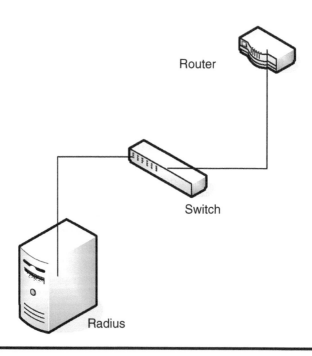

Figure 3.2 A Very Simple Network.

The following is a portion of a configuration very similar to what was implemented on the switch using IOS 12.1. It should be noted that this version of IOS is based upon the original specifications for EAP and 802.1X. This means that some features and functions contained, usually as optional characteristics, are not available. However, for our purposes, the capabilities available are sufficient. IOS versions containing additional capabilities will be reviewed as necessary when a discussion of the newer features is pertinent.

For brevity, only a portion of the configuration and a few of the ports are displayed in the configuration, but all remaining ports can be considered to have similar configurations.

```
aaa new-model
aaa authentication dot1x default group RADIUS none
aaa authorization network default group RADIUS none
!
dot1x system-auth-control
!
interface FastEthernet0/1
   switchport access VLAN 10
   switchport mode access
   no ip address
!
interface FastEthernet0/2
   switchport access VLAN 10
   switchport mode access
   no ip address
!
interface FastEthernet0/3
   switchport access VLAN 30
   switchport mode access
   no ip address
   dot1x port-control auto
   dot1x Guest vlan 20
!
interface VLAN 1
   no ip address
   shutdown
!
interface VLAN 10
   ip address 10.46.10.2 255.255.255.0
!
interface VLAN 20
   ip address 10.46.20.2 255.255.255.0
   ip access-group Internet in
```

```
!
interface VLAN 30
   ip address 10.46.30.2 255.255.255.0
!
ip access-list extended Internet
   deny ip any 10.46.10.0 0.0.0.255
   permit ip any any
!
RADIUS-server host 10.46.10.70 auth-port 1645 acct-port 1646
RADIUS-server retransmit 3
RADIUS-server key Fl1nt50n#
!
```

Most of this configuration is straightforward. Several VLANs are established, but only 30 and 20 are relevant to 802.1X. VLAN 30 is defined as the data VLAN and VLAN 20 is defined as the Guest VLAN on ports utilizing 802.1X authentication. The Guest VLAN is intended to allow unauthenticated devices access to the Internet only by denying access to VLAN 30. A span port, FastEthernet0/24, was defined to replicate traffic in and out of port FastEthernet0/3.

It is obvious that the bare minimum was configured for 802.1X. Only sufficient configuration was coded to allow a supplicant to connect to the switch and be authenticated or be placed in a Guest VLAN. 802.1X was enabled globally on the switch with the following command: dot1x system-auth-control.

Port FastEthernet0/3 was configured to implement 802.1X with the following commands:

```
dot1x port-control auto
dot1x Guest VLAN 20
```

The following command was configured to direct 802.1X authentication requests to RADIUS: aaa authentication dot1x default group RADIUS none

Finally, three commands were configured to identify and allow connection to a specific RADIUS server. The ports identified are the standard default ports used by RADIUS.

```
RADIUS-server host 10.52.34.70 auth-port 1645 acct-port 1646
RADIUS-server retransmit 3
RADIUS-server key Fl1nt50n#
```

The configuration is the absolute minimum necessary to implement 802.1X on the port and probably is the way in which many implementations on a very simple network would be constructed initially.

3.2.3   What Happens If Everything Works Right?

The following example details what happens when a device with a Supplicant is authenticated. This is ultimately what is desired—authenticated devices are allowed onto the network. Of course we configure Guest VLANs for situations where a device attempting to connect to the network is allowed some access but not full. The Guest VLAN will be discussed in greater detail in a subsequent section.

The port on the switch that the device was plugged into was monitored and full debugs for RADIUS, 802.1X, and AAA were run on the switch. The following is the output from the show debug command:

General OS:
AAA Authentication debugging is on
RADIUS protocol debugging is on
dot1x:
Dot1x registry info debugging is on
Dot1x packet info debugging is on
Dot1x events debugging is on
Dot1x State machine transitions and actions debugging is on
Dot1x Errors debugging is on

Note that the debug was issued on the switch, monitoring of the port was enabled, and the test laptop was fully booted prior to the Ethernet cable being inserted into the 802.1X enabled port. The debug output below shows what happens on the Authenticator as soon as a cable is plugged into a port with 802.1X enabled:

23:50:13: dot1x-registry:dot1x_port_linkchange invoked on interface
    FastEthernet0/3
23:50:13: dot1x-registry:dot1x_port_linkcomingup invoked on interface
    FastEthernet0/3

The prior two statements show that the change in the electrical state has occurred at the physical layer on the port. In short, the link is coming up.

23:50:13: dot1x-ev:dot1x_port_enable: set dot1x ask handler on inter-
    face FastEthernet0/3
23:50:13: dot1x_auth Fa0/3: initial state auth_initialize has enter
23:50:13: dot1x-sm:Fa0/3:0000.0000.0000:auth_initialize_enter called
23:50:13: dot1x-ev:auth_initialize_enter:0000.0000.0000: Current ID=0

Immediately, 802.1X processing is initiated on the port.

23:50:13: dot1x_auth Fa0/3: during state auth_initialize, got event
    0(cfg_auto)

23:50:13: @@@ dot1x_auth Fa0/3: auth_initialize -> auth_disconnected
23:50:13: dot1x-
sm:Fa0/3:0000.0000.0000:auth_disconnected_enter_action called
23:50:13: dot1x-sm: dot1x_update_port_status called with port_status =
DOT1X_PORT_STATUS_UNAUTHORIZED

As shown by the output from the debug shown above, the port is immediately moved into an unauthorized status. At this point, if a show VLAN is executed, the port will be shown to be in VLAN 30 which is the access VLAN configured for the port. However, if the interface is actually displayed, it is clear that the port is not connected.

A sequence of debug messages will continue to be displayed. These will be mostly unintelligible to all but the most die-hard geeks. They are meaningless strings of characters to most of us, so they will not be duplicated just to take up white space in this book. The messages have to do with the initialization of the two state machines, etc. After skipping over them, the next interesting debug messages are shown below:

23:50:13: dot1x-ev:dot1x_post_message_to_auth_sm:0000.0000.0000:
Sending TX_FAIL
23:50:13: dot1x-ev:dot1x_post_message_to_auth_sm:0000.0000.0000:
Current ID = 1
23:50:13: dot1x-ev:dot1x_tx_eap: EAP Ptk
23:50:13: dot1x-ev:EAP-code = FAILURE
23:50:13: dot1x-ev:EAP Type = IDENTITY
23:50:13: dot1x-ev:ID = 0

Note that the first packet sent is an EAP-Failure. This packet forces a reset of any 802.1X processing that may have been initiated on the Supplicant. Also, look at the Identity field in this packet. It is a 0, which seems to be outside the expected value, but it will be used again on a subsequent request. However, there should never have been a conversation to this point, so a value Identity has not been established. The capture of the EAP-Failure is shown below. Again, this packet was sent immediately upon detection of the Link coming up.

Frame 1 (60 bytes on wire, 60 bytes captured)
Arrival Time: Oct 13, 2005 07:18:19.305425000
Time delta from previous packet: 0.000000000 seconds
Time since reference or first frame: 0.000000000 seconds
Frame Number: 1
Packet Length: 60 bytes
Capture Length: 60 bytes
Ethernet II, Src: 00:0f:f7:96:14:03, Dst: 01:80:c2:00:00:03
Destination: 01:80:c2:00:00:03 (Spanning-tree-(for-bridges)_03)

Source: 00:0f:f7:96:14:03 (00:0f:f7:96:14:03)
Type: 802.1X Authentication (0x888e)
Trailer: 00000000000000000000000000000000...
802.1X Authentication
Version: 1
Type: EAP Packet (0)
Length: 4
Extensible Authentication Protocol
Code: Failure (4)
Id: 0
Length: 4

0000 01 80 c2 00 00 03 00 0f f7 96 14 03 88 8e 01 00   ....

0010 00 04 04 00 00 04 00 00 00 00 00 00 00 00 00 00   ....

0020 00 00 00 00 00 00 00 00 00 00 00 00 00 00 00 00   ....

0030 00 00 00 00 00 00 00 00 00 00 00 00 00   ....

Notice the destination address of the packet. It is the group address reserved for 802.1X in 802.1D bridging. Of course, at this point the Authenticator cannot know the MAC address for the "thing" at the other end of the link, but this address is used by the Authenticator and the Supplicant for all exchanges—long after it is possible for each to know the MAC address of the other. Every exchange between the Supplicant and the Authenticator while 802.1X is "active" will show this as the destination address. This makes it simple for both the Authenticator and the Supplicant to identify messages intended for them. It also makes it more difficult to sort through messages when more than one Supplicant is on the same cable. This particular subject will be discussed in more detail in the Section entitled Unplanned Expansion.

The switch does a minimal amount of housekeeping as shown in the debug output below. The EAP-Failure packet will be immediately followed by an EAP-Request Identity packet. The debug shows that the supplicant MAC address is still unknown and set to 0000.0000.0000. This means that the group address must still be used in the transmission. Note that all of the processing thus far has taken less than a second.

23:50:13: dot1x-registry:registry:dot1x_ether_macaddr called
23:50:13: dot1x-ev:dot1x_post_message_to_auth_sm: cleanup author
    from interface FastEthernet0/3
23:50:13: dot1x-ev:dot1x_post_message_to_auth_sm: Tx for req_id for
    supplicant 0000.0000.0000
23:50:13: dot1x-ev:dot1x_tx_eap: EAP Ptk
23:50:13: dot1x-ev:EAP-code=REQUEST
23:50:13: dot1x-ev:EAP Type=IDENTITY

23:50:13: dot1x-ev:ID=1
23:50:13: dot1x-registry:registry:dot1x_ether_macaddr called
23:50:15: %LINK-3-UPDOWN: Interface FastEthernet0/3, changed state
   to up

At this point the physical connection, the LINK Layer, between the Authenticator and the Supplicant has been established. The message at 23:50:15 shows this status being reported on the switch. This message is a little late in being displayed because the initial EAP-Failure, followed by an EAP-Request, was sent on 23:50:13. The following is a capture of the second packet seen on the link. This is the EAP-Request Identity referenced in the debug statements above. The switch is ready for "normal" sequencing of exchanges and has set the Identity to 1.

Frame 2 (60 bytes on wire, 60 bytes captured)
Arrival Time: Oct 13, 2005 07:18:19.306117000
Time delta from previous packet: 0.000692000 seconds
Time since reference or first frame: 0.000692000 seconds
Frame Number: 2
Packet Length: 60 bytes
Capture Length: 60 bytes
Ethernet II, Src: 00:0f:f7:96:14:03, Dst: 01:80:c2:00:00:03
Destination: 01:80:c2:00:00:03 (Spanning-Tree-(for-bridges)_03)
Source: 00:0f:f7:96:14:03 (00:0f:f7:96:14:03)
Type: 802.1X Authentication (0x888e)
Trailer: 00000000000000000000000000000000...
802.1X Authentication
Version: 1
Type: EAP Packet (0)
Length: 5
Extensible Authentication Protocol
Code: Request (1)
Id: 1
Length: 5
Type: Identity [RFC2284] (1)

```
0000  01 80 c2 00 00 03 00 0f f7 96 14 03 88 8e 01 00   ...............

0010  00 05 01 01 00 05 01 00 00 00 00 00 00 00 00 00   ...............

0020  00 00 00 00 00 00 00 00 00 00 00 00 00 00 00 00   ...............

0030  00 00 00 00 00 00 00 00 00 00 00 00               ...........
```

The Supplicant responds with an EAPOL-Start frame. This seems to be fairly silly. It would seem that the Supplicant should respond with an EAP-Response packet. The reason why this seemed to happen is that the

Supplicant was not really aware of the two packets from the Authenticator. In at least some cases where a Windows Supplicant is not configured to issue EAPOL packets—as described in the section on configuration—the Supplicant does not respond to the first Request Identity but waits until the Authenticator retransmits—usually after 30 seconds. This implies that it did not recognize those first two packets issued by the Authenticator. There are several possible reasons for this situation, but they are somewhat irrelevant. The fact that this happens is the issue.

The following is the capture of the third packet on the Link. This packet is the EAPOL-Start from the Supplicant to the Authenticator. Note the times between this packet and the previous one. Approximately three seconds have elapsed.

> Frame 3 (60 bytes on wire, 60 bytes captured)
> Arrival Time: Oct 13, 2005 07:18:22.924056000
> Time delta from previous packet: 3.617939000 seconds
> Time since reference or first frame: 3.618631000 seconds
> Frame Number: 3
> Packet Length: 60 bytes
> Capture Length: 60 bytes
> Ethernet II, Src: 00:0d:56:b7:6f:c2, Dst: 01:80:c2:00:00:03
> Destination: 01:80:c2:00:00:03 (Spanning-tree-(for-bridges)_03)
> Source: 00:0d:56:b7:6f:c2 (169.254.101.32)
> Type: 802.1X Authentication (0x888e)
> Trailer: 000000000000000000000000000000000000...
> 802.1X Authentication
> Version: 1
> Type: Start (1)
> Length: 0
>
> 0000 01 80 c2 00 00 03 00 0d 56 b7 6f c2 88 8e 01 01   ....V.o.....
>
> 0010 00 00 00 00 00 00 00 00 00 00 00 00 00 00 00 00   ....
>
> 0020 00 00 00 00 00 00 00 00 00 00 00 00 00 00 00 00   ....
>
> 0030 00 00 00 00 00 00 00 00 00 00 00 00   ....

The debug below shows that the Authenticator received the EAPOL-Start and reacts to it. It recognizes the MAC address as a new one on the port—000d.56b7.6fc2—and initiates processing for that one. It forces the port into an unauthorized status. This is redundant because the debug never shows the port having ever left the unauthorized state. After performing a variety of housekeeping functions, it issues an EAP-Request Identity.

> 23:50:17: dot1x-packet:Received an EAPOL frame on interface
>   FastEthernet0/3

23:50:17: dot1x-ev:Received pkt saddr=000d.56b7.6fc2, daddr= 0180.c200.0003,pae-ether-type=34958

23:50:17: dot1x-ev:Couldn't find a supplicant block for mac 000d.56b7.6fc2

23:50:17: dot1x-ev:Found a supplicant block for mac 0000.0000.0000 10B9CB0

23:50:17: dot1x_auth Fa0/3: initial state auth_initialize has enter

23:50:17: dot1x-sm:Fa0/3:000d.56b7.6fc2:auth_initialize_enter called

23:50:17: dot1x-ev:auth_initialize_enter:000d.56b7.6fc2: Current ID=0

23:50:17: dot1x_auth Fa0/3: during state auth_initialize, got event 0(cfg_auto)

23:50:17: @@@ dot1x_auth Fa0/3: auth_initialize -> auth_disconnected

23:50:17: dot1x-sm:Fa0/3:000d.56b7.6fc2:auth_disconnected_enter_action called

23:50:17: dot1x-sm:

dot1x_update_port_status called with port_status=DOT1X_PORT_-STATUS_ UNAUTHORIZED

At this point the debugs show that 802.1X is formally placing the port in an UNAUTHORIZED state. I suppose it is unauthorized because it is not allowed to transmit traffic across it. The device connected is unauthenticated and its authorization is indeterminate.

23:50:17: dot1x-ev:dot1x_port_cleanup_author: cleanup author on interface FastEthernet0/3

23:50:17: dot1x-ev:dot1x_update_port_status: Called with host_mode= 0 state UNAUTHORIZED

23:50:17: dot1x-ev:dot1x_update_port_status: using mac 000d.56b7.6fc2 to send port to unauthorized on vlan 0

23:50:17: dot1x-ev:Found a supplicant block for mac 000d.56b7.6fc2 10BB294

23:50:17: dot1x-ev:dot1x_port_unauthorized: Host-mode=0 RADIUS/-guest vlan=0

23:50:17: dot1x-ev: GuestVlan configured=0

23:50:17: dot1x-ev:supplicant 000d.56b7.6fc2 is last

23:50:17: dot1x-ev:dot1x_port_cleanup_author: cleanup author on interface FastEthernet0/3

23:50:17: dot1x_auth Fa0/3: idle during state auth_disconnected

At this point the Authenticator is preparing itself for connectivity with the backend, identified by bend in the debug messages. There is nothing to communicate to the Authentication Server, but preparations in AAA (@@@ debug messages) and RADIUS are made. Finally, a Request Identity in response to the EAPOL-Start is sent.

23:50:17: @@@ dot1x_auth Fa0/3: auth_disconnected -> auth_connecting

23:50:17: dot1x-sm:Fa0/3:000d.56b7.6fc2:auth_connecting_enter called

23:50:17: dot1x_bend Fa0/3: initial state dot1x_bend_initialize has enter

23:50:17: dot1x-sm:Dot1x Initialize State Entered

23:50:17: dot1x_bend Fa0/3: initial state dot1x_bend_initialize has idle

23:50:17: dot1x_bend Fa0/3: during state dot1x_bend_initialize, got event 16383(idle)

23:50:17: @@@ dot1x_bend Fa0/3: dot1x_bend_initialize -> dot1x_bend_idle

23:50:17: dot1x-sm:Dot1x Idle State Entered

23:50:17: dot1x-ev:Created port supplicant block 000d.56b7.6fc2 expected_id=1 current_id=1

23:50:17: dot1x-ev:dot1x_post_message_to_auth_sm: cleanup author from interface FastEthernet0/3

23:50:17: dot1x-ev:dot1x_post_message_to_auth_sm: cleanup author from interface FastEthernet0/3

23:50:17: dot1x-ev:dot1x_post_message_to_auth_sm: Tx for req_id for supplicant 000d.56b7.6fc2

23:50:17: dot1x-ev:dot1x_tx_eap: EAP Ptk

23:50:17: dot1x-ev:EAP-code=REQUEST

23:50:17: dot1x-ev:EAP Type=IDENTITY

23:50:17: dot1x-ev:ID=0

Notice that an EAPOL frame is received in response to the Request Identity almost immediately. This is not what happened with the first Request Identity. This seems to support the premise that the Supplicant indeed did miss that particular packet.

23:50:17: dot1x-registry:registry:dot1x_ether_macaddr called

23:50:17: dot1x-packet:Received an EAPOL frame on interface FastEthernet0/3

23:50:17: dot1x-ev:Received pkt saddr=000d.56b7.6fc2, daddr=0180.c200.0003,pae-ether-type=34958

23:50:17: dot1x-ev:Found a supplicant block for mac 000d.56b7.6fc2 10BB294

All of this activity has occurred in less than a second. The Supplicant responds within the same second. Again, notice that the destination MAC address is the group address associated with 802.1X; the Ethertype is 888e, as identified earlier. In short, the packet conforms to the encapsulation mechanisms described in an earlier section in the technology chapter. It is interesting to note the Identity field. The response shown below performs a lock-step with the previous packet from the Authenticator that contained an Identity of 0. The Authenticator can readily associate the response from the Supplicant with the request because of this value. However, it does open certain issues with security. A Denial Of Service attack can be mounted that mimics the packet, except for the value of Identity, causing the process to be aborted.

```
Frame 5 (60 bytes on wire, 60 bytes captured)
Arrival Time: Oct 13, 2005 07:18:22.933771000
Time delta from previous packet: 0.004035000 seconds
Time since reference or first frame: 3.628346000 seconds
Frame Number: 5
Packet Length: 60 bytes
Capture Length: 60 bytes
Ethernet II, Src: 00:0d:56:b7:6f:c2, Dst: 01:80:c2:00:00:03
Destination: 01:80:c2:00:00:03 (Spanning-Tree-(for-bridges)_03)
Source: 00:0d:56:b7:6f:c2 (169.254.101.32)
Type: 802.1X Authentication (0x888e)
Trailer: 00000000000000000000000000000000...
802.1X Authentication
Version: 1
Type: EAP Packet (0)
Length: 21
Extensible Authentication Protocol
Code: Response (2)
Id: 0
Length: 21
Type: Identity [RFC2284] (1)
Identity (16 bytes): CCCC\edwin.brown


0000  01 80 c2 00 00 03 00 0d 56 b7 6f c2 88 8e 01 00   ........V.o.....

0010  00 15 02 00 00 15 01 4b 43 49 4e 5c 65 64 77 69   .......CCCC\edwi

0020  6e 2e 62 72 6f 77 6e 00 00 00 00 00 00 00 00 00   n.brown.........

0030  00 00 00 00 00 00 00 00 00 00 00 00               ............
```

The debug below reflects the receipt of the response. Notice that various timers are initiated. For the first time in the debug, AAA (@@@) activity is seen. The user is setup in AAA and RADIUS is invoked.

```
23:50:17: dot1x-packet:Received an EAP packet on interface
    FastEthernet0/3
23:50:17: dot1x_auth Fa0/3: during state auth_connecting, got event
    6(rxRespId)
```

23:50:17: @@@ dot1x_auth Fa0/3: auth_connecting -> auth_
authenticating

23:50:17: dot1x-sm:Fa0/3:000d.56b7.6fc2:auth_connecting_exit alled

23:50:17: dot1x-sm:Fa0/3:000d.56b7.6fc2:auth_authenticating_enter
called

23:50:17: dot1x-ev:sending AUTH_START to BEND for supp_info=
10BB294

23:50:17: dot1x-sm:Fa0/3:000d.56b7.6fc2:auth_connecting_authentica-
ting_action called

23:50:17: dot1x-ev:Received AuthStart from Authenticator for
supp_info=10BB294

23:50:17: dot1x_bend Fa0/3: during state dot1x_bend_idle, got event
1(auth_start)

23:50:17: @@@ dot1x_bend Fa0/3: dot1x_bend_idle ->
dot1x_bend_response

23:50:17: dot1x-sm:Dot1x Response State Entered for supp_info=
10BB294 hwidb=D39480, swidb=D3A7BC on intf=Fa0/3

23:50:17: dot1x-ev:Managed Timer in sub-block attached as leaf
to master

23:50:17: dot1x-sm:Started the ServerTimeout Timer

23:50:17: dot1x-ev:Going to Send Request to AAA Client on RP for id=0
and length=21

23:50:17: dot1x-ev:Got a Request from SP to send it to RADIUS with id 35

23:50:17: dot1x-ev:Couldn't Find a process that's already handling the
request for this id 0

23:50:17: dot1x-ev:Inserted the request on to list of pending requests

23:50:17: dot1x-ev:Found a free slot at slot 0

23:50:17: dot1x-ev:Found a free slot at slot 0

23:50:17: dot1x-ev:Request id=35 and length=21

23:50:17: dot1x-ev:The Interface on which we got this AAA Request is
FastEthernet0/3

23:50:17: dot1x-ev:Username is CCCC\edwin.brown

23:50:17: dot1x-ev:MAC Address is 000d.56b7.6fc2

23:50:17: AAA: parse name=FastEthernet0/3 idb type=−1 tty=−1

23:50:17: AAA: name=FastEthernet0/3 flags=0x15 type=7 shelf=0
slot=0 adapter=0 port=3 channel=0

23:50:17: AAA: parse name= <no string> idb type=−1 tty=−1

23:50:17: AAA/MEMORY: create_user (0xD553C4) user='CCCC\edwin.-
brown' ruser='CCCC\edwin.brown' port='FastEthernet0/3' rem_
addr=" authen_type=EAP service=802.1X priv=1

23:50:17: dot1x-ev:MAC Address copied is 000d.56b7.6fc2

23:50:17: AAA/AUTHEN/START (4083091005): port='FastEthernet0/3'
list='Dot1x Acc List' action=LOGIN service=802.1X

23:50:17: AAA/AUTHEN/START (4083091005): using "default" list

23:50:17: AAA/AUTHEN/START (4083091005): Method=RADIUS (RADIUS)

The Authenticator initiates contact with the Authentication Server. It constructs an Access-Request packet. This is documented in the debug output shown below.

23:50:17: RADIUS: ustruct sharecount=1
23:50:17: RADIUS: EAP-login: NAS Port=00-0d-56-b7-6f-c2 RemAddr= 000d.56b7.6fc2
23:50:17: RADIUS: EAP-login: length of RADIUS packet=122 code=1
23:50:17: RADIUS: Initial Transmit FastEthernet0/3 id 35 10.92.30.39: 1645, Access-Request, len 122
23:50:17: Attribute 4 6 0A5C025A
23:50:17: Attribute 61 6 00000000
23:50:17: Attribute 1 18 43434343
23:50:17: Attribute 6 6 00000002
23:50:17: Attribute 12 6 000005DC
23:50:17: Attribute 31 19 30302D30
23:50:17: Attribute 79 23 02000015
23:50:17: Attribute 80 18 FD614A78

Notice the attributes sent to the Authentication Server. The packet developed by the Authenticator contains the following: User Name, NAS-IP-Address, Service-Type, Framed-MTU, Calling-Station-ID, NAS-Port-Type, EAP Message, and Message Authenticator. The User Name is supplied by the Supplicant in its Response. The EAP Message is a response, as indicated by the "02" as the first byte, and the required Message Authenticator is present. Remember that the Message Authenticator is derived from the content of the message and the shared secret.

23:50:17: RADIUS: Received from id 35 10.92.30.39:1645, Access-Challenge, len 77
23:50:17: Attribute 79 8 01050006
23:50:17: Attribute 24 31 43495343
23:50:17: Attribute 80 18 3F8E740C

The debug output shown above indicates an Access-Challenge response from the Authentication Server. This is the expected sequence of events as described previously. The Authentication Server issues an EAP Request. The content includes the required Message Authenticator along with a State attribute.

23:50:17: RADIUS: EAP-login: length of eap packet=6
23:50:17: RADIUS: EAP-login: got challenge from RADIUS

23:50:17: AAA/AUTHEN (4083091005): status=GETDATA

23:50:17: dot1x-ev: going to send to backend on SP, length=6

23:50:17: dot1x-ev:Received VLAN is No VLAN

23:50:17: dot1x-ev:Enqueued the response to backend

23:50:17: dot1x-ev:Sent to Bend

23:50:17: dot1x-ev:Received QUEUE EVENT in response to AAA Request

23:50:17: dot1x-ev:Dot1x matching request-response found

23:50:17: dot1x-ev:Length of recv eap packet from RADIUS=6

23:50:17: dot1x-ev:Received VLAN Id -1

23:50:17: dot1x_bend Fa0/3: during state dot1x_bend_response, got event 0(areq)

23:50:17: @@@ dot1x_bend Fa0/3: dot1x_bend_response -> dot1x_bend_request

23:50:17: dot1x-sm:Dot1x Request State Entered

23:50:17: dot1x-ev:dot1x_bend_request_enter:000d.56b7.6fc2: Current ID=5

23:50:17: dot1x-ev:Managed Timer in sub-block attached as leaf to master

23:50:17: dot1x-ev:dot1x_bend:Sending RADIUS Response to Supplicant of length 6

23:50:17: dot1x-ev:dot1x_tx_eap: EAP Ptk

23:50:17: dot1x-ev:EAP-code=REQUEST

23:50:17: dot1x-ev:EAP Type=Unknown

23:50:17: dot1x-ev:ID=5

The Authenticator processes the information from the Authentication Server and issues another Request Identity to the Supplicant. It is interesting to look at the Identity field contained in the packet. It would be normal to assume a sequential progression, but this is not the case. The previous ID was 0 and this one is 5. It follows the prescribed rule of being an increasing value, but is not sequential.

Frame 6 (60 bytes on wire, 60 bytes captured)
Arrival Time: Oct 13, 2005 07:18:22.948536000
Time delta from previous packet: 0.014765000 seconds
Time since reference or first frame: 3.643111000 seconds
Frame Number: 6
Packet Length: 60 bytes
Capture Length: 60 bytes
Ethernet II, Src: 00:0f:f7:96:14:03, Dst: 01:80:c2:00:00:03
Destination: 01:80:c2:00:00:03 (Spanning-Tree-(for-bridges)_03)
Source: 00:0f:f7:96:14:03 (00:0f:f7:96:14:03)
Type: 802.1X Authentication (0x888e)
Trailer: 0000000000000000000000000000000000...
802.1X Authentication

Version: 1
Type: EAP Packet (0)
Length: 6
Extensible Authentication Protocol
Code: Request (1)
Id: 5
Length: 6
Type: PEAP [Palekar] (25)
Type-Data (1 byte) Value: 21

```
0000  01 80 c2 00 00 03 00 0f f7 96 14 03 88 8e 01 00   ...............

0010  00 06 01 05 00 06 19 21 00 00 00 00 00 00 00 00   .......!........

0020  00 00 00 00 00 00 00 00 00 00 00 00 00 00 00 00   ...............

0030  00 00 00 00 00 00 00 00 00 00 00 00               ............
```

When the captured packet is parsed, it can be seen that the Authentication Server is proposing the use of PEAP as the EAP-Method.

23:50:17: dot1x-registry:registry:dot1x_ether_macaddr called
23:50:17: dot1x-packet:Received an EAPOL frame on interface FastEthernet0/3
23:50:17: dot1x-ev:Received pkt saddr=000d.56b7.6fc2, daddr= 0180.c200.0003,pae-ether-type=34958

The Supplicant responds with the following packet. It is fairly obvious that the Supplicant agrees to use PEAP as the method because it responds with that EAP-Method.

Frame 7 (130 bytes on wire, 130 bytes captured)
Arrival Time: Oct 13, 2005 07:18:22.949445000
Time delta from previous packet: 0.000909000 seconds
Time since reference or first frame: 3.644020000 seconds
Frame Number: 7
Packet Length: 130 bytes
Capture Length: 130 bytes
Ethernet II, Src: 00:0d:56:b7:6f:c2, Dst: 01:80:c2:00:00:03
Destination: 01:80:c2:00:00:03 (Spanning-tree-(for-bridges)_03)
Source: 00:0d:56:b7:6f:c2 (169.254.101.32)
Type: 802.1X Authentication (0x888e)
802.1X Authentication
Version: 1
Type: EAP Packet (0)
Length: 112

Extensible Authentication Protocol
Code: Response (2)
Id: 5
Length: 112
Type: PEAP [Palekar] (25)
Type-Data (107 bytes) Value: 80000000661603010061010000 5D0301…

```
0000  01 80 c2 00 00 03 00 0d 56 b7 6f c2 88 8e 01 00   ........V.o.....
0010  00 70 02 05 00 70 19 80 00 00 00 66 16 03 01 00   .p...p.....f....
0020  61 01 00 00 5d 03 01 43 4e 50 8e b6 92 ab 94 b7   a...]..CNP......
0030  a4 c4 7d 72 e1 51 87 65 68 3a e3 71 f3 17 96 17   ..}r.Q.eh:.q....
0040  f8 ed 32 ec 7f 0b 35 20 25 be 7c af da 69 10 e3   ..2...5 %.l..i..
0050  14 3c bc d8 97 f3 11 98 83 b8 5f 5d 06 0a 36 a2   .<........_]..6.
0060  13 89 85 a8 00 65 19 97 00 16 00 04 00 05 00 0a   .....e..........
0070  00 09 00 64 00 62 00 03 00 06 00 13 00 12 00 63   ...d.b.........c
0080  01 00                                             .    ..
```

The response from the Supplicant initiates a TLS tunnel to the Authentication Server and that is why the EAP-Method data is incomprehensible. The Authenticator receives the packet and constructs one to send to the Authentication Server with the contents of the EAP field from the Supplicant. Also, several timers are reinitialized. All of this is shown in the debug output below.

23:50:17: dot1x-ev:Found a supplicant block for mac 000d.56b7.6fc2 10BB294
23:50:17: dot1x-ev:RECEIVED mac=000d.56b7.6fc2 and Stored MAC= 000d.56b7.6fc2
23:50:17: dot1x-packet:Received an EAP packet on interface FastEthernet0/3
23:50:17: dot1x-ev:Received RxResp from Authenticator
23:50:17: dot1x_bend Fa0/3: during state dot1x_bend_request, got event 4(rxresp)
23:50:17: @@@ dot1x_bend Fa0/3: dot1x_bend_request -> dot1x_bend_response
23:50:17: dot1x-sm:Dot1x Response State Entered for supp_info= 10BB294 hwidb=D39480, swidb=D3A7BC on intf=Fa0/3
23:50:17: dot1x-ev:Managed Timer in sub-block attached as leaf to master
23:50:17: dot1x-sm:Started the ServerTimeout Timer
23:50:17: dot1x-ev:Going to Send Request to AAA Client on RP for id=5 and length=112

23:50:17: dot1x-ev:Got a Request from SP to send it to RADIUS with id 36

23:50:17: dot1x-ev:Found a process that's already handling the request for this id 5

23:50:17: dot1x-ev:Username is CCCC\edwin.brown; eap packet length=112

23:50:17: AAA/AUTHEN/CONT (4083091005): continue_login (user= 'CCCC\edwin.brown')

23:50:17: AAA/AUTHEN (4083091005): status=GETDATA

23:50:17: AAA/AUTHEN (4083091005): Method=RADIUS (RADIUS)

23:50:17: RADIUS: ustruct sharecount=1

23:50:17: RADIUS: EAP-login: NAS Port=00-0d-56-b7-6f-c2 RemAddr= 000d.56b7.6fc2

23:50:17: RADIUS: EAP-login: length of RADIUS packet=244 code=1

23:50:17: RADIUS: Initial Transmit FastEthernet0/3 id 36 10.92.30.39:1645, Access-Request, len 244

23:50:17: Attribute 4 6 0A5C025A

23:50:17: Attribute 61 6 00000000

23:50:17: Attribute 1 18 43434343

23:50:17: Attribute 6 6 00000002

23:50:17: Attribute 12 6 000005DC

23:50:17: Attribute 31 19 30302D30

23:50:17: Attribute 24 31 43495343

23:50:17: Attribute 79 114 02050070

23:50:17: Attribute 80 18 EBE85A7B

The Authentication Server received the packet from the Authenticator and responded with one of its own. The debug shows that it sent 134 bytes of EAP data. This information will complete the TLS tunnel and initiate credentials transfer.

23:50:17: RADIUS: Received from id 36 10.92.30.39:1645, Access-Challenge, len 203

23:50:17: Attribute 79 134 01060084

23:50:17: Attribute 24 31 43495343

23:50:17: Attribute 80 18 D754ABDC

23:50:17: RADIUS: EAP-login: length of eap packet=132

23:50:17: RADIUS: EAP-login: got challenge from RADIUS

23:50:17: AAA/AUTHEN (4083091005): status=GETDATA

23:50:17: dot1x-ev:going to send to backend on SP, length=132

23:50:17: dot1x-ev:Received VLAN is No VLAN

23:50:17: dot1x-ev:Enqueued the response to backend

23:50:17: dot1x-ev:Sent to Bend

23:50:17: dot1x-ev:Received QUEUE EVENT in response to AAA Request

23:50:17: dot1x-ev:Dot1x matching request-response found

23:50:17: dot1x-ev:Length of recv eap packet from RADIUS=132

23:50:17: dot1x-ev:Received VLAN Id -1

23:50:17: dot1x_bend Fa0/3: during state dot1x_bend_response, got event 0(areq)

23:50:17: @@@ dot1x_bend Fa0/3: dot1x_bend_response -> dot1x_bend_request

23:50:17: dot1x-sm:Dot1x Request State Entered

23:50:17: dot1x-ev:dot1x_bend_request_enter:000d.56b7.6fc2: Current ID=6

23:50:17: dot1x-ev:Managed Timer in sub-block attached as leaf to master

23:50:17: dot1x-ev:dot1x_bend: Sending RADIUS Response to Supplicant of length 132

23:50:17: dot1x-ev:dot1x_tx_eap: EAP Ptk

23:50:17: dot1x-ev:EAP-code=REQUEST

23:50:17: dot1x-ev:EAP Type=Unknown

23:50:17: dot1x-ev:ID=6

This is the packet sent to the Supplicant from the Authenticator. It contains the EAP data sent to the Authenticator from the Authentication Server. The Authenticator did not manipulate the content of the EAP-Method data. It simply forwarded the information after decrypting it.

Frame 8 (150 bytes on wire, 150 bytes captured)

Arrival Time: Oct 13, 2005 07:18:22.960875000

Time delta from previous packet: 0.011430000 seconds

Time since reference or first frame: 3.655450000 seconds

Frame Number: 8

Packet Length: 150 bytes

Capture Length: 150 bytes

Ethernet II, Src: 00:0f:f7:96:14:03, Dst: 01:80:c2:00:00:03

Destination: 01:80:c2:00:00:03 (Spanning-Tree-(for-bridges)_03)

Source: 00:0f:f7:96:14:03 (00:0f:f7:96:14:03)

Type: 802.1X Authentication (0x888e)

802.1X Authentication

Version: 1

Type: EAP Packet (0)

Length: 132

Extensible Authentication Protocol

Code: Request (1)

Id: 6

Length: 132

Type: PEAP [Palekar] (25)

Type-Data (127 bytes) Value: 800000007A160301004A020000460301…

```
0000  01 80 c2 00 00 03 00 0f f7 96 14 03 88 8e 01 00   ...............
0010  00 84 01 06 00 84 19 80 00 00 00 00 7a 16 03 01 00   ..........z....
0020  4a 02 00 00 46 03 01 43 4e 50 45 62 1d 25 9b ed   J...F..CNPEb.%..
0030  73 e8 95 9b 89 ae a2 2a b5 c2 ba 31 79 e8 30 87   s......*...1y.0.
0040  83 df 0c e2 ae 00 26 20 25 be 7c af da 69 10 e3   ......& %.l..i..
0050  14 3c bc d8 97 f3 11 98 83 b8 5f 5d 06 0a 36 a2   .<.........]..6.
0060  13 89 85 a8 00 65 19 97 00 04 00 14 03 01 00 01   .....e.........
0070  01 16 03 01 00 20 4c b8 82 3c 44 0e 23 f7 fe 35   ..... L..<D.#..5
0080  65 6b 30 d1 a1 e8 67 44 04 03 ad 9f 67 ed 3e e9   ek0...gD....g.>.
0090  14 98 a4 12 83 28                                  .....(
```

The Supplicant immediately responds with the following packet. This packet contains credential information. This information may be a certificate, username/password, or even machine credentials. That is entirely up to the parameters specified within the EAP-Method. There is no way to tell what the actual content is because it is being tunneled. It would defeat the EAP-Method used here to be able to capture and decrypt the content.

Frame 9 (71 bytes on wire, 71 bytes captured)
Arrival Time: Oct 13, 2005 07:18:22.962029000
Time delta from previous packet: 0.001154000 seconds
Time since reference or first frame: 3.656604000 seconds
Frame Number: 9
Packet Length: 71 bytes
Capture Length: 71 bytes
Ethernet II, Src: 00:0d:56:b7:6f:c2, Dst: 01:80:c2:00:00:03
Destination: 01:80:c2:00:00:03 (Spanning-tree-(for-bridges)_03)
Source: 00:0d:56:b7:6f:c2 (169.254.101.32)
Type: 802.1X Authentication (0x888e)
802.1X Authentication
Version: 1
Type: EAP Packet (0)
Length: 53
Extensible Authentication Protocol
Code: Response (2)
Id: 6
Length: 53
Type: PEAP [Palekar] (25)

Type-Data (48 bytes) Value: 800000002B1403010001011603010020...

```
0000  01 80 c2 00 00 03 00 0d 56 b7 6f c2 88 8e 01 00  ........V.o.....
0010  00 35 02 06 00 35 19 80 00 00 00 2b 14 03 01 00  .5...5.....+....
0020  01 01 16 03 01 00 20 7f 4f 06 b1 80 ce 76 4c 59  ...... .O....vLY
0030  56 9a e9 c1 b6 2f 8e 26 52 03 28 fb fb 15 2c b0  V..../.&R.(...,.
0040  4a 48 28 ed 99 10 30                             JH(...0
```

The debug shows the Authenticator receiving the packet, resetting timers, manipulating the information from the Supplicant, and forwarding a packet to the Authentication Server.

23:50:17: dot1x-registry:registry:dot1x_ether_macaddr called

23:50:17: dot1x-packet:Received an EAPOL frame on interface FastEthernet0/3

23:50:17: dot1x-ev:Received pkt saddr=000d.56b7.6fc2, daddr=0180.c200.0003,pae-ether-type=34958

23:50:17: dot1x-ev:Found a supplicant block for mac 000d.56b7.6fc2 10BB294

23:50:17: dot1x-ev:RECEIVED mac=000d.56b7.6fc2 and Stored MAC=000d.56b7.6fc2

23:50:17: dot1x-packet:Received an EAP packet on interface FastEthernet0/3

23:50:17: dot1x-ev:Received RxResp from Authenticator

23:50:17: dot1x_bend Fa0/3: during state dot1x_bend_request, got event 4(rxresp)

23:50:17: @@@ dot1x_bend Fa0/3: dot1x_bend_request -> dot1x_bend_response

23:50:17: dot1x-sm:Dot1x Response State Entered for supp_info=10BB294 hwidb=D39480, swidb=D3A7BC on intf=Fa0/3

23:50:17: dot1x-ev:Managed Timer in sub-block attached as leaf to master

23:50:17: dot1x-sm:Started the ServerTimeout Timer

23:50:17: dot1x-ev:Going to Send Request to AAA Client on RP for id=6 and length=53

23:50:17: dot1x-ev:Got a Request from SP to send it to RADIUS with id 37

23:50:17: dot1x-ev:Found a process that's already handling the request for this id 6

23:50:17: dot1x-ev:Username is CCCC\edwin.brown; eap packet length=53

23:50:17: AAA/AUTHEN/CONT (4083091005): continue_login (user='CCCC\edwin.brown')

23:50:17: AAA/AUTHEN (4083091005): status = GETDATA

23:50:17: AAA/AUTHEN (4083091005): Method = RADIUS (RADIUS)

23:50:17: RADIUS: ustruct sharecount = 1

23:50:17: RADIUS: EAP-login: NAS Port = 00-0d-56-b7-6f-c2 RemAddr = 000d.56b7.6fc2

23:50:17: RADIUS: EAP-login: length of RADIUS packet = 185 code = 1

23:50:17: RADIUS: Initial Transmit FastEthernet0/3 id 37 10.92.30.39:1645, Access-Request, len 185

23:50:17:   Attribute 4 6 0A5C025A

23:50:17:   Attribute 61 6 00000000

23:50:17:   Attribute 1 18 43434343

23:50:17:   Attribute 6 6 00000002

23:50:17:   Attribute 12 6 000005DC

23:50:17:   Attribute 31 19 30302D30

23:50:17:   Attribute 24 31 43495343

23:50:17:   Attribute 79 55 02060035

23:50:17:   Attribute 80 18 724D2361

Even though this seems to be a huge amount of effort and a lot of information has been exchanged, it has taken less than a second of real time. The packet, back from the Authentication server, is shown below. Again, it is a very simple packet with all pertinent data encapsulated in attribute 79. There is almost nothing for the Authenticator to work with except to validate attribute 80 and then repackage the contents of attribute 79 and forward the result to the Supplicant.

23:50:17: RADIUS: Received from id 37 10.92.30.39:1645, Access-Challenge, len 109

23:50:17:   Attribute 79 40 01070026

23:50:17:   Attribute 24 31 43495343

23:50:17:   Attribute 80 18 56D38FFE

23:50:17: RADIUS: EAP-login: length of eap packet = 38

23:50:17: RADIUS: EAP-login: got challenge from RADIUS

23:50:17: AAA/AUTHEN (4083091005): status = GETDATA

23:50:17: dot1x-ev:going to send to backend on SP, length = 38

23:50:17: dot1x-ev:Received VLAN is No VLAN

23:50:17: dot1x-ev:Enqueued the response to backend

23:50:17: dot1x-ev:Sent to Bend

23:50:17: dot1x-ev:Received QUEUE EVENT in response to AAA Request

23:50:17: dot1x-ev:Dot1x matching request-response found

23:50:17: dot1x-ev:Length of recv eap packet from RADIUS = 38

23:50:17: dot1x-ev:Received VLAN Id -1

23:50:17: dot1x_bend Fa0/3: during state dot1x_bend_response, got event 0(areq)

23:50:17: @@@ dot1x_bend Fa0/3: dot1x_bend_response -> dot1x_bend_request

23:50:17: dot1x-sm:Dot1x Request State Entered

23:50:17: dot1x-ev:dot1x_bend_request_enter:000d.56b7.6fc2: Current ID=7

23:50:17: dot1x-ev:Managed Timer in sub-block attached as leaf to master

23:50:17: dot1x-ev:dot1x_bend: Sending RADIUS Response to Supplicant of length 38

23:50:17: dot1x-ev:dot1_tx_eap: EAP Ptk

23:50:17: dot1x-ev:EAP-code=REQUEST

23:50:17: dot1x-ev:EAP Type=Unknown

23:50:17: dot1x-ev:ID=7

This is the packet sent to the Supplicant that was derived from what the Authentication Server sent. This packet is telling the Supplicant that the credential exchange was a success. The Authentication Server is not notifying the Authenticator because the Supplicant must acknowledge the successful authentication before that notification will take place.

Frame 10 (60 bytes on wire, 60 bytes captured)
Arrival Time: Oct 13, 2005 07:18:22.972566000
Time delta from previous packet: 0.010537000 seconds
Time since reference or first frame: 3.667141000 seconds
Frame Number: 10
Packet Length: 60 bytes
Capture Length: 60 bytes
Ethernet II, Src: 00:0f:f7:96:14:03, Dst: 01:80:c2:00:00:03
Destination: 01:80:c2:00:00:03 (Spanning-Tree-(for-bridges)_03)
Source: 00:0f:f7:96:14:03 (00:0f:f7:96:14:03)
Type: 802.1X Authentication (0x888e)
Trailer: 00000000
802.1X Authentication
Version: 1
Type: EAP Packet (0)
Length: 38
Extensible Authentication Protocol
Code: Request (1)
Id: 7
Length: 38
Type: PEAP [Palekar] (25)

Type-Data (33 bytes) Value: 00170301001BF7F82506C758D1691DE6...

```
0000  01 80 c2 00 00 03 00 0f f7 96 14 03 88 8e 01 00   ...............
0010  00 26 01 07 00 26 19 00 17 03 01 00 1b f7 f8 25   .&...&.........%
0020  06 c7 58 d1 69 1d e6 fe 5e 37 48 a2 42 2f 13 a9   ..X.i...^7H.B/..
0030  66 7d 5d 75 1e cb cb e8 00 00 00 00               f}]u........
```

The Supplicant immediately responds with the packet below. This packet contains the acknowledgement that the Authentication Server is looking for. Of course, this acknowledgement is in the EAP-Method data and is not available for perusal. The number of exchanges between the Supplicant and the Authentication Server will vary and the content of those exchanges will also vary depending on how the authentication process is defined for the particular EAP-Method employed. This has been an example of an exchange based in PEAP MSCHAPV2. This method requires the acknowledgment imbedded in the response from the Supplicant before the Authentication Server will declare success. Other methods may or may not require this acknowledgement.

Frame 11 (60 bytes on wire, 60 bytes captured)
Arrival Time: Oct 13, 2005 07:18:22.974513000
Time delta from previous packet: 0.001947000 seconds
Time since reference or first frame: 3.669088000 seconds
Frame Number: 11
Packet Length: 60 bytes
Capture Length: 60 bytes
Ethernet II, Src: 00:0d:56:b7:6f:c2, Dst: 01:80:c2:00:00:03
Destination: 01:80:c2:00:00:03 (Spanning-tree-(for-bridges)_03)
Source: 00:0d:56:b7:6f:c2 (169.254.101.32)
Type: 802.1X Authentication (0x888e)
Trailer: 00000000
802.1X Authentication
Version: 1
Type: EAP Packet (0)
Length: 38
Extensible Authentication Protocol
Code: Response (2)
Id: 7
Length: 38
Type: PEAP [Palekar] (25)

Type-Data (33 bytes) Value: 00170301001BF69F4A6889C97FAA8086...

```
0000  01 80 c2 00 00 03 00 0d 56 b7 6f c2 88 8e 01 00   ........V.o.....
0010  00 26 02 07 00 26 19 00 17 03 01 00 1b f6 9f 4a   .&...&.........J
0020  68 89 c9 7f aa 80 86 69 ab 1a f5 c8 91 49 d0 2a   h......i.....I.*
0030  47 47 eb 2d 6c c2 96 e1 00 00 00 00               GG.-l.......
```

The Authenticator continues to do with this packet what it has done with all the previous packets. It finally constructs a RADIUS packet derived from what was sent by the Supplicant and forwards that packet to the Authentication Server. All of the debug messages are not shown leading up to that event. Shown below is the debug output regarding the packet being sent and the response back from the Authentication Server.

```
23:50:17: RADIUS: ustruct sharecount=1
23:50:17: RADIUS: EAP-login: NAS Port=00-0d-56-b7-6f-c2 RemAddr=
   000d.56b7.6fc2
23:50:17: RADIUS: EAP-login: length of RADIUS packet=170 code=1
23:50:17: RADIUS: Initial Transmit FastEthernet0/3 id 38
   10.92.30.39:1645, Access-Request, len 170
23:50:17:   Attribute 4 6 0A5C025A
23:50:17:   Attribute 61 6 00000000
23:50:17:   Attribute 1 18 43434343
23:50:17:   Attribute 6 6 00000002
23:50:17:   Attribute 12 6 000005DC
23:50:17:   Attribute 31 19 30302D30
23:50:17:   Attribute 24 31 43495343
23:50:17:   Attribute 79 40 02070026
23:50:17:   Attribute 80 18 48E552B0
23:50:17: RADIUS: Received from id 38 10.92.30.39:1645, Access-Accept,
   len 211
23:50:17:   Attribute 8 6 FFFFFFFF
23:50:17:   Attribute 79 6 03070004
23:50:17:   Attribute 26 58 000001371034BE18
23:50:17:   Attribute 26 58 0000013711348467
23:50:17:   Attribute 25 45 43495343
23:50:17:   Attribute 80 18 63F21546
```

Up to this point all packets from the Authentication Server were Access-Challenge packets requesting information. This packet is an Access-Accept. Now the Authenticator has something to do. It has been notified that the Supplicant has been successfully authenticated. Shown below are the debug output messages caused by the Access-Accept. Note that the configuration of the Authentication Server, CiscoACS in this case, was very simple. No special attributes, such as VLAN, Access-List, or any authorizations were configured. If they had been, they would have been passed back to the Authenticator and the Authenticator would have taken appropriate actions. The RADIUS debug messages shown below reflect that situation.

> 23:50:17: RADIUS: EAP-login: length of eap packet=4
>
> 23:50:17: RADIUS: EAP-login: RADIUS didn't send any VLAN
>
> 23:50:17: AAA/AUTHEN (4083091005): status=PASS
>
> 23:50:17: RADIUS: unrecognized Microsoft VSA type 16
>
> 23:50:17: RADIUS: unrecognized Microsoft VSA type 17
>
> 23:50:17: RADIUS: no appropriate authorization type for user.
>
> 23:50:17: dot1x-ev:dot1x_port_cleanup_author_atonce: cleanup author on interface FastEthernet0/3
>
> 23:50:17: RADIUS: allowing negotiated framed address
>
> 23:50:17: RADIUS: unrecognized Microsoft VSA type 16
>
> 23:50:17: RADIUS: unrecognized Microsoft VSA type 17
>
> 23:50:17: RADIUS: no appropriate authorization type for user.
>
> 23:50:17: dot1x-ev:Successfully applied per-user IP ACL on interface FastEthernet0/3
>
> 23:50:17: RADIUS: unrecognized Microsoft VSA type 16
>
> 23:50:17: RADIUS: unrecognized Microsoft VSA type 17
>
> 23:50:17: RADIUS: no appropriate authorization type for user.
>
> 23:50:17: dot1x-ev:Successfully applied per-user MAC ACL on interface FastEthernet0/3
>
> 23:50:17: dot1x-ev:Received VLAN is No VLAN
>
> 23:50:17: dot1x-ev:Enqueued the response to backend
>
> 23:50:17: AAA/MEMORY: free_user (0xD553C4) user='CCCC\edwin.-brown' ruser='CCCC\edwin.brown' port='FastEthernet0/3' rem_addr=" authen_type=EAP service=802.1X priv=1
>
> 23:50:17: dot1x-ev:Received QUEUE EVENT in response to AAA Request
>
> 23:50:17: dot1x-ev:Dot1x matching request-response found
>
> 23:50:17: dot1x-ev:Length of recv eap packet from RADIUS=4
>
> 23:50:17: dot1x-ev:Received VLAN Id -1
>
> 23:50:17: dot1x_bend Fa0/3: during state dot1x_bend_response, got event 2(asuccess)
>
> 23:50:17: @@@ dot1x_bend Fa0/3: dot1x_bend_response -> dot1x_bend_success
>
> 23:50:17: dot1x-sm:Dot1x Success State Entered
>
> 23:50:17: dot1x-ev:dot1x_bend_success_enter:000d.56b7.6fc2: Current ID=7

Thus, in less than a second, the authentication process has been completed successfully. There are a couple of interesting statements in the above debug that should be explored a little further. They seem a little cryptic until they are considered in terms of the configuration and the expected behavior of 802.1X. The first is:

23:50:17: dot1x-ev:Successfully applied peruser MAC ACL on interface FastEthernet0/3

What access list is the switch talking about? There is no access list in the configuration, so what the heck is this? Remember that by default only one Supplicant is allowed to connect to any port. This must be enforced, somehow, and this is how it is accomplished. A per-user access list identifying the MAC address of the successfully authenticated Supplicant is created and applied. This access list is internal and cannot be readily displayed The next statement occurs a little earlier in the debug and also seems just a bit cryptic:

23:50:17: RADIUS: EAP-login: RADIUS didn't send any VLAN

The VLAN assigned can be controlled by RADIUS upon a successful authentication. The debug statement is simply indicating that there was no VLAN configured on the Authentication Server for the user. This situation will be explored in more detail in just a couple of paragraphs. But let us finish with this scenario first. The debug messages below show the formation of a notification to the Supplicant that the Authenticator recognizes as the successful authentication.

23:50:17: dot1x-ev:dot1x_bend: Sending RADIUS Response to Supplicant of length 4
23:50:17: dot1x-ev:dot1x_tx_eap: EAP Ptk
23:50:17: dot1x-ev:EAP-code = SUCCESS
23:50:17: dot1x-ev:EAP Type = Unknown
23:50:17: dot1x-ev:ID = 7

This is the actual packet sent to the Supplicant. It is an EAP packet, technically an EAPOL packet, but it contains no EAPOL information because it is a Type 0 that indicates a successful authentication to the Supplicant.

Frame 12 (60 bytes on wire, 60 bytes captured)
Arrival Time: Oct 13, 2005 07:18:22.990822000
Time delta from previous packet: 0.016309000 seconds
Time since reference or first frame: 3.685397000 seconds
Frame Number: 12
Packet Length: 60 bytes
Capture Length: 60 bytes
Ethernet II, Src: 00:0f:f7:96:14:03, Dst: 01:80:c2:00:00:03
Destination: 01:80:c2:00:00:03 (Spanning-tree-(for-bridges)_03)

Source: 00:0f:f7:96:14:03 (00:0f:f7:96:14:03)
Type: 802.1X Authentication (0x888e)
Trailer: 0000000000000000000000000000000000...
802.1X Authentication
Version: 1
Type: EAP Packet (0)
Length: 4
Extensible Authentication Protocol
Code: Success (3)
Id: 7
Length: 4

```
0000  01 80 c2 00 00 03 00 0f f7 96 14 03 88 8e 01 00   ...............

0010  00 04 03 07 00 04 00 00 00 00 00 00 00 00 00 00   ...............

0020  00 00 00 00 00 00 00 00 00 00 00 00 00 00 00 00   ...............

0030  00 00 00 00 00 00 00 00 00 00 00 00                   ...........
```

The debug below continues on to show that the Authenticator has cleaned up the 802.1X process on the port and placed it in an authorized state. The last debug message shows the line protocol coming up. The Supplicant now can begin what the user would consider "normal" activity.

23:50:17: dot1x-registry:registry:dot1x_ether_macaddr called
23:50:17: dot1x_bend Fa0/3: idle during state dot1x_bend_success
23:50:17: @@@ dot1x_bend Fa0/3: dot1x_bend_success -> dot1x_bend_idle
23:50:17: dot1x-sm:Dot1x Idle State Entered
23:50:17: dot1x_auth Fa0/3: during state auth_authenticating, got event 7(authSuccess)
23:50:17: @@@ dot1x_auth Fa0/3: auth_authenticating -> auth_authenticated
23:50:17: dot1x-sm:Fa0/3:000d.56b7.6fc2:auth_authenticated_enter called
23:50:17: dot1x-sm:
dot1x_update_port_status called with port_status=DOT1X_PORT_STATUS_AUTHORIZED
23:50:17: dot1x-ev:dot1x_update_port_status: using mac 000d.56b7.6fc2 to send port to authorized
23:50:17: dot1x-ev:dot1x_update_port_status: using mac 000d.56b7.6fc2 to send port to authorized
23:50:17: dot1x-ev:Found a supplicant block for mac 000d.56b7.6fc2 10BB294

23:50:17: dot1x-ev:dot1x_port_authorized:supplicant 000d.56b7.6fc2 is first, old VLAN 1, new VLAN 0

23:50:17: dot1x-ev:dot1x_port_authorized: Host-mode=0 RADIUS/-Guest VLAN=0

23:50:17: dot1x-ev: GuestVLAN configured=0

23:50:17: dot1x-registry:** dot1x_vp_statechange:

23:50:17: dot1x-ev:VLAN 30 vp is added on the interface FastEthernet0/3

23:50:17: dot1x-registry:dot1x_port_modechange invoked on interface FastEthernet0/3

23:50:17: dot1x-ev:dot1x_port_authorized: clearing HA table from VLAN 1

23:50:17: dot1x-ev:dot1x_port_authorized: Added 000d.56b7.6fc2 to HA table on VLAN 30

23:50:17: dot1x-sm:Fa0/3:000d.56b7.6fc2:auth_authenticating_authenticated_action called

23:50:18: %LINEPROTO-5-UPDOWN: Line protocol on Interface FastEthernet0/3, changed state to up

A partial output from a "show VLAN" confirms that the port is in the VLAN established for an authenticated Supplicant. Specifically port Fastethernet 0/3 is in VLAN 30.

VLAN Name	Status	Ports
1 default	active	Fa0/17, Fa0/18, Fa0/19, Fa0/20
		Fa0/21, Fa0/22, Fa0/24, Gi0/1
		Gi0/2
2 management	active	
3 VLAN0003	active	
7 VLAN0007	active	Fa0/12
10 VLAN0010	active	Fa0/1, Fa0/2, Fa0/8, Fa0/9, Fa0/10, Fa0/11
20 VLAN0020	active	
30 VLAN0030	active	Fa0/3

And a "show interface FA0/3" confirms that the port is fully "up."

FastEthernet0/3 is up, line protocol is up (connected)
Hardware is Fast Ethernet, address is 000f.f796.1403 (bia 000f.f796.1403)
MTU 1500 bytes, BW 100000 Kbit, DLY 100 usec,
Reliability 255/255, txload 1/255, rxload 1/255
Encapsulation ARPA, loopback not set

Keepalive set (10 seconds)
Full-duplex, 100 Mb/s

Now the Supplicant is connected to the network and the poor user behind the keyboard is none the wiser. The Supplicant is in the access VLAN coded for the port and working just fine. Now suppose that this user is part of a small group that requires special control and privilege. That is probably a stretch, considering that our network is only a few ports and consists of a router and a RADIUS server, but assume that anyway.

As discussed briefly a couple of paragraphs earlier, it is viable to configure the RADIUS server in such a way that a specific user or user group is placed in a specific VLAN. This configuration takes place entirely on the RADIUS server and will be subject to the format of the specific server implemented.

In CiscoACS, as described in the section on configuration, this is accomplished by identifying that RADIUS (IETF) is the form to be taken and attributes 64, 65, and 81 are correctly configured. This was done in our very simple network. In the debug statement shown below, those special attributes are returned by the Authentication Server. If a comparison is made to the earlier Access-Accept packet returned by the server, they are the same except for the inclusion of these attributes. Also, it should be noted and expected that these attributes are returned outside of the EAP-Method data.

```
2w2d: RADIUS: Received from id 82 10.92.30.39:1645, Access-Accept,
    len 228
2w2d:   Attribute 64 6 0100000D
2w2d:   Attribute 65 6 01000006
2w2d:   Attribute 81 5 01323008
2w2d:   Attribute 8 6 FFFFFFFF
2w2d:   Attribute 79 6 03090004
2w2d:   Attribute 26 58 000001371034C916
2w2d:   Attribute 26 58 000001371134F16D
2w2d:   Attribute 25 45 43495343
2w2d:   Attribute 80 18 6FC14F60
```

This debug continues by showing the evaluation of the contents of those particular attributes associated with the modification of the VLAN to be assigned. It ultimately identifies that VLAN 20 is to be assigned to the port for as long as the authentication of the Supplicant is in effect.

```
2w2d: RADIUS: EAP-login: length of EAP packet=4
2w2d: AAA/AUTHEN (3028732558): status=PASS
2w2d: RADIUS: Tunnel-Type, [01] 00 00 0D
2w2d: RADIUS: TAS(1) created and enqueued.
2w2d: RADIUS: Tunnel-MType, [01] 00 00 06
2w2d: RADIUS: Tunnel-GID, [01] 20
```

The debug continues to output a plethora of messages that have not been included but ultimately show that VLAN 20 was received from the Authentication Server and the authentication was successful.

2w2d: dot1x-ev:Received VLAN Id 20
2w2d: dot1x_bend Fa0/3: during state dot1x_bend_response, got event
   2(asuccess)
2w2d: @@@ dot1x_bend Fa0/3: dot1x_bend_response ->
   dot1x_bend_success
2w2d: dot1x-sm:Dot1x Success State Entered
2w2d: dot1x-ev:dot1x_bend_success_enter:000d.56b7.6fc2: Current
   ID=9
2w2d: dot1x-ev:dot1x_bend: Sending RADIUS Response to Supplicant
   of length 4
2w2d: dot1x-ev:dot1x_tx_eap: EAP Pkt
2w2d: dot1x-ev:EAP-code=SUCCESS
2w2d: dot1x-ev:EAP Type=Unknown
2w2d: dot1x-ev:ID=9

The Authenticator places the port into VLAN 20 and issues a Success packet to the Supplicant. This can be a point of confusion for someone attempting to manage the device because a "show config" will not indicate that the port should have any type of association with VLAN 20. However, a "show VLAN" will clearly show the port to be in VLAN 20. If the VLAN identified by the Authentication Server is not defined on the Authenticator, then an error message will be displayed and the authentication process will continue with the port remaining in an unauthorized state. A partial output of the "show VLAN" is included below.

VLAN Name	Status	Ports
1 default	active	Fa0/17, Fa0/18, Fa0/19, Fa0/20
		Fa0/21, Fa0/22, Fa0/24, Gi0/1
		Gi0/2
2 management	active	
3 VLAN0003	active	
7 VLAN0007	active	Fa0/12
10 VLAN0010	active	Fa0/8, Fa0/9, Fa0/10, Fa0/11
20 test-dynamic-8021x	active	Fa0/3
30 test-ipt	active	Fa0/1, Fa0/2

A very similar situation happens when a per-user access-list has been coded on the RADIUS server. Like the VLAN information, the access list is sent to the Authenticator and is applied to the port for the duration in which the port is authenticated. Just as with the dynamically applied VLAN, the port is the recipient of the application and not the user. Should more than one user be active on the port, then there can be very unpredictable results. The last authentication resets the port to values associated with it. The actual configuration is not modified so that this information cannot get permanently "stuck."

3.2.4   What Happens If They Logoff?

One of the options to end a user session in Windows 2000 is to logoff rather than shutting down or restarting a personal computer. A shutdown or a restart drops the link and 802.1X is reinitiated on the port. So what happens when a user logs off? There are two possible situations here. The Supplicant can be an active participant in 802.1X—meaning that it will have issued an EAPOL-Start when it first became active. Or it may be passive—meaning that it relied on the Authenticator to initiate the process and did not send an EAPOL-Start. If it was passive, then nothing will happen when a user logs off because the physical connection is maintained. This means that the authentication state of the port will be maintained. This is not the case for an active participant.

Let us use the same type of debug that has been used throughout the book: Full debugging of dot1x, AAA authentication, and RADIUS. Looking at the statements below, it is easy to see that the Supplicant became active and the expected output from the authentication took place at 00:22:24. Then there is a gap until 00:22:41—this was a short session, but it was a session—when the Supplicant issues an EAPOL frame.

```
00:22:24 @@@ dot1x_auth Fa0/3:auth_connecting->auth_connecting
00:22:24 dot1x-
    sm:Fa0/3:0000.0000.0000:auth_connecting_connecting_action called
00:22:24 dot1x-ev:dot1x_post_message_to_auth_sm: Skipping tx for
    req_id for default supplicant
00:22:24 dot1x-packet:Received an EAPOL frame on interface
    FastEthernet0/3
00:22:24 dot1x-ev:Received pkt saddr=000d.56b7.6fc2,daddr=
    0180.c200.0003,pae-ether-type=34958
00:22:24 dot1x-ev:Found a supplicant block for mac
    00d.56b7.6fc2 110C210
```

The next portion of the debug, beginning at 00:22:41, is interesting. It would be normal to assume that the frame sent upon a user logoff would be an EAPOL-Stop, but it is an EAPOL-Start instead. Consider the implications of issuing a Start rather than a Stop. A Stop will end processing on the port, causing it to go into an unauthorized state. This means that when a user logs back into the device, an EAPOL-Start would be required in order for the authentication process to be initiated. Remember that the port is up, so the Authenticator will not reinitiate the process. It is entirely possible that the new user will not have an active Supplicant. This will leave the new user with no network connectivity. However, if the device issues an EAPOL-Start instead of an EAPOL-Stop upon logging off, then the Authenticator will restart the authentication process immediately. Let us continue with the debug at 00:22:41 when the user logs off.

00:22:41 dot1x-ev:RECEIVED mac -000d.56b7.6fc2 and Stored MAC= 00d.56b7.6fc2

00:22:41 dot1x-packet:Received   EAPOL_START   on   interface FastEthernet0/3

00:22:41 dot1x_auth Fa0/3: during state auth_authenticated, got event 4(eapStart)

00:22:41 @@@ dot1x_auth Fa0/3: auth_authenticated->auth_connecting

00:22:41 dot1x-sm:Fa0/3,000d.56b7.6fc2:auth_authenticated_exit_action called

00:22:41 dot1x-sm:Fa0/3,000d.56b7.6fc2:auth_connecting_enter called

00:22:41 dot1x-sm:Fa0/3,000d.56b7.6fc2:auth_authenticated_connecting_action called

00:22:41 dot1x-ev:dot1x_post_message_to_auth_sm:Tx for req_id for supplicant 00d.56b7.6fc2

00:22:41 dot1x-ev:dot1x_tx_eap: EAP Pkt

00:22:41 dot1x-ev:EAP-code=REQUEST

00:22:41 dot1x-ev:EAP Type=IDENTITY

00:22:41 dot1x-ev:ID=22

Of course, the Supplicant does not respond to the request and during this time the port remains in a "connected" state. The Authenticator will continue to attempt to communicate, but there is no response from the Supplicant. Eventually the Authenticator will place the port in an unauthorized state and will issue an EA-Failure to the Supplicant. This will cause the port to be placed into a Guest VLAN, if one has been configured. This is an optimal state for the port, awaiting when there is no user logged into the Supplicant. This way, if the new user does not participate in 802.1X, then he will be able to attach to the network as desired. On the other hand, if the new user does participate in 802.1X, the Supplicant will issue an EAPOL-Start to initiate authentication.

The debug output shown below illustrates the final actions taken by the Authenticator when a user logs off.

00:22:41: dot1x-sm:Fa0/3:000d.56b7.6fc2:auth_disconnected_enter_action called

00:22:41: dot1x-sm:

dot1x_update_port_status called with port_status= DOT1X_PORT_STATUS_UNAUTHORIZED

00:22:41: dot1x-ev:dot1x_port_cleanup_author: cleanup author on interface FastEthernet0/3

00:22:41: dot1x-ev:dot1x_update_port_status: Called with host_mode= 0 state UNAUTHORIZED

00:22:41: dot1x-ev:dot1x_update_port_status: using mac 000d.56b7.6fc2 to send port to unauthorized on VLAN 0

00:22:41: dot1x-ev:Found a supplicant block for mac 000d.56b7.6fc2 110C210

00:22:41: dot1x-ev:dot1x_port_unauthorized: Host-mode=0 RADIUS/Guest VLAN=0

00:22:41: dot1x-ev: Guest Vlan configured=0

Up to this point in the debug the output is very similar to that displayed during an initial connection when the link became active. However, in this case the port was already active and authenticated. Some additional cleanup is required and this is shown below.

00:22:41 dot1x-registry:**dot1x_vp_statechange

00:22:41 dot1x-ev:VLAN 30 vp is removed on the interface FastEthernet0/3

00:22:41 dot1x-registrydot1x_port_unauthorized:Host-mode=0 RADIUS/guest=0

00:22:41: dot1x-ev:supplicant 000d.56b7.6fc2 is last

00:22:41 dot1x-ev:dot1x_port_unauthorized: removing feature 000d.56b7.6fc2 to HA table on VLAN 30

00:22:41: dot1x-ev:dot1x_port_cleanup_author: cleanup author on interface FastEthernet0/3

00:22:41: dot1x_auth Fa0/3: idle during state auth_disconnected

00:22:41 @@@ dot1x_auth Fa0/3: auth_disconnected->auth_connecting

00:22:41: dot1x-sm:Fa0/3:000d.56b7.6fc2:auth_connecting_enter called

00:22:41: dot1x-ev:Found a supplicant block for mac 0000.0000.0000 FB9134

00:22:41 dot1x-ev:dot1x_auth_connecting_action: Updating default supplicant block with expected/current id=22/22 from 000d.56b7.6fc2 block

00:22:41: dot1x-sm:dot1x_auth_connecting_action:000d.56b7.6fc2 Posting reAuthMax_exceeded event

00:22:41: dot1x-ev:dot1x_post_message_to_auth_sm: 000d.56b7.6fc2: sending TX_FAIL

00:22:41: dot1x-ev:dot1x_post_message_to_auth_sm: 000d.56b7.6fc2: Current ID=23

00:22:41: dot1x-ev:dot1x_tx_eap: EAP Pkt

00:22:41: dot1x-ev:EAP-code=REQUEST

00:22:41: dot1x-ev:EAP Type=IDENTITY
00:22:41: dot1x-ev:ID=22

Here the port becomes "not connected" and the normal authentication process will continue. The Supplicant does not respond, so the port eventually is placed in a Guest VLAN, if one has been configured.

The port on the Authenticator is in an entirely reasonable state as far a 802.1X is concerned. It will continue the normal authentication process. The next 802.1X events will either be an EAPOL-Start from a new user logging in or the port will attempt authentication when the configured quiet period has expired.

That is what happens when it works the way it is supposed to work, or at least the way we want it to work. Surely there are additional situations where it will work differently, but in a way that is still desirable. Still, when a user that is supposed to have access to the network plugs in, then a process similar to those discussed above is the desired and expected outcome. It can happen in the background and the user may never be aware that she has been scrutinized and finally allowed access. The timeframe in which this has taken place is probably not even noticeable by the user, as it will frequently take place while a device is being booted. The total time that elapsed was less than four seconds and most of the actual processing took place in less than one second of real time.

While all of the examples shown utilize IOS on a small switch, both larger switches and switches implementing CAT-OS will exhibit the same functionality and similar output. In a very simple network, the implementation of 802.1X in a wired environment is clean and simple. But what happens when the process does not really work as desired?

3.3 WHAT IF IT DIDN'T WORK RIGHT?

3.3.1 Section Summary

Even though in the vast majority of instances a connection on an 802.1X enabled port will function as described in the previous section, there are common situations where everything does not work as desired. This section will discuss a variety of them.

There is one situation that could be considered a failure, but really is not. That is the connection of a machine that does not house a Supplicant. The fact that an entity connecting to an 802.1X enabled port does not get placed on an authenticated VLAN does not constitute a failure. That is a situation covered by the specifications for 802.1X. Most frequently, the lack of a functioning Supplicant will be why an individual machine is placed into a Guest VLAN. And, most frequently, the lack of a Supplicant is because the client machine attempting to attach belongs to a true guest.

There is one additional situation that is frequently the result of a guest attempting to attach to the network and that is the presentation of invalid credentials. This situation may take one of two directions and most frequently will appear as an EAP-Method mismatch. Not as common for guests is the presentation of invalid credentials. The presentation of invalid credentials is discussed in this section and the mismatch of an EAP-Method is presented in the next section dedicated to "guests."

It is difficult to diagnose whether invalid credentials have been supplied or there is an EAP-Methods mismatch because in debugs both situations develop the same output. Frequently, the only place to actually diagnose the reason why the Authentication Server rejected the authentication attempt is in the logs on the RADIIUS server.

The last situation discussed in this section is the absence of an Authentication Server. This is the last situation of a missing component to be discussed. If there is no Authenticator, then 802.1X does not even get started. If there is no Supplicant, then the client will be placed in the Guest VLAN. If there is no Authentication Server, then the situation becomes very awkward because, generally, the port never becomes active in any VLAN. The Authenticator has a Supplicant that is supplying credentials, but it has no authority that validates them. Thus, the Authenticator continues to attempt to validate the credentials while keeping the port in an unauthorized state.

There may be additional side conditions where things are not working properly, but for the most part the conditions explored in this section and the next one on guests are the most common. There are situations that occur with the use of hubs or unauthorized devices that require support, but they are not strictly situations where something has gone wrong. Several of these types of situations will be discussed in subsequent sections.

3.3.2 What Happens If There Is No Active Supplicant?

Why would a situation where there is no active Supplicant arise? There a couple of immediate scenarios where this would occur. The most common reason for this is that 802.1X is not enabled as a service on a Windows machine. This could have been done purposely or it could have happened accidentally. The more common situation is where an individual from a different organization than the one to whose network he is attempting to attach is not using 802.1X. In this situation, it will be unlikely that the Windows service enabling 802.1X was actually started. Anyway, this common situation may be reported as a problem. Shown below is the output from various sources that describes what happens in this instance. Of course, this assumes that a Guest VLAN has been configured on the Supplicant.

It starts at the point where a port on an Authenticator is made active. The Authenticator acts in the normal fashion described in detail in the previous section. It will do some background housekeeping and eventually will send an EAP Failure. Immediately following that it will send an EAP Request Identity. This is shown in the debug below.

```
00:03:04: dot1x-ev:dot1x_tx_eap: EAP Pkt
00:03:04: dot1x-ev:EAP-code=FAILURE
00:03:04: dot1x-ev:EAP Type=IDENTITY
00:03:04: dot1x-ev:ID=0
00:03:04: dot1x-registry:registry:dot1x_ether_macaddr called
00:03:04: dot1x-ev:dot1x_post_message_to_auth_sm: cleanup author
    from interface FastEthernet0/3
00:03:04: dot1x-ev:dot1x_post_message_to_auth_sm: Tx for req_id for
    supplicant 0000.0000.0000
00:03:04: dot1x-ev:dot1x_tx_eap: EAP Pkt
00:03:04: dot1x-ev:EAP-code=REQUEST
00:03:04: dot1x-ev:EAP Type=IDENTITY
00:03:04: dot1x-ev:ID=1
```

At this point, the output begins to deviate from that shown in the situation where the Supplicant responds to the request. The Authenticator initiated a timer upon the transmission of the Request Identity. In the default state, the timer will expire in thirty seconds and a second EAP Request Identity will be transmitted. This is shown in the following debug. Note the time stamp in the last debug statement above and the first statement below.

```
00:03:34: dot1x-sm:Fa0/3:0000.0000.0000:dot1x_process_txWhen_ex-
    pire called
00:03:34: dot1x_auth Fa0/3: during state auth_connecting, got event
    18(txWhen_expire)
```

The debug statement above identifies that the timer has expired and that a retransmission is required. The following debug statement indicates the current state of the port and the state to which it is transitioning. In this case, the state does not change.

```
00:03:34: @@@ dot1x_auth Fa0/3: auth_connecting -> auth_connecting
```

The following statements are exactly the same as those surrounding the transmission of the first EAP Request Identity. They reflect the fact that an EAPOL packet was transmitted on the Ethernet connection to the Supplicant.

```
00:03:34: dot1x-sm:Fa0/3:0000.0000.0000:auth_connecting_connectin-
    g_action called
00:03:34: dot1x-ev:dot1x_post_message_to_auth_sm: Tx for req_id for
    supplicant 0000.0000.0000
```

```
00:03:34: dot1x-ev:dot1x_tx_eap: EAP Pkt
00:03:34: dot1x-ev:EAP-code=REQUEST
00:03:34: dot1x-ev:EAP Type=IDENTITY
00:03:34: dot1x-ev:ID=1
```

If the status of the port is queried during the thirty seconds separating the issuance of the two Request Identity packets, the port will be shown to be up, but the line protocol will be down. The following messages are also likely to be displayed.

```
00:03:06: %LINK-3-UPDOWN: Interface FastEthernet0/3, changed state
  to up
00:03:07: %LINEPROTO-5-UPDOWN: Line protocol on Interface
  FastEthernet0/3, changed state to down
```

It can be slightly confusing because the port will be shown to be in the VLAN assigned if a display of VLANs is conducted. The key here is that the display of the VLANs shows what VLAN a port has been configured to be placed into under normal processing. 802.1X does not allow the port to be active until authenticated, so it does not matter that the port is assigned to a VLAN.

The Authenticator has issued a Request Identity, waited thirty seconds, and issued another Request Identity. It has waited another thirty seconds after transmitting the second Request Identity. The debug below shows that the timer has expired and continues to show that the maximum number of attempts has now been exceeded. Remember that the default is two attempts and the count is now three.

```
00:04:04: dot1x-
  sm:Fa0/3:0000.0000.0000:dot1x_process_txWhen_expire called
00:04:04: dot1x_auth Fa0/3: during state auth_connecting, got event
  18(txWhen_expire)
00:04:04: @@@ dot1x_auth Fa0/3: auth_connecting -> auth_connecting
00:04:04: dot1x-
  sm:Fa0/3:0000.0000.0000:auth_connecting_connecting_action called
00:04:04: dot1x-sm:dot1x_auth_connecting_action:0000.0000.0000
  reauth_count=3 exceeded DOT1X_DEFAULT_REAUTH_MAX
```

So what happens now? The Authenticator must determine whether or not a Guest VLAN has been coded. The following debug statement shows that it has begun that evaluation.

```
00:04:04: dot1x-ev:Default and only instance. evaluation for Guest
  VLAN move
```

The next debug statements indicate that a Guest VLAN was found and the Authenticator proceeds to authorize the port.

```
00:04:04: dot1x_auth Fa0/3: during state auth_connecting, got event
    7(authSuccess)
00:04:04: @@@  dot1x_auth  Fa0/3:  auth_connecting  ->
    auth_authenticated
00:04:04: dot1x-sm:Fa0/3:0000.0000.0000:auth_connecting_exit alled
00:04:04: dot1x-
    sm:Fa0/3:0000.0000.0000:auth_authenticated_enter called
00:04:04: dot1x-sm:
dot1x_update_port_status  called  with  port_status=
    DOT1X_PORT_STATUS_AUTHORIZED
00:04:04: dot1x-ev:dot1x_update_port_status: using mac 0000.0000.0000
    to send port to authorized
00:04:04: dot1x-ev:dot1x_update_port_status: using mac 0000.0000.0000
    to send port to authorized
```

The port is assigned a new VLAN as indicated by the configured Guest VLAN. Note that the debug below also shows that the MIB element indicating that the port is in the Guest VLAN is set.

```
00:04:04: dot1x-ev:Found  a  supplicant  block  for  mac
    0000.0000.0000 10B9CB0
00:04:04: dot1x-ev:dot1x_port_authorized:supplicant 0000.0000.0000 is
    first, old VLAN 1, new VLAN 10
00:04:04: dot1x-ev:dot1x_port_authorized: Host-mode=0 radius/Guest
    VLAn=10
00:04:04: dot1x-ev: Guest Vlan configured=1
00:04:04: dot1x-registry:** dot1x_vp_statechange:
00:04:04: dot1x-ev:VLAn 10 vp is added on the interface FastEthernet0/3
```

Finally, the port becomes fully active as show below.

```
00:04:04: dot1x-registry:dot1x_port_modechange invoked on interface
    FastEthernet0/3
00:04:04: dot1x-ev:dot1x_port_authorized: clearing HA table from
    VLAN 1
00:04:05: %LINEPROTO-5-UPDOWN: Line protocol on Interface
    FastEthernet0/3, changed state to up
```

It should be obvious that if a Guest VLAN had not been configured the following statement in the debug would have indicated failure instead of success and the port would not have been authorized.

> 00:04:04: dot1x_auth Fa0/3: during state auth_connecting, got event 7(authSuccess)

Notice that there is never any attempt to contact the Authentication Server. That would be futile because there is no information to send. All of the processing in this situation is confined to the Authenticator.

If there is no Supplicant on a port that is enabled for 802.1X, then the port either remains unauthorized or is placed in a configured Guest VLAN, depending on the coding of the Guest VLAN for the port on the Authenticator.

What we have seen is the expected behavior of 802.1X. There is nothing that is out of spec or unusual. However, it does point out that there are some considerations in the design and implementation of 802.1X that must be made with regard to the presence or absence of a Supplicant and the docking of a Guest VALN on the port.

When everything works as planned, the implementation of 802.1X is nearly invisible. A laptop with a Supplicant using valid credentials is readily admitted and the user probably will never notice that the process has occurred. She is authenticated and placed into the anticipated VLAN. Life is good.

But when there is no Supplicant present on the laptop, then life has the potential to go awry. The amount of time required to be placed into a VLAN increases to 60 seconds or more. Some applications may be affected and the Help Desk might be called. Life will be better if this situation is recognized, accepted, and good processes are defined for the Help Desk.

3.3.3 What Happens If There Is a Supplicant but There Is No Authentication Server?

For whatever reason, the Authentication Server is not available in our very simple Network. It may have crashed, or a misconfiguration is not allowing communication between the Authenticator and the Authentication Server. This scenario was discussed in the section entitled How Does It Work.

Thus, a Supplicant connects to the network and has a successful exchange of EAP/EAPOL frames with the Authenticator. The Authenticator now attempts to contact the RADIUS server just as it did in the previous example. Again, debugs and traces were made and some of the debug information is shown below.

> 00:25:42: AAA: parse name=FastEthernet0/3 idb type=−1 tty=−1
> 00:25:42: AAA: name=FastEthernet0/3 flags=0x15 type=7 shelf=0
>   slot=0 adapter=0 port=3 channel=0
> 00:25:42: AAA: parse name=<no string> idb type=−1 tty=−1

00:25:42: AAA/MEMORY: create_user (0xFC82A8) user='CCCC\Ed-win.Brown' ruser='CCCC\Edwin.Brown' port='FastEthernet0/3' rem_addr=" authen_type=EAP service=802.1X priv=1

00:25:42: dot1x-ev:MAC Address copied is 000d.56b7.6fc2

00:25:42: AAA/AUTHEN/START (3281315797): port='FastEthernet0/3' list='Dot1x Acc List' action=LOGIN service=802.1X

00:25:42: AAA/AUTHEN/START (3281315797): using "default" list

00:25:42: AAA/AUTHEN/START (3281315797): Method=radius (radius)

00:25:42: RADIUS: ustruct sharecount=1

00:25:42: RADIUS: EAP-login: NAS Port=00-0d-56-b7-6f-c2 RemAddr= 000d.56b7.6fc2

00:25:42: RADIUS: EAP-login: length of radius packet=122 code=1

00:25:42: RADIUS: Initial Transmit FastEthernet0/3 id 7 10.92.30.39:1645, Access-Request, len 122

00:25:42:   Attribute 4 6 0A5C025A

00:25:42:   Attribute 61 6 00000000

00:25:42:   Attribute 1 18 43434343

00:25:42:   Attribute 6 6 00000002

00:25:42:   Attribute 12 6 000005DC

00:25:42:   Attribute 31 19 30302D30

00:25:42:   Attribute 79 23 02000015

00:25:42:   Attribute 80 18 17E6E4B5

Up to this point the debug and packet captures will show the exact same situation and sequence of events as would occur in a successful authentication. The exchange has been entirely normal and as expected. However, the next sequence from the debug illustrates the problem. The Authenticator is retransmitting packets and finally marks the Authentication Server as dead.

00:25:47: RADIUS: Retransmit id 7

00:25:52: RADIUS: Retransmit id 7

00:25:57: RADIUS: Retransmit id 7

00:26:02: RADIUS: Marking server 10.92.30.39:1645,1813 dead

In the configuration used for this example, only one RADIUS server was defined. The Authenticator has just placed that server into a status indicating that it cannot be contacted. If additional servers had been configured, the Authenticator would have continued to attempt to contact them in the order in which they were configured. If they, too, were dead, then the Authenticator would reach the point shown below where it has entered a state where no Authentication Server is available.

00:26:02: RADIUS: Tried all servers.

00:26:02: RADIUS: No valid server found. Trying any viable server

00:26:02: RADIUS: Tried all servers.

00:26:02: RADIUS: No response for id 7
00:26:02: AAA/AUTHEN (3281315797): status=ERROR

AAA has now entered a state where the primary method of authentication has failed. If a secondary method has been identified, in this case NONE, it would normally continue with that method. In this case, an attempt was made to mitigate the situation the Authenticator is now in. A secondary method of NONE was included to stop the authentication process, as the RADIUS server is not contactable. As shown in the debug statements below, it does not work and another round of attempted contact to the RADIUS server is initiated.

00:26:02: AAA/AUTHEN/START (3281315797): Method=NONE
00:26:02: AAA/AUTHEN (3281315797): status=PASS
00:26:02: dot1x-err:EAP packet not recvd
00:26:02: RADIUS: authenticating to get author data
00:26:02: RADIUS: ustruct sharecount=2
00:26:02: RADIUS: EAP-login: NAS Port=00-0d-56-b7-6f-c2 RemAddr=
    000d.56b7.6fc2
00:26:02: RADIUS: EAP-login: length of radius packet=101 code=1
00:26:02: RADIUS: Initial Transmit FastEthernet0/3 id 8 10.92.30.39:1645,
    Access-Request, len 101
00:26:02:   Attribute 4 6 0A5C025A
00:26:02:   Attribute 61 6 00000000
00:26:02:   Attribute 1 18 43434343
00:26:02:   Attribute 6 6 00000002
00:26:02:   Attribute 12 6 000005DC
00:26:02:   Attribute 31 19 30302D30
00:26:02:   Attribute 79 2 5012BFEE
00:26:02:   Attribute 80 18 BFEECB49
00:26:07: RADIUS: Retransmit id 8

Again, there is no response. Notice the timestamps on the debug output. It has taken twenty seconds of real time for this sequence of events. That can seem like an eternity to a frustrated user. But the worst event is yet to occur, in terms of user frustration. The Authenticator now notifies the Supplicant that the process has failed and does not place the port into any VLAN, but leaves it in an unauthorized state.

00:26:08: dot1x-
    sm:Fa0/3:0000.0000.0000:dot1x_process_txWhen_expire called
00:26:08: dot1x_auth Fa0/3: during state auth_connecting, got event
    18(txWhen_expire)

00:26:08: @@@ dot1x_auth Fa0/3: auth_connecting -> auth_connecting

00:26:08: dot1x-sm:Fa0/3:0000.0000.0000:auth_connecting_connecting_action called

00:26:08: dot1x-ev:dot1x_post_message_to_auth_sm: Skipping tx for req_id for default supplicant

00:26:12: dot1x-ev:Received TIMER EVENT

00:26:12: dot1x_bend Fa0/3: during state dot1x_bend_response, got event 7(awhile_expire)

00:26:12: @@@ dot1x_bend Fa0/3: dot1x_bend_response -> dot1x_bend_timeout

00:26:12: dot1x-sm:Dot1x Timeout State Entered

00:26:12: dot1x-ev:AAA Session on RP for this Interface FastEthernet0/3 terminated because of timeout on SP

00:26:12: dot1x-ev:dot1x_tx_eap: EAP Ptk

00:26:12: dot1x-ev:EAP-code=FAILURE

00:26:12: dot1x-ev:EAP Type=IDENTITY

00:26:12: dot1x-ev:ID=0

The captured Failure packet is shown below. Notice the elapsed time. More than 60 seconds have passed since the first packet was issued by the Authenticator.

Frame 18 (60 bytes on wire, 60 bytes captured)
Arrival Time: Oct 12, 2005 07:25:31.321893000
Time delta from previous packet: 0.062371000 seconds
Time since reference or first frame: 63.660745000 seconds
Frame Number: 18
Packet Length: 60 bytes
Capture Length: 60 bytes
Ethernet II, Src: 00:0f:f7:96:14:03, Dst: 01:80:c2:00:00:03
Destination: 01:80:c2:00:00:03 (Spanning-Tree-(for-bridges)_03)
Source: 00:0f:f7:96:14:03 (00:0f:f7:96:14:03)
Type: 802.1X Authentication (0x888e)
Trailer: 000000000000000000000000000000000...
802.1X Authentication
Version: 1
Type: EAP Packet (0)
Length: 4
Extensible Authentication Protocol
Code: Failure (4)
Id: 1

Length: 4

```
0000  01 80 c2 00 00 03 00 0f f7 96 14 03 88 8e 01 00    ...............
0010  00 04 04 01 00 04 00 00 00 00 00 00 00 00 00 00    ...............
0020  00 00 00 00 00 00 00 00 00 00 00 00 00 00 00 00    ...............
0030  00 00 00 00 00 00 00 00 00 00 00 00                ...........
```

The Authenticator will continue to try to authenticate the port by ascertaining the identity of the Supplicant. Who knows? It might have changed. The Quiet Timer will identify how long the Authenticator will wait before restarting the Authentication process. Thus, the entire process will repeat itself ad infinitum. The Supplicant will never be allowed to connect to the network.

Obviously, this is a totally undesirable situation.

Life becomes a lot worse when there is no Authentication Server available for the Authenticator to access when a Supplicant is present. This situation becomes untenable and fairly drastic measures must be taken. In some cases, this will require intervention on the Authenticator to remove 802.1X either globally or on a port-by-port basis. This is not a good situation for the Help Desk or the Network Administrator. There are no parameters that are effective in remediating the functionality of 802.1X in this situation. The only thing that can be effectively implemented as global solution across switch types and IOS versions is to have a backup Authentication Server. Hopefully, this reduces the probability of both failing simultaneously to nearly zero. We blithely can dismiss the remaining risk by taking the attitude that should both Authentication Servers fail, then we have bigger problems anyway. Of course, there are additional time factors that must be considered and additional Help Desk processes required.

Because 802.1X is dynamically controlling the admission of devices onto the network and dynamically controlling the VLAN in which they are placed, the Management, Troubleshooting, and Help Desk processes will probably wind up determining the final success or failure of this implementation. The key words are "dynamically" and "controlling." Even though the result of the authentication process can be accurately predicted, the number of factors involved will almost certainly preclude most users from being able to do so. It will be incumbent upon personnel charged with supporting both the network and the users to be able to do so.

Thus, even with potential problems, the implementation of 802.1X in this very simple environment is pretty easy.

3.4   GUESTS

3.4.1   Section Summary

It would be nice to assume that everyone wishing to attach to the network is actually authenticatable—meaning, everyone that connects to the network has current and valid credentials. Unfortunately, that is not the case. There will be situations where access is granted to visitors. The problem of how to support visitors needing access to resources that are on your corporate network or are available across the internet is one that has been pertinent for years. This problem is exacerbated by the implementation of 802.1X, unless it is recognized as a design issue to be considered during implementation.

There are really two issues around guest access that must be considered. The obvious one is that of visitors coming into your environment and requiring access to information via your network. The one that is less obvious is the issue of your users going to other environments and requiring access from them. If 802.1X has not been implemented, then there is no greater issue than has always existed. However, if it has been implemented in one or the other environments, then the complexity of allowing access increases.

Assume that 802.1X has been implemented in your network and a visitor arrives from an environment without 802.1X. This should mean that he does not have a Supplicant on his computer. Through the normal process of attempting authentication, the visitor will be placed in a Guest VLAN if one has been coded.

What if the visitor comes from an environment that has implemented 802.1X? This can be a serious issue because he will have an active Supplicant. This situation quickly devolves into the issue of a Supplicant either not being able to participate in the desired EAP-Method or of appearing to supply bad credentials. In the previous section, these situations indicated that "it was not working right." However, in this case, it is working right. Both parties are doing exactly what they are supposed to do.

In newer versions of IOS that support the 2004 version of the specifications, the visitor can be placed in a guest VLAN in this type of situation. However, in versions of IOS that are based on the 2001 specifications, the user will never be allowed access. In this situation, the only alternative is to remove the Supplicant prior to attempting to connect.

This issue does not really arise in wireless because of the separation of authenticated users and guests into distinct SSIDs. Because a SSID does not really have the capability to support multiple VLANs, a SSID to support authentication and a SSID with open credentials are usually constructed. Visitors are usually instructed to connect to the Guest SSID.

This leads to one of the significant design concerns. A consideration of who will likely be placed in a Guest VLAN and for what reason must be made. It is obvious that guests probably will wind up there, but who else might, as well? Are there situations where legitimate corporate users could wind up there? This is a question that should have been answered in the concept phase of the design. Will every legitimate corporate user actually have a Supplicant on his computer? There are a lot of questions of that nature that need to be asked and resolved while designing the Guest VLAN. It would be optimistic to envision only guests going onto that VLAN, and then only allowing Internet access to that VLAN.

For the purposes of this section, it will be assumed that the design issue has been adequately addressed. That leaves the issue of what happens if the user, in some fashion, supplies invalid material for authentication. This could be the EAP-Method or the credentials themselves.

3.4.2   What Happens If the Supplicant Supplies Bad Credentials?

This is not an uncommon situation. Passwords expire, new machines are commissioned, and both of these situations can lead to an out-of-sync environment between the Supplicant and the Authentication Server. It is also possible for a guest, using an EAP-Method that is supported, to attempt to attach and be rejected with bad credentials.

Some EAP-Methods will allow the Authentication Server to identify the situation to the Supplicant and allow the Supplicant to take remedial action. Others will not. The specific IOS implemented will affect the outcome of this situation, as well. IOS is loosely built to conform to specifications in effect at the time of construction. The IEEE specifications of 2004 allow for more flexibility than the 2001 specifications. Most of this flexibility is defined as optional rather than required. Thus, the selection of an IOS is important.

The presentation is based on the original 2001 specifications. The Authenticator configuration, debugs, etc. are essentially the same as used in previous examples.

The normal and expected situation applies. The Authenticator and the Supplicant establish communication, then the Authenticator contacts the Authentication Server. Let us pick up with the Authenticator receiving the first Access Challenge back from the Authentication Server. As expected, the packet is very similar to the one shown in the debug for a successful authentication.

```
00:58:32: RADIUS: Received from id 49 10.92.30.39:1645, Access-Chal-
    lenge, len 83
00:58:32:   Attribute 79 8 01090006
00:58:32:   Attribute 24 37 43495343
00:58:32:   Attribute 80 18 766DC7FE
00:58:32: RADIUS: EAP-login: length of EAP packet=6
00:58:32: RADIUS: EAP-login: got challenge from radius
```

The Authenticator constructs an EAPOL packet, inserts the EAP-Data, and forwards the packet to the Supplicant.

00:58:32: dot1x-ev:dot1x_bend: Sending Radius Response to Supplicant
   of length 6
00:58:32: dot1x-ev:dot1x_tx_eap: EAP Pkt
00:58:32: dot1x-ev:EAP-code=REQUEST
00:58:32: dot1x-ev:EAP Type=Unknown
00:58:32: dot1x-ev:ID=9

The Supplicant immediately responds and the Authenticator constructs a RADIUS packet and stuffs the EAP-Data from the Supplicant into it.

00:58:32: dot1x-registry:registry:dot1x_ether_macaddr called
00:58:32: dot1x-packet:Received an EAPOL frame on interface
   FastEthernet0/3
00:58:32: dot1x-ev:Received pkt saddr=000d.56b7.6fc2, daddr=
   0180.c200.0003,pae-ether-type=34958
00:58:32: dot1x-ev:Found a supplicant block for mac
   000d.56b7.6fc2 FB6CDC
00:58:32: dot1x-ev:RECEIVED mac=000d.56b7.6fc2 and Stored MAC=
   000d.56b7.6fc2
00:58:32: dot1x-packet:Received an EAP packet on interface
   FastEthernet0/3
00:58:32: dot1x-ev:Received RxResp from Authenticator
00:58:32: dot1x_bend Fa0/3: during state dot1x_bend_request, got event
   4(rxresp)
00:58:32: @@@ dot1x_bend Fa0/3: dot1x_bend_request ->
   dot1x_bend_response
00:58:32: dot1x-sm:Dot1x Response State Entered for supp_info=
   FB6CDC hwidb=D3703C, swidb=D38378 on intf=Fa0/3
00:58:32: dot1x-ev:Managed Timer in sub-block attached as leaf
   to master
00:58:32: dot1x-sm:Started the ServerTimeout Timer
00:58:32: dot1x-ev:Going to Send Request to AAA Client on RP for id=9
   and length=80
00:58:32: dot1x-ev:Got a Request from SP to send it to Radius with id 46
00:58:32: dot1x-ev:Found a process that's already handling the request
   for this id 9
00:58:32: dot1x-ev:Username is CCCC\Edwin.Brown; EAP packet
   length=80
00:58:32: RADIUS: ustruct sharecount=1
00:58:32: RADIUS: EAP-login: NAS Port=00-0d-56-b7-6f-c2 RemAddr=
   000d.56b7.6fc2
00:58:32: RADIUS: EAP-login: length of radius packet=218 code=1

```
00:58:32: RADIUS:   Initial   Transmit   FastEthernet0/3   id   50
   10.92.30.39:1645, Access-Request, len 218
00:58:32:   Attribute 4 6 0A5C025A
00:58:32:   Attribute 61 6 00000000
00:58:32:   Attribute 1 18 43434343
00:58:32:   Attribute 6 6 00000002
00:58:32:   Attribute 12 6 000005DC
00:58:32:   Attribute 31 19 30302D30
00:58:32:   Attribute 24 37 43495343
00:58:32:   Attribute 79 82 02090050
00:58:32:   Attribute 80 18 67A0DDD8
```

The Authentication Server responds immediately with an Access Challenge. Notice that there is a large amount of EAP-Data. There are four
Attribute 79 elements in the packet. This deviates somewhat from what was
seen earlier, but there is no way of actually interpreting that data because of
the encryption—using the shared secret.

```
00:58:32: RADIUS: Received from id 50 10.92.30.39:1645, Access Chal-
   lenge, len 971
00:58:32:   Attribute 79 255 010A0378
00:58:32:   Attribute 79 255 EAC6063E
00:58:32:   Attribute 79 255 0C060355
00:58:32:   Attribute 79 131 263B5845
00:58:32:   Attribute 24 37 43495343
00:58:32:   Attribute 80 18 1D8918BB
00:58:32: RADIUS: EAP-login: length of EAP packet=888
00:58:32: RADIUS: EAP-login: got challenge from radius
```

Following the normal process, the Authenticator sends the information
to the Supplicant, the Supplicant responds, the Authenticator sends to the
Authentication Server, and the server responds. This is where the deviation
from the anticipated occurs. The response from the Authentication Server is
an Access-Reject.

```
00:58:32: RADIUS: Received from id 51 10.92.30.39:1645, Access-Reject,
   len 56
00:58:32:   Attribute 79 6 040B0004
00:58:32:   Attribute 18 12 52656A65
00:58:32:   Attribute 80 18 0AD585CE
00:58:32: RADIUS: EAP-login: length of EAP packet=4
00:58:32: RADIUS: EAP-login: got reject from radius
00:58:32: dot1x-ev:going to send to backend on SP, length=4
00:58:32: dot1x-ev:Received VLAN is No VLAN
00:58:32: dot1x-ev:Enqueued the response to backend
```

00:58:32: dot1x-ev:Received QUEUE EVENT in response to AAA Request

00:58:32: dot1x-ev:Dot1x matching request-response found

00:58:32: dot1x-ev:Length of recv EAP packet from radius=4

00:58:32: dot1x-ev:Received VLAN Id −1

The Authenticator realizes that the authentication has failed and notes the situation in the debug. It immediately notifies the Supplicant with an EAP-Failure packet and leaves the port in an unauthorized state.

00:58:32: dot1x_bend Fa0/3: during state dot1x_bend_response, got event 3(afail)

00:58:32: @@@ dot1x_bend Fa0/3: dot1x_bend_response -> dot1x_bend_fail

00:58:32: dot1x-sm:Dot1x Failure State Entered

00:58:32: dot1x-ev:dot1x_bend_fail_enter:000d.56b7.6fc2: Current ID= 11

00:58:32: dot1x-ev:dot1x_bend: Sending Radius Response to Supplicant of length 4

00:58:32: dot1x-ev:dot1x_tx_eap: EAP Pkt

00:58:32: dot1x-ev:EAP-code=FAILURE

00:58:32: dot1x-ev:EAP Type=Unknown

00:58:32: dot1x-ev:ID=11

00:58:32: dot1x-registry:registry:dot1x_ether_macaddr called

00:58:32: dot1x_bend Fa0/3: idle during state dot1x_bend_fail

00:58:32: @@@ dot1x_bend Fa0/3: dot1x_bend_fail -> dot1x_bend_idle

00:58:32: dot1x-sm:Dot1x Idle State Entered

00:58:32: dot1x_auth Fa0/3: during state auth_authenticating, got event 8(authFail)

00:58:32: @@@ dot1x_auth Fa0/3: auth_authenticating -> auth_held

00:58:32: dot1x-sm:Fa0/3:000d.56b7.6fc2:auth_held_enter called

00:58:32: dot1x-sm:

dot1x_update_port_status called with port_status=DOT1X_PORT_-STATUS_ UNAUTHORIZED

Shown below is the capture of the failure packet sent to the Supplicant.

Frame 13 (60 bytes on wire, 60 bytes captured)

Arrival Time: Oct 10, 2005 15:54:24.707691000

Time delta from previous packet: 0.089379000 seconds

Time since reference or first frame: 3.780468000 seconds

Frame Number: 13

Packet Length: 60 bytes

Capture Length: 60 bytes

Ethernet II, Src: 00:0f:f7:96:14:03, Dst: 01:80:c2:00:00:03

Destination: 01:80:c2:00:00:03 (Spanning-Tree-(for-bridges)_03)

Source: 00:0f:f7:96:14:03 (00:0f:f7:96:14:03)
Type: 802.1X Authentication (0x888e)
Trailer: 00000000000000000000000000000000...
802.1X Authentication
Version: 1
Type: EAP Packet (0)
Length: 4
Extensible Authentication Protocol
Code: Failure (4)
Id: 9
Length: 4

```
0000  01 80 c2 00 00 03 00 0f f7 96 14 03 88 8e 01 00  ................

0010  00 04 04 09 00 04 00 00 00 00 00 00 00 00 00 00  ................

0020  00 00 00 00 00 00 00 00 00 00 00 00 00 00 00 00  ................

0030  00 00 00 00 00 00 00 00 00 00 00 00              ............
```

At this point, the Supplicant cannot communicate except with the Authenticator using EAPOL packets. Anything else it attempts to do will be ignored. After the quiet period timer expires, the Authenticator will initiate another round of attempted authentication. This will continue ad infinitum. Authenticators that cannot learn from past failures are condemned to repeat them, so to speak.

An Authenticator using an IOS that is based on the 2001 specifications never will allow a Supplicant with invalid credentials to enter the network. Also, an Authenticator using an IOS based on the 2004 specifications may be able to place this Supplicant into a Guest VLAN. This will depend on the specific capability of the IOS, because this is an optional feature under the 2004 specs, and it will also depend on the configuration applied to the Authenticator. The specific command in some Cisco version of IOS to enable this is:

dot1x guest-vlan-supplicant

This is configured as a global command; thus, if the port is configured to support a Guest VLAN, then the Supplicant would be placed into it.

3.4.3 What Happens If There Is an EAP-Method Mismatch?

This scenario is difficult to describe using traces or debug statements on the Authenticator. The reason is simple: It will appear to be an authentication failure. Remember that the EAP-Data is encrypted in all but the most primitive of methods. This means that only the Supplicant and the Authentication Server really know why the authentication failed. It is likely that the

Authentication Server will have—or at least will have the capability to have—logged the reason why the failure occurred. An analysis of the RADIUS logs probably will be required to detail what failed in the authentication process. From the perspective of logs and traces, the failure will look similar to that shown in the previous section discussing what happens when a Supplicant provides bad credentials.

This is a likely event when a visitor attempts to connect to a wired environment enabled for 802.1X. Although the number of possible methods is fairly small, the likelihood of two networks implementing the same methods in the same way is relatively uncommon. When a visitor complains about not being able to connect to your corporate wired network, then this should be one of the first areas included in the troubleshooting process.

3.4.4 What Happens When My Users Go to Someone Else's Network?

This is potentially a nasty situation. It will shake out more in the future as IOS releases catch up with the current specifications. Here are the possible scenarios. If the other network has not implemented 802.1X, then there is no problem. The user will attempt to find an Authenticator and, when none responds, she will attach as "normal" within that network.

If 802.1X has been implemented on that network, then, hopefully, a Guest VLAN has been implemented and the Authenticator is functioning with the option of having users with invalid credentials being placed in a Guest VLAN. In that case, everyone is happy because your user gets the anticipated access on the foreign network.

But if the foreign network is not functioning under the 2004 specifications, then the only real recourse is to have your user incapacitate 802.1X temporarily, disconnect from the network, and then reconnect. That is: Unless the administrator of the foreign network is willing to provide credentials for guest access and your Supplicant is configured in a way that will allow an EAP-Method to take advantage of them. Which is not likely. But in either case, your user will either need specific training in the issue or your Help Desk may get a lot of calls. And remember the issue of the returning visitor not re-enabling the Supplicant and being placed in a Guest VLAN on your networks. That situations will generate a lot of phone calls as well.

3.4.5 Guests and Wireless

This is probably the best scenario for guests and 802.1X. To connect to your network, either with a SSID that requires 802.1X authentication or with a SSID that has open authentication, the guest will need to access a new SSID. This means that there is a conscious process of connecting, and control can be exerted to ensure correct configuration.

It is interesting that the new standards for wireless security included in 802.11i require the use of 802.1X. Thus, the entire foundation for security, going forward, will have 802.1X included as a basic requirement. This has been discussed in previous sections and will be discussed again in the section on Wireless implementation.

Usually, there will be a SSID that is specifically configured to support guest connectivity. It will be configured with open authentication and frequently will not have any encryption associated. This SSID is associated then with either the guest configured on the wired network or one very similar to it. This makes wireless a nice mechanism to use in an 802.1X environment to support visitors, especially in an 2001 specifications-based implementation.

It is fairly certain that 802.1X will become ubiquitous in a wireless environment. It is less so in a wired. However, the issue of guests will remain for sometime—both in your network and when your users attempt to connect to a foreign network.

3.5   WHAT DO I DO WITH MY PRINTERS AND SERVERS?

3.5.1   Section Summary

The network we have worked with so far has been simple, but somewhat unrealistic in that it has not included functions that are found uniformly on networks. These functions are some form of server to support data storage or an application and a printing capability.

Printers and servers are special classes of devices on a network. They are client rather than infrastructure devices, in the same way that a personal computer is a client device, but they are unattended. Certainly, someone can walk away from a personal computer and leave it connected to the network. That is really not what I mean by unattended. These types of devices are meant to be attached to the network and then perform their functions without requiring an individual to be in attendance.

The special thing about these devices is that many of them do not have Supplicants. There are some printers that have Supplicant capabilities, but the feature is far from ubiquitous. But servers do not really fall into this category, do they? Well, yes and no. Many servers have a special network connection for management. This port frequently does not support a Supplicant.

Even if these devices do support the use of a Supplicant, it can be awkward to implement 802.1X on the ports housing them. Remember that these devices quite often are unattended, meaning that there is no individual available to enter credentials should it be required. This means one of three things happens. Either credentials are imbedded on the device, such as certificates, or the device cannot complete authentication and is not allowed on the network, or it is placed in the Guest VLAN. None of these choices is always satisfactory.

This situation extends into the network infrastructure itself. If 802.1X is intended to provide the foundation for Port-Based Authentication, then what about the ports that are used to interconnect the infrastructure? How can you be certain that those connections are legitimate?

Thus, how do you protect your network when devices without a Supplicant must be attached? There are two common methods. Either restrict the port to a MAC address that corresponds to that on the NIC of the specific device, or, if generic functionality can be defined and restricted to a specific set of IP ports, then restrict the devices to a VLAN and implement a filter for the VLAN.

In any case, the implementation of 802.1X to restrict access to the network means that corresponding care must be taken with ports that cannot readily be included in the 802.1X authentication process.

3.5.2 The Simple Network

The very simple network is really too simple. Except in the sparsest of circumstances, it does not represent a network that really might be in existence. Therefore, let us expand the very simple network slightly by adding a couple of devices that are common on most networks. In fact, most networks would not be networks without them: Servers, Printers, and Routers. Figure 3.3 shows an expanded version of the network making it a simple network.

There are two classes of devices that must be considered. There are network infrastructure components such as routers, switches, and wireless access points; and then there are client devices that utilize the network infrastructure. If a serious effort is directed at Port-Based Authentication, then both classes of devices must be addressed. Let us begin with client devices.

What is special about this class of devices? This might be an over-simplification, but they are endpoints on the network similar to user computers except that they are unattended. This essentially means that they must be capable of entering the network in a functional manner without requiring intervention. In a Windows environment when a person connects and activates a computer, a certain amount of credentials are expected to be entered. This class of endpoint devices usually does not have that option.

In many cases, this class of endpoint device does not have the capability to support a Supplicant. That is not true in all cases. Some printers definitely have the capability and most servers also have the capability for a Supplicant to be implemented. The obvious solution is to not implement 802.1X on ports housing these devices. But this defeats the purpose of implementing Port-Based Authentication. After all, George, the janitor, can come in at night, unplug a printer, and have full access to the network. Every network

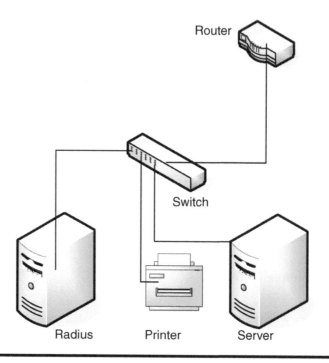

Figure 3.3 A Simple Network.

has an elusive George on the janitorial staff that lucratively moonlights by stealing confidential and sensitive information. Therefore, in addition to implementing 802.1X, it is highly advisable to run deep background checks on all janitorial staff. Seriously, the intent of implementing 802.1X is compromised if any ports are left unguarded by some mechanism. The goal is to know the status of all devices on the network. 802.1X supports this goal by providing a mechanism to authenticate devices at the port level. It should not be considered to be the only mechanism, or naively assumed to be implementable on all ports.

This becomes a significant design issue and should be considered prior to any excursion into implementation. The tasks are simple. Define the Requirements, develop a Concept, create an Architecture, develop a Design, and, finally, Implement. Each step builds upon information gathered or constructed in the previous step. Ultimately, this must be accomplished for the entire 802.1X project and not just for printers and servers. Think about how to be able to connect those devices and still protect the network in your specific environment. It becomes a much simpler task when broken down and formalized as show above.

At this point, a Printer and a Server have been added to our very simple network. The result is the enhancement of the capabilities and the evolution to a Simple Network. These two devices either are not capable of housing a

Supplicant or the implementation of a Supplicant and the resulting authentication process would be very difficult. This means that the implementation of 802.1X on the ports housing these devices is not desirable—probably not feasible. So what are the requirements?

We have added a printer. The users are so happy now that they fail to realize that they cannot print. The printer was simply plugged into the switch on any available port. The switch and that particular port were enabled for 802.1X. The switch promptly issued an EAP Request for Identity that was ignored, and ultimately the printer was placed in the Guest VLAN. Actually, all the guests are happy because they now have a printer.

As indicated, this is a design issue. It should have been identified in the Requirements definition and addressed in Concept and Architecture. There are several alternatives, and a couple will be addressed here. There is the option of only implementing printers with Supplicants and utilizing an appropriate EAP-Method to support them. That is certainly a viable option in a closely controlled environment. But not all environments are as strict.

It is certainly possible to envision an environment where the staff go to the local computer store, find a printer that looks pretty, verify that it has an Ethernet connector, purchase it using the corporate card (since it falls into the petty cash category), throw it in the back seat of the car, haul it into the office, and plug it into the network. If 802.1X has been implemented, then this printer is probably going to wind up on the Guest VLAN. Is that bad? Not necessarily. Access lists can be fairly easily implemented that will allow printing to be initiated from a different VLAN. This is certainly a viable alternative.

Then there are the middle ground scenarios. If more corporate control is desired, but replacement of all printers is not fiscally possible, then there are at least two possible solutions that allow robust printing but ensure that some form of protection is implemented.

In both cases, the port to which the printer is going to attach must be identified. In the first case, once the port is identified it can be placed in a special VLAN that has been established to house all printers. Why might this scenario be implemented? If printers are supported by a centralized group and only specific printers are allowed, this method could provide a mechanism to support security and policy. Alternatively, in the second solution, each port could be protected through the use of a mechanism like a MAC address filter to allow only the printer to attach to a particular port. This might be implemented to allow the printer to remain in a specific VLAN. Or perhaps the printer is a multi-function device that requires special connectivity capabilities.

Common garden variety printers are generally passive devices that only talk when spoken to and then on specific TCP ports. They essentially accept information, a print stream, usually acknowledge the receipt, and transfer the data stream to paper. Because most networked printers can operate using an IP address, and, commonly, personal computer operating systems can construct a TCP/IP definition for a printer, it is reasonable to consolidate all printers into a general category. This category then becomes a VLAN for printers, and an access list restricting communication outbound from the VLAN can be constructed.

The same does not always hold true for devices like servers. In many ways, servers are the brains of the outfit. Unless a stringent review of communication allowed to each server has been conducted, then it should be assumed that virtually any IP port could be used to communicate with the device. In many instances, servers, unlike printers, initiate conversations. This is especially true for servers hosting applications. A multi-tiered approach to application development is a common practice. Trying to design alternative protection for servers is different than with printers because their behavior is different.

Supplicant code almost always can be located that could be installed on a Server. However, some code will only work with specific encryption or a specific EAP-Method—or some other issue could exist that will make authentication difficult. As an example, the decision is made that all authentication will make use of tokens. This might be difficult to implement with servers or constitute a high risk to availability. Or even worse, it might place the server on the Guest VLAN, thus exposing highly sensitive information if it is inadvertently rebooted.

How do you protect the network in this situation? The number of IP ports that must be "open" across all of the servers implemented is large and potentially unmanageable if all servers are placed in a single VLAN. A couple of alternatives would be first to use multiple VLANs or to restrict connectivity to individual ports through a MAC address filter. Individual networks will require individual solutions designed to meet the specific requirements.

There is also the situation where "lights out" management of the servers is implemented through the use of a special network connection. This connection is special in that it allows for control of the server to be assumed remotely. This is a huge risk; yet, in most cases, this connection will not support any form of Supplicant. This situation might require that a specific VLAN be implemented while access to that VLAN is restricted to a very small number of addresses that can be controlled. The situation might also require that MAC address filters be implemented within the VLAN to ensure that a port within the VLAN cannot be hijacked. Again, the specific implementation will vary with the individual corporate circumstances.

Of course, all of those possibilities depend on the functional capabilities and the configuration of 802.1X on the network. The intent of the discussion was simply to point out once again that knowledge of what is supposed to be occurring on the network is critical in defining how the network is implemented. Servers play a significant role on most networks and, therefore, the functions that they and the applications housed on them perform must be documented prior to charging off and implementing 802.1X.

There are additional devices that might be connected to a network and those will need to be identified, as well—and possibly have implemented alternative mechanisms for protection. A couple of examples are secondary NICs in servers, such as integrated lights out (ILO) boards, that do not support supplicants and NICs in some UPS devices.

The same type of protection identified for printers can be applied to all of these types of devices. MAC address filters can be applied to specific ports to ensure that only the device that is supposed to be on the port is allowed to communicate. Or special VLANs can be established with whatever restrictions on communication are required for the particular situation.

It is key to ensure that devices of this nature are identified and a plan of action has been defined that takes them into account. The essential information in developing the plan is to know what communication is anticipated for each type of device. Selection of the appropriate mechanism to protect the network then can be made. It might include enabling 802.1X for the particular device type, or it might be something else.

What about the infrastructure itself? Almost every network will have at least two devices that should be considered as infrastructure. There will be a switch that allows users to connect and a router that allows connectivity to devices not connected to the switch—usually the Internet. The router must connect to the switch or vice versa. This means that a port on the switch and a port on the router require some form of authentication when connected. These devices, too, do not generally have user credentials, nor do they usually have Supplicants.

Remember that in the technology chapter the section entitled Management identified that a port on an Authenticator must also support Supplicant functions. This begins to make more sense now. An infrastructure connection is somewhat different than the connection of a client to a switch. It is not uncommon for each appliance in that type of connection to be an Authenticator. In that case, each appliance will need to authenticate the other. This means that each appliance or, more correctly, each port must simultaneously act as an Authenticator and a Supplicant.

When a link is accomplished, each side of the connection must authenticate the other side. Each will issue an EAPOL Request Identity that must be acknowledged. An asynchronous mutual authentication must occur. What does this mean? Take the simple network diagrammed at the beginning of the chapter. It means that the router connected to the switch has no guarantee that it is really the authentic switch that it is communicating with. Similarly, there is no guarantee to the switch that it is the authentic router on the port. Because these devices do not house Supplicant capable code, it is not possible to utilize 802.1X to authenticate the port. Mechanisms similar to those defined for endpoint devices must be implemented where possible.

To reiterate once again a statement made several times earlier, the capability for infrastructure devices to mutually authenticate one another is optional in the 2004 specifications. However, that capability is not implemented in any Cisco operating system at the time of the writing of this book.

It is not possible to implement Layer 2 security, MAC address filtering, or 802.1X on ports performing trunking. So now what? Probably just throw your hands in the air and tell whoever asks that the risk to have those ports unsecured must be taken until the Supplicant function is available to secure those devices utilizing trunks. There are alternatives, but almost certainly they are going to be cumbersome and potentially difficult to manage.

This makes the definition of anticipated traffic patterns even more important on a global scale. Either the individual ports must be secured through mechanisms like MAC address filters or a full Layer 3 security, such as was defined for printer VLANs earlier, must be attempted. Implementing Layer 3 security on this scale is apt to be so cumbersome that it will become a nonviable alternative in all but the most secure environments.

Thus, the simple network really is not so simple after all. There are a number of devices, both client and infrastructure, that cannot easily support a Supplicant, yet must be connected to the network. There are holes in the authentication process that must be addressed outside of a strict 802.1X implementation. In at least one case, that of implementing trunks, there is no easy solution for authentication. The maturity level of 802.1X implementations has not caused solutions to be defined and ubiquitously applied for these types of devices. That will come in the future. In the mean time, alternative mechanisms must be designed and implemented to supplement an 802.1X implementation.

3.6   UNPLANNED EXPANSION

3.6.1   Section Summary

It always seems that there are never enough ports in at least one location in the network. One of the most dread sounds is the knock on the cube wall. One of the most dread sights is the hangdog looking co-worker standing in the cube doorway. Invariably, this means that someone wants some more ports. The need for temporary network expansion is one of the bugaboos that is the bane of a network administrator.

In situations where 802.1X has not been implemented, network expansion is a simple thing to accomplish. All it takes is to plug in a small switch, hub, or wireless access point. This has the effect of expanding one port in a particular VLAN into a much larger number. It is almost like feeding a multitude from a single loaf. This is not the case when 802.1X has been implemented. The default functionality on an 802.1X enabled port is to allow exactly one MAC address. This means that one and only one device can utilize the hub. There is no benefit to attaching a hub to an 802.1X enabled port in its default state.

Similar situations exist when small switches and wireless access points are attached to an 802.1X enabled port. In both of these situations, the device attaching does have a MAC address associated with its port. Technically, this means that only that MAC address will be allowed to communicate. However, the way in which the address is used can allow other devices to utilize it. The issue that arises is that the rogue device does not have a Supplicant. Remember that we just explored this situation in the previous section. The specifications will allow for mutual authentication of infrastructure devices, but no devices exist to accomplish that authentication. This means that, at best, the switch or access point will be placed in the Guest VLAN and anything attached or associated with it will exist in the Guest VLAN. This may be only adequate connectivity, but it is the best that is going to happen.

The best expansion is going to be establishing a new device within the designed 802.1X environment. Allowing unplanned, random expansion of the network is risky and goes against the intent of 802.1X.

3.6.2   Connecting a Hub

The default state of 802.1X is to allow only a single MAC address to be active on an enabled port in the wired environment. This immediately causes problems with hubs. A single device can become active using a hub, but attempting to connect a second one just does not work.

The obvious thought is to install that spare switch or hub that is collecting dust in the closet. What happens when one of these devices is plugged into any old port that happens to be available? Assume, at this point, that the port in which this device is plugged is an Ethernet port that has 802.1X enabled and configured on it.

Even if the defaults have been implemented, this might work. Remember: The default is one MAC address per port. Thus, the Authenticator will attempt authentication. The second switch will not have a Supplicant, so the best that will happen is that the second will be placed in a Guest VLAN if one is coded. Then users will plug into the new switch with the anticipation of being able to connect to the network. The key factor in communication is whether or not a Guest VLAN has been configured on the port of the primary switch. If one has not been configured, then the second switch will not be able to connect. Therefore, assume that one has been configured.

The users will connect to the second switch and, depending on the configuration of that switch, might be able to get a DHCP address. They might be able to converse with one another locally on the second switch and will be able to cross the connection onto the original switch. The reason for this is that the registered MAC address is that of the second switch, and all traffic crossing the link will be assigned that switch's Layer 2 address. Of course, the additional users on the second switch will be able to access only the Guest VLAN. The situation of a second MAC address attempting to use a port will be discussed in more detail later. But right now let us stay with the higher level discussion of unplanned expansion.

The option of using the switch in the closet that is a configurable Cisco switch is not bad, but it is not the only situation likely to happen. Users have an unforgivable tendency to do things without ever contacting the support organization. One will frequently act like an evil Santa Claus, reach into his laptop bag, extract a device, and plug it into any convenient network port with the intent of allowing locally expanded network access. Usually this device is an Ethernet hub, a small nonconfigurable switch, or a small inexpensive wireless access point.

Follow what happens when a hub is connected to the Authenticator. First, these devices usually have an uplink port. The uplink ports crossover the send and receive signals so that a normal Ethernet cable may be used to establish connectivity. There is one further characteristic they frequently share. They are nonconfigurable. This is the key issue when attaching one to an 802.1X enabled port.

This means that the device itself does not contain a MAC address. It only establishes physical connectivity. When the device is connected to the Authenticator, the physical link becomes active and the Authenticator will begin attempting to authenticate the device. The hub will not respond and will be placed in the Guest VLAN, if one has been configured, just as anticipated. But because the device does not have an address, the Authenticator will not be able to restrict any conversation. Shown below is the output from a show dot1x statistics interface FastEthernet0/3. A small hub has been connected to this port and no other device is connected yet to the hub.

PortStatistics Parameters for Dot1x

TxReqId = 2 TXReq = 0	TxTotal = 2	
RxStart = 0 RxLogoff = 0	RxRespId = 0	RxResp = 0
RxInvalid = 0 RxLenErr = 0	RxTotal = 0	
RxVersion = 0	LastRxMac 0000.0000.0000	

This output shows that the Authenticator has issued two packets. This is consistent with the expected Request Identity packets that the specifications require the Authenticator to issue. What is interesting is that, in fact, three packets have been transmitted by the Authenticator—One Failure and two Request Identity packets. The first packet, the Failure, does not appear in the statistical information displayed above.

At this point, the Authenticator has not yet received a packet from the attached switch or hub. This is confirmed in the information shown above.

Therefore, no MAC address is known for the port. The port becomes active and, because the new device cannot participate in the authentication process as a Supplicant, the port is placed in an unauthorized state. The next device to converse over the link must use the Guest VLAN. But because the Authenticator has not yet seen a MAC address for the port, if the computer attaching has the capability of issuing an EAPOL-Start, it can successfully request that 802.1X be restarted. The authentication process then will proceed as normal and the port on the Authenticator will be reassigned to the appropriate VLAN, based on the outcome of the process. This may be a Guest VLAN, an authenticated VLAN, or a VLAN associated with the user in RADIUS.

Let us examine the connection of a second computer to the hub. Assume that the Authenticator has been left in the default configuration of allowing a single MAC address on the 802.1X enabled port. To illustrate this, look what happens when a Supplicant with the capability of issuing an EAPOL-Start attaches. The debug output below begins when the Authenticator receives that frame.

> 1d23h: dot1x-packet:Received an EAPOL frame on interface TastEthernet0/3
> 1d23h: dot1x-ev:Received pkt saddr = 000f:1f43:682a, daddr = 0180.c200.0003, pae-ether-type = 34958
> 1d23h: dot1x-ev:Couldn't find a supplicant block for mac 000f.1f43.682a

That is the entire output from the debug. The Authenticator recognizes the fact that an EAPOL frame has been issued, but does not do anything with it. The only real clue as to what has happened is the last line. It indicates that the Supplicant has not been set up on the Authenticator. There is one interesting thing to note in this situation. Because this is a hub, unplugging the original Supplicant does not destroy the authentication for that Supplicant. The MAC address of the device that first attached is the only address that will be allowed to communicate. The Authenticator will not allow a different device to usurp the role. Even if the second device is 802.1X enabled, it will not be allowed to communicate. The original Supplicant will need to have issued an EAPOL-Logoff prior to the new device issuing an EAPOL-Start in order for the second device to be recognized.

Now go back to the debug output. As just discussed, there is little to go on when attempting to identify what happened. If the debug is expanded to include port security, which would be expected to be involved in restricting the MAC addresses allowed on a port, no additional information is displayed. In the previous section, A Very Simple Network, the debugs show that 802.1X has constructed a MAC address filter to restrict communication. This filter is not displayable. It will be difficult to diagnose this situation without understanding the topology of what has been connected to the Authenticator and reviewing the configuration of 802.1X for the port.

Thus, it really depends on the characteristics of the infrastructure device being attached as to whether or not communication is allowed. Under the default configuration of 802.1X, if the device is configurable, like a small Cisco switch, the Authenticator port will be placed in a Guest VLAN, and other devices attached to that switch will be allowed to communicate across the link. Remember that the MAC address recognized is that of the second switch. All communication from the network is directed to that MAC address. However, if a hub or a nonconfigurable switch is used, then one device attached to the hub will be allowed to communicate across the link.

3.6.3 Allowing Multiple Hosts

How can unplanned expansion be supported? First, unplanned expansion should utilize configurable devices that can be quickly incorporated into the network and participate fully in the authentication process. This is less a technical issue than one of management and design. Processes and equipment necessary to expand the network quickly to meet local needs should be implemented. From a technical perspective, the new switch should be attached with a trunk port to the network. This means that 802.1X must be removed from the port that requires expansion and the new switch should be configured to be an Authenticator. This can be a simple set of tasks that are accomplishable in a relatively short amount of time.

If the switch in the closet is not going to be implemented to expand the network, and small, inexpensive switches pulled from user's bags are going to be allowed, then how can 802.1X be implemented to provide the connectivity for random expansion? This option is to reconfigure the port on the Authenticator to support multiple MAC addresses. This is the configuration a port on a Layer 3 switch could utilize to accomplish this.

```
interface FastEthernet0/3
switchport access VLAN 30
switchport mode access
no ip address
dot1x port-control auto
dot1x host-mode multi-host
dot1x max-rEquation 6
dot1x Guest-VLAN 10
Spanning-Tree portfast
```

The number of hosts can be controlled through the configuration of port security. That is the only mechanism available to control the connectivity to the port once it has been configured for multi-host.

This command was discussed briefly in the section on configuration. Its use opens a great deal of uncertainty into the connectivity of a given port. All of that depends on which MAC is the last to attach and how it participated in the authentication process. Let us go through a couple of scenarios.

Consider the situation when a hub has been connected to the Authenticator and a single computer has connected to the new hub. At this point, assume that a Guest VLAN has been configured and the first device to connect is a computer without an active Supplicant—meaning that it did not issue an EAPOL-Start. There is no authentication to take place because the port has already been authorized and will allow multiple MAC addresses. The device is placed in the Guest VLAN. Any subsequent devices without an active Supplicant will also be placed in the Guest VLAN.

Now look at the situation when a different device is attached to the hub that houses a population already using the hub in the Guest VLAN. This new device is a Windows 2000 machine configured with an active Supplicant. This machine issues an EAPOL-Start. And this is where life becomes interesting because there are multiple possibilities.

As soon as the EAPOL-Start is received by the Authenticator, the port will revert to an unauthorized state. That packet causes the authentication process to begin anew. This is illustrated in the debug output shown below.

> 1d00h: dot1x-sm: dot1x_update_port_status called with port-status= DOT1X_PORT_STATUS_UNAUTHORIZED
> 1d00h: dot1x-ev:dot1x_port_cleanup_author: cleanup author on interface FastEthernet0/3
> 1d00h: dot1x-ev:dot1x_update_port_status: Called with host_mode=0 state UNAUTHORIZED
> 1d00h: dot1x-ev:dot1x_update_port_status: using mac 0000.0000.0000 to send port to unauthorized on VLAN 0
> 1d00h: dot1x-ev:Found a supplicant block for mac 0000.0000.0000 FB9134
> 1d00h: dot1x-ev:dot1x_port_unauthorized: Host-mode=0 radius/Guest VLAN=0

The devices that were attached to the hub prior to the issuing of the EAPOL-Start can no longer communicate across the port. Any conversation with an application that was in progress is interrupted. The device that issued the EAPOL-Start continues the authentication process according to the rules established for the EAP-Method employed.

If the authentication is successful, it is highly likely that the port on the Authenticator will be placed in a different VLAN. All of the original devices are addressed for the Guest VLAN. They can no longer communicate with anything. The subnet associated with the port on the Authenticator has changed. The original computers, the ones without a Supplicant, now can request a new DHCP address and obtain one, presumably, in the VLAN associated with the computer that just successfully authenticated. Now, for all practical purposes, all users—ones that did not authenticate and ones that did—have access to the "authenticated" resources on the network. Suddenly, there is the potential for one or more unauthorized devices to have access to the secured network. This is not a good thing.

But that is what happens in some cases. What if the original device was configured for 802.1X but was not active? Remember the flow. The EAPOL-Start tells the Authenticator to issue a Request Identity packet. That packet is addressed to a group address. This means that all devices on the hub that are configured for 802.1X will receive the packet and act upon it. Potentially multiple devices will attempt to join the authentication process. In this situation, it is unpredictable which device, if any, will be authenticated. It is possible that the Authenticator will receive multiple responses to the single Request Identity and either discard them or restart the process.

This random situation continues in unpredictable ways. Assume that the first device that attached to the hub actually had an active Supplicant and was successful in its authentication. This means that the port is in an authorized state with access to secured resources. Because 802.1X does not limit the number of MAC addresses in this scenario, any number of devices without an active Supplicant now can attach and have the same level of access as the authenticated device.

The port on the Authenticator is not a trunk and can support only one VLAN. That VLAN can be the Guest VLAN configured, the authorized VLAN for the port, or a VLAN associated with the user in the Authentication Server. It depends entirely on the sequence in which computers attach to the hub/switch as to what VLAN will be active and what capabilities will be allowed. Needless to say, this can cause some confusion with anyone attempting to utilize this new hub.

3.6.4 Connecting a Small Switch or an Access Point

What happens if, instead of a hub, a small configurable switch is pulled from the user's bag? Well, everyone winds up in the Guest VLAN just like in the situation where the Cisco switch was dug out of the closet. Remember that 802.1X is a Layer 2 process and that Layer 2 is not carried across switch ports. Therefore, any Supplicant attempting to initiate authentication will not find an Authenticator. It will quit trying to authenticate and finally just get a DHCP address in the Guest VLAN.

There is a second situation that frequently will occur when an unauthorized expansion of the network is attempted. That is when, instead of a hub being attached to a port, a small wireless access point is used. In some ways, this is preferable to the use of a hub. This is because the access point will be placed in a Guest VLAN and, because it does not have 802.1X enabled, all connections will be assigned to the Guest VLAN no matter what their capabilities are. Any Supplicant communicating with the access point will recognize quickly that the access point is not functioning as an Authenticator and will cease attempting to initiate an 802.1X authentication.

The use of access points and small switches is preferable to the use of hubs. At least in those situations it is known where all connections will be assigned. In general, the default configuration for 802.1X allowing only a single MAC address is the best scenario. This does not allow the randomness or open the vulnerabilities associated with allowing multiple hosts. The new specifications allow for multiple hosts on a port and require each host to be authenticated. If this is employed, then many of the situations described above are mitigated. There are certainly situations where the use of a "multiple host" configuration can be effective in tightly designed and controlled circumstances.

3.7 EXPANDING TO WIRELESS

3.7.1 Section Summary

Our simple network needs even more expansion, but the cost is pretty high. Business has been great and some new space has been acquired, as well as remodeling in the existing space. A whole bunch of new people have been hired. To provide the necessary ports, additional cabling and switches will be required. All the basic network infrastructure is going to change and will necessitate a redesign. All of this is expensive. Other big problems associated with this type of expansion are the inconvenience the cabling work causes and the amount of time necessary to complete the network modifications. Thus, the decision has been made to go with wireless instead.

The cost associated with implementing wireless can be significantly less than that required for a wired infrastructure. Although the inconvenience around the addition of access points is not necessarily trivial, it is less than that of adding a new physical switchport for every new required connection. The other significant advantage to wireless is that of mobility.

Mobility does not necessarily mean the constant movement from one location to another across access points. It does mean the flexibility to gather a group together in an ad hoc fashion and have enough bandwidth and connectivity to support the gathering. It also means the capability to maintain connectivity with an application while moving. In terms of Port-Based Authentication, this means being able to establish and secure the exchange of credentials for authentication and to reestablish an existing authentication quickly when the association with an access point moves from one to another.

Cisco has two wireless offerings—Aironet and Airespace. Both are viable products, but each operates from a different philosophy. Aironet is primarily a peer-to-peer implementation and requires some effort to implement a centralized control system. This makes Aironet easy and inexpensive to install in small environments. In fact, an Aironet access point can be installed out of the box and will immediately be able to allow associations using the default SSID. Airespace on the other hand is a centralized implementation where the access points require a controller to function. More effort is required to enable an access point in Airespace. However, as the size of the implementation grows, it is easier to add access points in a coordinated fashion.

There are some additional aspects of communication that must be considered. Aironet requires the use of trunk connections if multiple SSIDs are implemented. Airespace does not. Instead, all traffic is tunneled from the access point back to a controller for distribution. This makes placement of controllers in the network, and deployment of VLANs for transport between controller and access points, key design features.

Both solutions are viable within an 802.1X based authentication scheme. If Aironet is implemented with a centralized control overlay, then both systems allow for fast reauthentication. Both solutions are implementable, but given the circumstances of an individual network, one may be preferable to the other.

3.7.2 Wireless Connectivity

So what does this really mean to our environment? In terms of 802.1X, from a technical perspective, it is not that significant. The same 802.1X flows seen in a wired environment also are seen in a wireless one. For all practical purposes, the access point performs the same functions as a switch when configured to be an Authenticator. That being said, the implementation of wireless, combined with 802.1X, is not insignificant. This book will digress somewhat from the strict implementation of 802.1X to discuss some of the issues that affect the implementation.

As a reminder, when operating in a wireless environment the Supplicant must associate with an access point prior to beginning an authentication. It is entirely possible to have associated without being authenticated. This can be confusing to an end user, and the Help Desk personnel should be explicitly trained to detect and correct this type of situation. Figure 3.4 illustrates the flow.

Wireless implies mobility and that is certainly a huge advantage when implementing the technology. The use of personal assistants and cell phones have made wireless connectivity an accepted function in everyday existence. But take a look at the use of wireless in an enterprise business environment. This is not the everyday environment we are accustomed to. The usual implementation of wireless in this environment is aimed at data connectivity with some voice. In a usual enterprise environment, neither of those requirements means significant mobility. At this point in time, it is not really customary for people to walk around frequently attempting to use a laptop. In an office, most phone calls, even those from cell phones, are

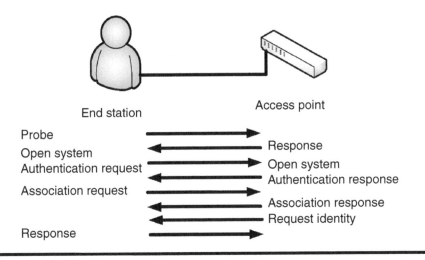

Figure 3.4   Wireless Association and Initial 802.1X Conversation.

made from stationary positions. People tend not to move around much. Wireless provides freedom of movement but does not force it on the office staff.

The major advantage that wireless offers is that of ubiquitous connectivity. Wireless means losing the leash that connects a user to the network—voice or data. An entire room can be filled with people without having to search for a switch or hub to expand the network—and each person can still connect. Wireless means that everyone can do their email during a meeting and not have to pay attention to what is being presented. While it is possible, wireless usually does not change the way people do business and, for the most part, people are stationary. That being said, one of the major considerations in wireless, and implementing Port-Based Authentication within wireless, is retention of connectivity when people do move from one location to another.

There are two different philosophies in wireless implementation. They differ as to where the "intelligence" of the implementation resides. It boils down to whether or not the access point is capable of operating independently. Is the system a peer-to-peer type of operation or is it centrally controlled? Cisco offers a solution in each philosophy. The legacy Aironet product line is essentially a peer-to-peer solution while the newer Airespace product line implements a central solution. Each of the solutions is capable of implementing 802.1X, but there are significant implications involved in making the choice.

Before discussing the individual solutions, the handling of 802.1X within wireless needs to be reviewed a little more. A couple of sections already have discussed wireless, so there is no need to recap issues in EAP-Method selection or how 802.1X functions within the association process. The authentication process essentially functions the same within a wireless environment as within a wired one. However, there is one significant difference in the handling of guests. Neither Cisco solution has the capability of assigning a Guest VLAN when no Supplicant is detected on the connecting device. The Guest VLAN is implemented as a specific SSID. This means that the user must make a conscious decision to connect to the Guest VLAN rather than being automatically redirected to it. This situation will have more significance in the Airespace implementation than it does within Aironet.

3.7.3 Aironet

Aironet is a peer-to-peer implementation. This solution can have a more centralized control imposed on it, but each access point is capable of operating as a standalone device. The access point can be configured using IOS or via a web interface. Rather than expand this book to discuss HTML, the capabilities of Aironet will be reviewed from an IOS perspective.

Because it is IOS based, the essential capabilities of the access point are very similar to those already discussed for switches in a wired environment. 802.1X can be implemented on an Aironet access point in much the same way that it is implemented on a Cisco switch. This means that each and every access point will function as an Authenticator in this system. The configuration of each access point will need to identify one or more Authentication Servers and have AAA defined. Shown below is a partial configuration illustrating the configuration of SSIDs intended for 802.1X authentication and a Guest VLAN.

```
ssid fred
VLAN 42
authentication open EAP EAP_Methods
authentication network-EAP EAP_Methods
!
ssid guest
VLAN 43
guest-mode
```

There is one very interesting tidbit of information that may be helpful here. There are two "authentication" statements for SSID "fred." At first glance, that seems to be a bit unusual. It would seem that only one would be necessary. The answer to why there are two lies in the construction and population of wireless LAN management frames. For our purposes, these frames are used when setting up an association. Imbedded within one of the management frames is an element called the Authentication Number. This number is a "0" for Open Authentication and a "1" for Cisco's Network-EAP. The configuration shown above ensures that the use of either a Cisco

Aironet card or a card from another vendor can have connectivity with SSID "fred." This affects the 802.1X configuration only in that EAP_Methods are defined to be the authentication mechanism for each of the two authentications. The term EAP_Methods implies that 802.1X is the transport.

This brings up a concern. Because Aironet access points each house intelligence, then configuration management becomes more complex. Each access point has the capability to be configured in a unique way. Different SSIDs can be configured on different access points. Even more importantly, the same SSID can be configured differently on one access point than on another. The VLAN for a particular SSID does not need to be consistent across an implementation of multiple access points, nor are the authentication statements for the SSID required to maintain consistency across the wireless domain. If consistency is not maintained, however, significant issues regarding mobility can arise.

Most obviously, the loss of connectivity due to a change in IP address is a real concern. But equally important is the concern that, should the authentication method for the particular SSID change, loss of connectivity altogether is a possibility. Thus, there is tremendous flexibility in the creation of the wireless domain. This is a mixed blessing, though, because of the more stringent management controls required to ensure that multiple access points are configured in the way intended.

Yet, all of this is somewhat peripheral to 802.1X. The real issues are how to ensure confidentiality within the infrastructure, how to protect connectivity from user to application, and how to preserve connectivity as a user moves from one access point to another.

The issue of confidentiality boils down to encryption methods and validation of credentials for a conversation. These issues are more a discussion of the EAP-Methods that can be deployed rather than the implementation of 802.1X. The proper selection of an EAP-Method is essential to a good implementation of security. It is more critical in a wireless environment than in a wired one because of the ease of eavesdropping. But the particular EAP-Method selected is peripheral to authentication until mobility is considered. A brief discussion of some methods available was conducted earlier in the technology chapter of this book and can be referenced. For the most part, the subject of confidentiality of a conversation is addressed in much the same way in either a wired or wireless environment. Confidentiality, as it applies to the connection from the access point to the network, is another matter.

The significant issue in an Aironet implementation is how to protect the wired connection between the access point and the rest of the network. This issue is the same as considering the protection of inter-switch connectivity. The fact is that the Cisco infrastructure, switches, and access points do not authenticate each other. Although the capability for mutual authentication is allowed by the specifications, it is not currently implemented. This means that an access point does not authenticate a switch to which it is attached and vice versa.

Take a look at the situation in more detail. This is a significant difference between the Aironet and Airespace implementations. Assume that there are two SSIDs implemented in the enterprise. One is intended to be used by guests for access to the Internet and does not participate in 802.1X. The other is intended to be used by authentic internal users and does participate in 802.1X. Each of these SSIDs is associated with a different VLAN. Also, the access point itself is probably addressed in a third VLAN. The only way that the full range of subnets needing support on the access point is to implement a trunk connecting the access point into the wired network. As discussed earlier, trunks cannot currently be 802.1X capable, nor can a MAC address filter be applied. This is a situation that can be fairly serious. In a robust wireless implementation, there will be tens or hundreds of ports that are distributed throughout the enterprise physical space that have no protection. Serious thought must be given to the situation during the design process. Figure 3.5 illustrates the Aironet trunk connection.

The configuration of the port on the Authenticator does not include any statements related to 802.1X because 802.1X. cannot be implemented on a trunk port. This was discussed briefly in a previous section. Shown below is a sample of a partial configuration that could have been implemented on the switch to support the network shown in Figure 3.5.

```
interface FastEthernet2/2
description Trunk to WAP
switchport trunk encapsulation dot1q
switchport native VLAN 2
switchport trunk allowed 2,5,7
switchport mode trunk
```

In this implementation, VLAN 5 might be the authenticated VLAN and 7 could be the Guest VLAN, with 2 being the VLAN in which the WAP is addressed. Once the traffic for those two VLANs arrives at the switched, wired infrastructure, it is up to configuration statements associated with

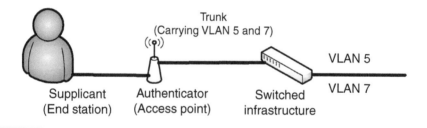

Figure 3.5 Aironet Trunk.

each VLAN to ensure that any required segregation of traffic is implemented. At that point, 802.1X has completed its function and it is up to the rest of the wired infrastructure to impose whatever restrictions—traffic flow, security, etc.—are necessary. This is not a good thing or a bad thing. It is simply the situation that exists in an implementation of 802.1X in an Aironet environment.

The last issue mentioned as being required in a wireless implementation was that of preserving connectivity when moving from one access point to another. The solution to this situation is pretty much imbedded in the particular wireless implementation selected. For the most part, the technology required to allow mobility between access points is available in any wireless solution. You will have to look hard to find a vendor that does not allow this type of mobility. However, this is the physical level that is provided; the logical connectivity is provided by configurations applied to the environment. This is where 802.IX enters the picture.

When wireless has been discussed throughout the book, there has been one issue of significant concern: Maintaining connectivity to an application during a reauthentication process that may be required when moving from one access point to another. This is a serious design issue. It has several components that must be integrated. Placement of Authentication Servers is one issue. Selection of the EAP-Method and the traffic patterns implied is another. The caching of credentials in the wireless domain is a big concern. This last one is of very serious concern in a peer-to-peer implementation such as Aironet. Fortunately, Cisco has provided an overlay for Aironet called Wireless Domain Services (WDS) that imposes this functionality on the peer-to-peer environment.

In a non-WDS environment, the Supplicant would be required to fully reauthenticate every time it moved from one Aironet access point to another. All of the discussion of authentication so far has pointed out that, depending on the EAP-Method employed, this can be a lengthy process in terms of machine time. In terms of human time, it is very quick; but machine time is much faster than human time, and a full authentication can be disruptive. Loss of connectivity to an application could conceivably occur. If an application that is very time sensitive, such as IPT, is in use during the transition and subsequent full reauthentication, then it is fairly likely that the quality of the connection will suffer. Caching of credentials makes full reauthentication unnecessary. A single device acts as a database housing the credentials for connections currently established and can validate a reassociation/reauthentication request very quickly. Of course the concern regarding latency associated with the WDS device still exists. However, if a "good" design has been accomplished, then mobility can take place quickly.

Thus, implementation of an Aironet solution is relatively simple from an 802.1X perspective. Configuration is fairly trivial, just as it is fairly trivial in a wired world. The main change in an Aironet implementation with 802.1X is the inclusion of WDS to support cached credentials. The network aspects of

Aironet can be pretty complex in terms of management and scalability, but there is minimal effort required to implement 802.1X on a single access point beyond what is required to implement a single access point in a non-802.1X environment.

3.7.4 Airespace

Airespace is a centralized wireless implementation. Where each access point is intelligent in an Aironet implementation, the reverse is true in an Airspace implementation. An Airespace access point houses just enough intelligence to obtain an address and find the device that will supply the rest of its configuration. This requires a new piece of equipment beyond what is required in an Aironet implementation. All the "intelligence" in Airespace is housed in something called a "controller." This device is much more complex than an Aironet access point because in controls a complete domain and not just the connection to an access point.

Thus, the Airespace access point obtains an address, locates a controller, and downloads a runtime configuration including all SSID information. The access point is still pretty stupid and relies heavily on the controller. An encrypted tunnel is built from the access point back to the controller. All of the traffic sent by the end user traverses this tunnel and ultimately is distributed by the controller rather than the access point itself. Thus, it is the controller that "interprets" the packets and places them on appropriate VLANs for distribution in the wired network.

It is interesting to note that the communication is not asynchronous. Traffic from the end user is tunneled to the controller where it is analyzed and distributed. Similarly, the recipient of the traffic, usually an application on the wired network, sends its portion of the conversation back to the controller. The controller then encrypts this traffic and forwards it to the access point to which the user is associated.

This causes an interesting situation in the network. The end user will "think" it owns a particular IP address. The rest of the network will see that address associated with a particular port on a controller. All traffic to or from the wireless client is tunneled between an access point and a controller. This situation has some huge advantages and also some huge disadvantages.

Follow what happens if a PING Trace is sent from the network to the wireless client. It will traverse the network to the controller where it is encapsulated and sent to the end station associated with an access point. The access point can be a significant distance, in terms of infrastructure, from the controller, but the trace will not report any of this infrastructure as having been traversed. As far as the PING is concerned, the end station is located at the controller. This has a significant impact on troubleshooting. Traditional tools probably will not be adequate in the Airespace environment. A new toolset utilizing Airespace management will be required to support the environment. This could have a very significant impact on the structure and processes of support organizations. Both the Help Desk and the Network Management functions will be affected.

That is the disadvantage. But look at what it provides. Because there is a single point that is fixed in the network that receives traffic destined for an end user, and that point will always know where the end user is, then IP addressing is simple. The problem of routing information to an end user becomes trivial. The route never changes as far as the traditional network is concerned—no matter where the user is. Movement between access points does not ever mean that the user needs to obtain a new address. Nor does it mean that the wired infrastructure between the access point and the controller must be modified if new subnets are implemented to support a new SSID. This is a huge advantage.

When configuring 802.1X in the Airspace environment, all that is necessary when establishing a SSID is to take the defaults. 802.1X must be explicitly disabled if it is not desired. This is consistent with the new specifications for 802.11i in which 802.1X provides the foundation for authenticating and encrypting wireless traffic.

The tunneled situation has some nice implications for 802.1X, as well as for IP addressing. The primary thing to remember is that SSIDs are not configured on an access point. They are configured on the controller and then distributed to each access point associated with that controller. However, the authentication process does not take place on the access point, it takes place on the controller. This means that the maintenance of the Authenticator/Authentication Server configurations can be reduced significantly. Only the controller must be configured for communication with the Authentication Server, rather than every single access point. The Authenticator is the controller rather than the access point and a controller may support hundreds of access points.

Because the controller is not tied to a physical location in the way that an access point is, it also can be strategically located for communication with the Authentication Server. Of course, the controller also must be strategically located to minimize latency for communication with the access point. The total concern regarding reauthentication is not eliminated, but the possibilities are significantly increased as far as design is concerned.

Furthermore, the tunneled connections between an access point and a controller can be useful when developing guest connectivity. The controller with which an access point communicates can be located anywhere in the infrastructure. It is possible to locate a controller for guest connections outside of the corporate firewalls and thus secure all communications for guests. Traffic from the guest would be tunneled through the network all the way to the "outside" where it would be placed on an appropriate LAN structure that allows communication with the Internet. There is no possibility then of a guest accidentally gaining access to secured corporate resources.

Tunnels also can be strategic in developing multiple layers of security and protecting internal traffic. The logical and physical placement of controllers can provide a mechanism for data protection across the wired corporate environment. It is a little strange to think that a wireless implementation can be used to extend security, but it is possible. This type of implementation, in conjunction with an appropriate EAP-Method, can be leveraged to construct a very secure communication path.

In the same way that WDS provides a central repository for credentials used to facilitate mobility, so does the Airespace implementation. Each controller is a natural location for the storage of credentials. It has not been mentioned before, but the controllers in an environment communicate with one another. Thus, sharing credential information, should a user move from one controller to another, is handled with minimal configuration required.

The centralized approach offers some nice advantages, but it must be carefully designed. There is definitely a trade-off, as most of the access point's communication must be with a controller. Management in some areas is reduced to the toolset associated with the product. The overall complexity of the environment can be much greater with Airespace than with Aironet, but the implementation of 802.1X is greatly simplified.

All in all, the implementation of wireless has larger issues within an organization than those specific to 802.1X. In fact, the issues related to the implementation of 802.1X in a wired environment can be pretty much the same as those that must be addressed in a wireless environment. The significant difference is that care must be taken when selecting an EAP-Method. Because wireless is a shared environment, the strength of encryption and vulnerability to various attacks is a major concern. From an 802.1X perspective, the length of time and effort an authentication requires combined with the process available for reauthentication are the primary concerns.

One of the major considerations regarding the implementation of wireless is the new specifications. 802.11i is a fairly new standard and requires the use of 802.1X. This means that any implementation of wireless will require a corresponding implementation of 802.1X in the relatively near future. This will have significance in selecting not only the wireless infrastructure but in selecting wireless drivers for the end stations.

So now the very simple network that we started with several sections ago has become a pretty complex environment.

3.8   IP TELEPHONY

3.8.1   Section Summary

Now that the corporation is finally making money and the network has been expanded to include wireless, the new project is to implement IP Tele-phony(IPT). The popular belief is that IP Telephony is a big money saver.

That may or may not be true in a given organization, but the application must be considered in terms of 802.1X. The two are not mutually exclusive, but IPT does affect an 802.1X implementation.

Most applications are relatively transparent as far as 802.1X is concerned. But any application, such as IPT, that requires the installation of special pieces of hardware on ports enabled for 802.1X can have a big impact. The connection of telephones to the network certainly qualifies. IPT phones usually consist of two Ethernet ports. One is used to connect the appliance to the network and the other is available to attach to a computer. This port is known as the phone data port.

Imbedded in the phone is a switch-like bus that allows the handset and the attached computer to communicate over the port attached to the network. This device has many characteristics of a hub, but is termed a switch by Cisco. Because voice is actually an IP application, the ports connecting the phone and the Authenticator are effectively a trunk if the voice and data is in separate VLANs. They do not have to be, but Cisco allows this. How this is accomplished is the consideration for 802.1X. It would seem that the port on the Authenticator would not have 802.1X enabled. This is not the case. A Cisco IP phone can be attached to an 802.1X enabled port.

Cisco phones implemented in conjunction with Cisco switches are able to "bypass" what normally would be expected for the 802.1X process. This is accomplished through the use of Cisco Discovery Protocol (CDP) exchanges. This exchange causes the phone to be placed in a voice VLAN associated with the port. The data portion of the port undergoes normal 802.1X processing and will eventually be placed in a Guest VLAN.

Any device with a Supplicant attaching to the data port on the phone must be an active partner and issue an EAPOL-Start to initiate authentication. This is because the port on the Authenticator is already up and will not recognize the attachment of another device in addition to the phone. As you would expect with the imbedded switch capability, the situation with the phone is similar to that of the hub discussed in the section, Unplanned Expansion. Newer firmware on some phones will monitor their data port and issue a gratuitous EAPOL packet as the link changes state. This allows the Authenticator to recognize the state change occurring on the phone and place the data portion of the port into an appropriate state.

3.8.2 Connecting a Phone

Phones do not currently house a Supplicant. In that sense, the phone is very much like any other dumb device attached to an Authenticator. But the way that a Cisco phone is treated by a Cisco Authenticator is entirely different. Before we discuss that, however, let us take a quick look at the implications of connecting a different vendor's IP phone to a Cisco network.

First, take a look at what a phone looks like from a network perspective. It obviously looks like a small hub or switch. It has at least three ports. One is an uplink port, one is a port for the handset, and the third is a port to which a computer can be attached. In previous sections we have discussed how devices like hubs and small switches must be attached to the network. The use of trunks was recommended and it would seem that this situation should be implemented for IP phones. This is absolutely true.

The phone will connect to either a port defined as a trunk, in which case 802.1X will not be enabled, or it will attach to an 802.1X enabled port. Remember that the phone does not have a Supplicant. This means that when the port on the Authenticator becomes active and the authentication process is initiated, the phone eventually will go into the Guest VLAN. Because the phone is addressable, then whether or not the bus in the phone acts like a switch or like a hub will determine whether or not the phone's port, available to be attached to a computer, can actually be used. If it acts like a hub, then the single address allowed by default will go to the handset and no computer can attach and communicate. If it acts like a switch, then both the handset and the computer will be placed in the Guest VLAN.

Is putting the phone on a Guest VLAN such a bad thing? That is a debatable point. Certainly it will be exposed to whatever viruses, etc. are dragged into the enterprise network by outsiders who connect. But the phones can be used and calls can be placed, right? Probably not. To place a call, phones must communicate with some form of Call Manager for call setup. It probably is customary to restrict the Guest VLAN to Internet access only. This means that calls to other sites across the internal corporate network cannot be placed. Furthermore, unless the Call Manager, gateways, etc are placed on the Guest VLAN, even local calls cannot be made.

Can the phone then be guaranteed to reside in the Guest VLAN? If the phone acts like a hub and the Authenticator is configured to allow multiple hosts then it is entirely possible that an active Supplicant attaching to the port on the phone could cause the phone to move to a different VLAN. The phone then will lose connectivity until it is readdressed. This is a bad situation for any application, but is really bad for IPT. All of the problems discussed earlier in the section, Unplanned Expansion, come home to roost here. Either special handling is required for IPT or 802.1X must be scrapped when using a non-Cisco phone on a Cisco network.

Cisco has chosen to take the second option—that of bypassing 802.1X authentication for the phone. Cisco leverages another special protocol— Cisco Discovery Protocol (CDP)—to avoid some of the problems. Each Cisco phone issues a CDP packet when it is activated. This packet is sensed by a Cisco Authenticator and receives special handling. The debug below shows what happens when a Cisco phone is plugged into a Cisco switch.

Note that this is a debug of CDP only and does not include 802.1X, RADIUS, or AAA as most of the other debug output shown in this book do.

```
00:04:52: %LINK-3-UPDOWN: Interface FastEthernet0/3,—changed
    state to up
00:04:52: CDP-AD: Interface FastEthernet0/3 coming up
00:04:52: CDP-PA: version 2 packet sent out on FastEthernet0/3
00:04:52: CDP-PA: version 2 packet sent out on FastEthernet0/3
00:04:52: CDP-PA: version 2 packet sent out on FastEthernet0/3
00:04:53: %LINEPROTO-5-UPDOWN: Line protocol on Interface
    FastEthernet0/3, changed state to up
00:04:55 CDP-PA: Packet received from SEP001120E30D8F on interface
    FastEthernet0/3
00:04:55: **Entry NOT found in cache**
00:04:55: CDP-PA: version 2 packet sent out on FastEthernet0/3
00:04:56: CDP-PA: Packet received from SEP001120E30D8F on interface
    FastEthernet0/3
00:04:56: **Entry found in cache**
00:04:56: CDP-PA: version 2 packet sent out on FastEthernet0/3
```

The debug statements shown above do not include all output for the phone to be installed, but do demonstrate that the phone is treated like any other Cisco device from a CDP perspective. After the phone has reached this point in the process, it attempts to derive an IP address and communicate with all necessary servers to obtain the remainder of its configuration. The data port on the phone is inactive during this process.

Look at that debug a little more closely. Notice that there is a significant amount of time that has elapsed. A total of four seconds were spent from the beginning of the debug until the point where the phone could begin to obtain its IP address. 802.1X has not been idle on the port during this time. The debug below has been expanded to include CDP as well as the debugs for 802.1X, AAA, and RADIUS seen in most other displays in the book. We will begin at the point in the process where the Authenticator attempts to communicate with a Supplicant.

```
*Aug 8 10:57:59:769 EDT: dot1x-ev:dot1x_tx_eap: EAP Pkt
*Aug 8 10:57:59:769 EDT: dot1x-ev:EAP-code=FAILURE
*Aug 8 10:57:59:769 EDT: dot1x-ev:EAP Type=IDENTITY
*Aug 8 10:57:59:769 EDT: dot1x-ev:ID=0
*Aug 8 10:57:59:769 EDT: dot1x-registry:registry: dot1x_ether_
    macaddr called
*Aug 8 10:57:59:769 EDT: dot1x-ev:dot1x_post_message_to_auth_sm:
    cleanup author from interface FastEthernet0/3
*Aug 8 10:57:59:769 EDT: dot1x-ev:dot1x_post_message_to_auth_sm:
    Tx for req_id for supplicant 0000.0000.0000
```

*Aug 8 10:57:59:769 EDT: dot1x-ev:dot1x_tx_eap: EAP Pkt
*Aug 8 10:57:59:769 EDT: dot1x-ev:EAP-code = REQUEST
*Aug 8 10:57:59:769 EDT: dot1x-ev:EAP Type = IDENTITY
*Aug 8 10:57:59:769 EDT: dot1x-ev:ID = 1
*Aug 8 10:57:59:769 EDT: dot1x-registry:registry:dot1x_ether_
macaddr called

Up to this point, the debug shows the expected activity for 802.1X. The Authenticator recognized that the port came up and issued a Request Identity. The next few lines of the output show the Authenticator receiving a CDP packet from the phone. This occurs within a second of the Request Identity packet being issued.

*Aug 8 10:58:00:649 EDT: CDP-PA: Packet received from SEP001120E30D8F on interface FastEthernet0/3
*Aug 8 10:58:00:649 EDT: **Entry found in cache**
*Aug 8 10:58:00:649 EDT: dot1x-ev:dot1x_cdp_receive_notify: install phone 0011.20b4.5dd1 on interface FastEthernet0/3 on VLAN 15
*Aug 8 10:58:00:649 EDT: dot1x-ev:Dot1x Querying CDP for 0011.20b4.5dd1 Mac

After a few more CDP exchanges, the debug below shows that the Authenticator is proceeding with the expected search for a Supplicant. Note that the debug time reported shows that this is the second Request Identity packet issued. All the CDP packets received have not caused any reset of 802.1X timers. For all practical purposes, all of this exchange is taking place outside the 802.1X authentication process.

*Aug 8 10:57:58:764 EDT: dot1x-ev:dot1x_tx_eap: EAP Pket
*Aug 8 10:57:58:764 EDT: dot1x-ev: EAP-code = REQUEST
*Aug 8 10:57:58:764 EDT: dot1x-ev: EAP Type = IDENTITY
*Aug 8 10:57:58:764 EDT: dot1x-ev: ID = 1

When no Response packet is received on the port, it is placed in a Guest VLAN. At this point, if the VLANs are displayed then the port will show up in the voice VLAN associated with the port and the Guest VLAN also associated with the port. The voice VLAN is identified in a special configuration command. Shown below is the IOS configuration for a port that will be used for IPT and 802.1X.

interface FastEthernet0/3
switchport access VLAN 15
switchport voice VLAN 115
dot1x port-control auto
dot1x Guest VLAN 10

qos trust qos
tx-queue 3
priority high
Spanning-Tree portfast

The Authenticator will place the phone in the voice VLAN when the proper CDP packets are received. It would seem that this would leave the port in a vulnerable state because that VLAN is unprotected by 802.1X. This is true to a certain extent. However, the exposure requires that an attacker be able to spoof a voice CDP connection. This is not impossible, but is not common either. Also, because the device that is expected to be connected to this VLAN is a phone, additional protection can be applied that will restrict access to specific IP ports or devices. In this way, voice VLANs can be constructed that provide similar Port-Based Authentication assurances similar to the way in which other devices that do not house a Supplicant are protected.

Potentially, there are two VLANs associated with this physical port in addition to the voice VLAN. They are the VLANs customarily seen on 802.1X enabled ports: The authenticated VLAN and the Guest VLAN. Although the voice VLAN is significant to IPT, the other two are of most interest in this book.

If a debug were to be continued here it would show that the phone is placed in the voice VLAN and the authentication would continue as normal. If a Supplicant had already been connected to the phone, then the Request Identity packets would cause it to issue a Response Identity packet. If there was not a Supplicant, then the device would be placed in the Guest VLAN.

The phone acts like a small switch or hub. In this way, voice and data connectivity are assured. This situation was discussed earlier in this section. The phone is in one VLAN and the data port is in a different one. This implies that trunking is being performed on the link. Yet, review of the configuration of the port shows that no trunk has been implemented. If the running configuration is displayed in some CATOS devices, the port will have become a trunk. The following line will have appeared, as if by magic, in the configuration for CATOS. There is no indication of trunking for IOS based devices.

Set trunk 4/4 auto negotiate 1-1005,1025-4094

This confirms how the port is able to handle more than one VLAN. Because there are two VLANs, some form of trunking must be implemented on the physical port. This creates an interesting situation. How can 802.1X be functional on a trunked port? Go back to the switch and display the trunks. The "show trunks" command will show that the port is not a trunk. But the configuration says that it is one. What it boils down to is that the physical port must utilize some trunk characteristics to be able to support multiple VLANs, but it is not "fully" a trunk.

Let us review a little. The phone is acting like a small hub/switch. Here are a couple of scenarios regarding the connectivity a device will exhibit when connected to the data port. If the phone was already active and a device is attached to its data port, then the functions discussed earlier regarding switches and hubs would apply. A non-Supplicant or a non-active Supplicant, one that does not issue an EAPOL-Start, will be placed in the Guest VLAN. An active Supplicant will issue an EAPOL-Start and the authentication will begin.

Cisco has recognized this as a serious problem and has increased the intelligence in the firmware for some phones to include monitoring of the Link status for the data port on the handset. The phone will recognize when the data port becomes active and issue a gratuitous EAPOL-Start on behalf of the device connected to the data port. This causes the data portion of the Authenticator port to be placed in an unauthorized state and for the authentication process to be initiated. This will cause all possible types of connectivity to be resolved correctly. Any type of Supplicant will function correctly, and if there is no Supplicant, then the physical port once again will be placed in the Guest VLAN.

This resolves the first half of the problem. The second half is when the device on the back of the phone leaves. At this point, the Authenticator does not recognize that the device is no longer there and potentially leaves the physical port in an authenticated state. This is the same situation with hubs discussed earlier. The new firmware resolves this by issuing a gratuitous EAPOL when the link status of the data port on the handset goes to a down state. This situation was illustrated in the second section of this chapter, A Very Simple Network. When the phone issues these EAPOL packets on behalf of the device attached to its data port, life once again becomes wonderful.

All in all, IPT can coexist with 802.1X without either causing serious concern from a technical standpoint. However, IPT does increase the complexity of the environment and introduces VLANs that cannot be guaranteed to have only authenticated devices attached in some situations. Currently, there is no guarantee that the device attempting to use the voice VLAN is actually a phone.

Network Management and Help Desk organizations will require significant process changes and education when IPT and 802.1X are implemented jointly. As was illustrated above, there are some significant status and events that are not fully documented when interrogating the switch.

3.9 A NOT SO SIMPLE NETWORK

3.9.1 Section Summary

Our network has evolved over the past several sections into a robust environment. The single switch has become a complex infrastructure with a variety of devices attached. The environment has grown from a single switch to multiple switches and the addition of IPT and Wireless. Effectively, it has become a large site or campus. About the only place left to go is to a multi-site network. There are multiple considerations that are present in virtually every network, but these become more obvious in a larger one. Ensuring continuity of service is one of those considerations. This includes the concept of redundancy.

Redundancy is usually a good thing to incorporate into a network. Planning for the hopefully rare events of failing devices is just good sense. For most infrastructures, failover to a redundant device is transparent. Not so with Authentication Servers. The Authentication Server is the only component in an 802.1X authentication system that can be redundant. The default state for contacting Authentication Servers actually produces a very cumbersome environment. The way in which the Authenticator contacts the Authentication Server is configurable, but, even so, the failover can produce lengthy wait times during the Authentication process. In a default state, the sequence of Authentication Servers is contacted for every request even though one or more of the servers is inactive.

A not so simple network usually reflects a not so simple organization. As the organization increases in size, it also tends to increase in complexity. This complexity is reflected in the number of VLANs implemented and the variety of restrictions placed on each one. 802.1X can be used to assign a very specific VLAN to an individual user. This in turn makes network management a much more complex task.

Sheer size of the environment creates complexities that would seem to be peripheral to Port-Based Authentication. Yet, the possibilities are enormous in terms of the granularity of managing user access—and they are equally enormous for potential failure in the authentication process itself.

3.9.2   Placement of the Authentication Server

The first consideration in a not so simple network is the placement of multiple Authentication servers. A multi-site environment becomes a balancing act of budget and performance. It will be a very uncommon environment indeed that is composed of homogonous sites. In almost every network there will be one or two large sites, a handful of mid-range sites, and a larger number of smaller satellite sites. The relative importance of individual locations will be variable. For smaller locations, the lack of connectivity will be an aggravation For larger locations or a core site, connectivity becomes more critical. Certainly, there are environments to which this paradigm does not apply and communication becomes absolutely critical in every situation. This is most common in financial industries. In any event, the linkage between sites introduces two factors for consideration in 802.1X. First is the possibility that connectivity to the Authentication Server will be lost, and the second is the latency involved in the communication with an Authentication Server across the WAN.

For the purposes of this book, assume that the network is composed of multiple sites. There are two processing centers acting in failover mode—essentially, one is an active disaster recovery site. There are Authentication Servers at each site. Figure 3.6 illustrates this scenario.

The local Authenticators have been configured in the following manner for redundancy. The primary Authentication Server is at the active processing center with a backup located at the disaster recovery site.

```
radius-server host 10.92.30.39 auth-port 1645 acct-port 1813
radius-server host 10.52.34.70 auth-port 1645 acct-port 1813
radius-server retransmit 3
radius-server key ^FoG@T4B!@5
```

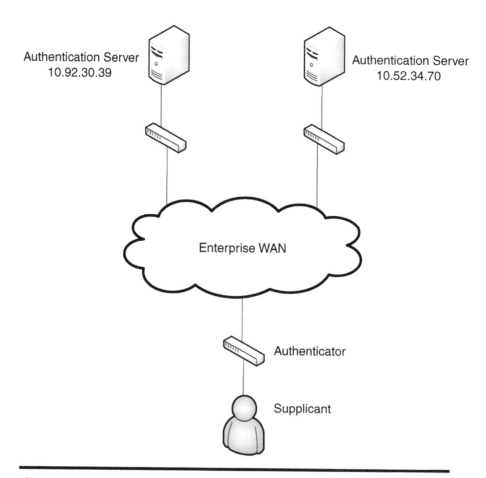

Figure 3.6 Network with Backup Authentication Server.

In the expected course of events, the Authenticator will connect to the primary Authentication Server and the latency is primarily that associated with the WAN. Normal latency associated with the LAN environments would be only a small fraction of the overall experience. Look at what happens when the primary server is no longer available. The following debug output shows that contact with the primary RADIUS server is attempted. Four distinct attempts to contact that Authentication Server are made and then an attempt to reach the next server is made. The first server is address 10.92.30.39 and the second server is 10.52.34.70.

```
00:01:41: RADIUS: EAP-login: length of radius packet=122 code=1
00:01:41: RADIUS: Initial Transmit FastEthernet0/3 id 1 10.92.30.39:1645,
    Access-Request, len 122
00:01:41: Attribute 4 6 0A5C0925A
00:01:41: Attribute 61 6 00000000
00:01:41: Attribute 1 18 4B4349E
00:01:41: Attribute 6 6 00000002
00:01:41: Attribute 12 6 000005DC
00:01:41: Attribute 31 19 30302D30
00:01:41: Attribute 79 23 02000015
00:01:41: Attribute 80 18 711585B0
00:01:46: RADIUS: Retransmit id 1
00:01:51: RADIUS: Retransmit id 1
00:01:56: RADIUS: Retransmit id 1
00:02:01: RADIUS: Marking server 10.92.30.39:1645,1813 dead
00:02:01: RADIUS: Re-signed packet (key:<HwG@TmB!@5;rctx:0x110
    AEC8)
00:02:01: RADIUS: Trying next server (10.52.34.70:1645,1813) for id1
00:02:01: RADIUS: Retransmit id 1
```

Notice that this has taken 20 seconds of real time. The secondary server responds quickly, as shown in the continuation of the debug output below.

```
00:02:01: RADIUS: Received from id 1 10.52.34.70:1645, Access-Chal-
    lenge, len 78
00:02:01: Attribute 79 8 01030006
00:02:01: Attribute 24 32 43495343
00:02:01: Attribute 80 18 5948F54E
00:02:01: RADIUS: EAP-login: length of EAP packet=6
00:02:01: RADIUS: EAP-login: got challenge from RADIUS
00:02:01: AAA/AUTHEN (745867): status=GETDATA
```

The authentication process continues in a normal fashion with the Authenticator exchanging packets with the Supplicant. When the Supplicant returns a response to the Request Identity that the contained information is from the Authentication Server, the Authenticator processes the information and again attempts to converse with the Authentication Server. There is just one problem. It starts with the first Authentication Server in the list. It starts with the primary, rather than continuing to access the secondary. This means that there is another 20 second lag in this exchange, just as there was in the first. Shown below is the debug output during that time.

```
00:02:01: AAA/AUTHEN/CONT (745867): continue_login (user=
   BBBB\Edwin.Brown)
00:02:01: AAA/AUTHEN (745867): status=GETDATA
00:02:01: AAA/AUTHEN (745867): Method=radius(radius)
00:02:01: RADIUS: unstruct sharecount=1
00:02:01: RADIUS: EAP-login: NAS Port=00-0f-1f-43-68-2a RemAddr=
   000f.1f43.682a
00:02:01: RADIUS: EAP-login: length of RADIUS packet=245 code=1
00:02:01: RADIUS: Initial Transmit FastEthernet0/3 id 1 10.92.30.39:1645,
   Access-Request, len 245
00:02:01:    Attribute 4 6 0A5C0925A
00:02:01:    Attribute 61 6 00000000
00:02:01:    Attribute 1 18 4B4349E
00:02:01:    Attribute 6 6 00000002
00:02:01:    Attribute 12 6 000005DC
00:02:01:    Attribute 31 19 30302D30
00:02:01:    Attribute 24 32 43495343
00:02:01:    Attribute 79 114 02030070
00:02:01:    Attribute 80 18 8E9D34FD
00:02:06: RADIUS: Retransmit id 2
00:02:07: dot1x-
   sm:Fa0/3:0000.0000.0000:dot1x_process_txWhen_expire called
00:02:07: dot1x_auth Fa0/3: during state auth_connecting_connecting
   got event 18(txWhen_expire)
00:02:07: @@@ dot1x_auth Fa0/3:auth_connecting-> auth_connecting
00:02:07: dot1x-
   sm:Fa0/3:0000.0000.0000:auth_connecting_connecting_action called
00:02:07: dot1x-ev:dot1x_post_message_to_auth_sm: Skipping tx for
   req_id for default supplicant
00:02:11:RADIUS: Retransmit id 2
00:02:16:RADIUS: Retransmit id 2
00:02:21: ADIUS: Marking server 10.92.30.39:1645,1813 dead
00:02:21:RADIUS: Re-signed packet (key: <HwG@TmB!@5;rctx:0x
   110AF08)
00:02:21:RADIUS: Trying next server (10.52.34.70:1645,1813) for id2
00:02:21:RADIUS: Retransmit id 2
```

```
00:02:21: RADIUS: Received from id 2 10.52.34.70:1645, Access-Chal-
    lenge, len 204
00:02:21:    Attribute 79 8 01040084
00:02:21:    Attribute 24 32 43495343
00:02:21:    Attribute 80 18 D6A32EA0
```

The authentication process is now approximately 40 seconds longer than anticipated in a "normal" environment and it has barely begun. Every exchange between the Authenticator and the Authentication Server follows this pattern. The Authenticator attempts to send the Access-Request to the primary RADIUS server, and only when it fails does it continue with the secondary. Finally, the Supplicant is authenticated and allowed access. This is illustrated in the final stages of the debug shown below.

```
00:04:22: dot1x_bend Fa0/3: during state dot1x_bend_response, got
    event 2(asuccess)
00:04:22:  @@@ dot1x_bend Fa0/3: dot1x_bend_response ->
    dot1x_bend_success
00:04:22: dot1x-sm:Dot1x Success State Entered
00:04:22: dot1x-ev:dot1x_bend_success_enter:000d.56b7.6fc2: Current
    ID=9
00:04:22: dot1x-ev:dot1x_bend: Sending RADIUS Response to Suppli-
    cant of length 4
00:04:22: dot1x-ev:dot1x_tx_eap: EAP Ptk
00:04:22: dot1x-ev:EAP-code=SUCCESS
00:04:22: dot1x-ev:EAP Type=Unknown
00:04:22: dot1x-ev:ID=9
```

The entire authentication has taken over two and a half minutes to complete. This is compared to the virtually instantaneous process when the primary server is accessible. There are a couple of issues that surface in this situation. First, the increased authentication time will probably cause some form of application problem. It is reasonable to assume that DHCP has expired and no address is available for the Supplicant. Even though the Supplicant has finally been authorized, it probably cannot communicate until DHCP has been restarted. This leads to the second likely issue: There is going to be a user support call. Very few users are going to wait for nearly 3 minutes to be allowed access even if they know what is happening—and it is highly unlikely that the garden variety user will understand what is happening. The user is going to call for support. This means that the support organizations must be able to diagnose this situation and resolve it quickly.

Now, it must be noted that there are some commands in IOS and CATOS that will allow a RADIUS server to be marked as "dead." However, these commands may not be available in every version or release. Furthermore, a typical command functions in terms of minutes rather than seconds. An example of the command in IOS is shown below.

radius-server deadtime <minutes>

This is a significant change in the anticipated state of affairs. In a wired environment, some applications, such as DHCP, will have timed out prior to authentication being completed. There is a second issue of mobility. Depending on the EAP-Method selected, connectivity to applications could be lost and would need to be re-established. This is more serious both in terms of support and in the effect of a failed application. If the implementation of wireless relies on the availability of a RADIUS server to be available when reauthenticating during a movement from one access point to another, then this will destroy applications such as IPT.

Of course, both of these situations should have been recognized from the very beginning. The overall design of the 802.1X environment should have taken into consideration the consequences of placement of the Authentication Server, as well as the effect on the EAP-Method chosen.

3.9.3 Significance of VLAN Design

The next thing that must be recognized as having significance is that of the VLAN design. Certainly this is a much larger issue than that of implementing Port-Based Authentication. However, the implementation of 802.1X brings this issue to the forefront. And as the scope of the network increases so does the complexity of the VLAN environment.

802.1X emphasizes who belongs on what VLAN—which is an oxymoron. That is the entire purpose of 802.1X. In a smaller environment, a single VLAN for authenticated users may be entirely appropriate. This will probably not be the case as the number of users increases. It is common to increase the differentiation of function, responsibility, and authority as the number of users increases. This will cause a corresponding increase in complexity of the environment. 802.1X both aggravates the situation and offers solutions.

While the state of the VLAN for any given port is entirely deterministic for an individual Supplicant, the overall perspective is that ports are randomly placed into a VLAN. That means, from a management perspective, any given port will seem to be in a fully variable and unpredictable state. Evaluation of the particular user attempting to connect is frequently the only way to determine whether or not a problem with connectivity exists. This certainly places an additional burden of detailed management on the environment. Any troubleshooting must involve detailed information regarding the configuration of the port, the state of authentication on all three participants, and any special per-user configuration applied by the Authentication Server.

This means that a level of sophistication that frequently is not available in Tier One Help Desk personnel must either be developed or supplemented with higher level personnel. This situation becomes more complex as the level of complexity increases in the network itself.

As stated a little earlier, the issues regarding VLAN assignment are fundamentally present in 802.1X but are most evident as the complexity of the network increases. In a smaller, or simpler, environment, there will be one or more VLANs, and frequently these are constructed to maintain a small broadcast domain rather than to segregate functions available on the network. In this type of environment, any user that can authenticate has complete access. This makes for a very tidy configuration.

However, as complexity increases so does the potential for VLAN assignment. Historically, more secured environments were localized. Meaning that if payroll functions were to be protected by Layer 3 functions, such as access lists, then the physical ports used by the Payroll Department were placed in a specific VLAN. This certainly is still an option and can make life simpler for those on the help desk. 802.1X in this situation is virtually transparent. If a user can authenticate, then he is placed on the access VLAN configured on the Authenticator. Troubleshooting then consists of two distinct tasks. First, can the user authenticate; second, is the configuration of the particular port satisfactory?

802.1X can be implemented in at least a couple of ways to enhance this effort. The intent of having ports restricted to specific VLANs implies that only a fraction of the user population should be allowed to have access to resources on that VLAN. The issue then is how can 802.1X restrict authentication to a subset of users? One possible way to do this is to separate the Authentication Server servicing the Authenticator housing the restricted ports and to authenticate only those users that should be allowed access. If this is done, then the Payroll Department will be granted access on those ports while other users will be placed in a Guest VLAN with considerably more restricted access. This is just one way to accomplish the physical segregation of ports. There are undoubtedly a large number of alternative mechanisms, but there is no need to attempt to design all alternatives in this section.

That being said, there is one alternative that must be discussed. Consider the situation where a subset of users should be allowed access to a set of resources controlled, at least partially, at Layer 3. Further assume that either the distribution of users is highly random in the environment or that security is such that no port should be allowed to have the VLAN configured as the default access VLAN. In this situation, the particular users that should be enabled to have access could have the per-user VLAN configured in the Authentication Servers. In this case, when the user is authenticated, she is placed in the special VLAN that allows access to the needed resources. Thus, a double level of security can be achieved through functionality available in 802.1X. First, there are no pre-defined ports available to access the protected resources; and second, only authenticated users are granted specific access to those resources. This is pretty neat.

However, consider the complexity that has been established as part of the configuration of the network. In a physically segregated environment, particular VLANs are configured on particular switches. In the more fluid environment, it may be necessary to configure those VLANs on every switch. Depending on a variety of other factors this could affect routing or even quality of service. The implementation of 802.1X as part of the overall security scheme can cause effects far beyond the simple authentication of a particular user. The entire configuration of access may need to be developed in conjunction with that of 802.1X. It is not out of line to believe that there are network scenarios that will require a complete revision if 802.1X is implemented in a robust manner.

Then consider the complexity that has been established regarding user management. Each user may potentially have a wide range of different access requirements. The maintenance of VLAN assignments at a user level can be fairly large, especially if the organization experiences a fair degree of churn. Then, as just indicated, the support issues for an individual VLAN assignment can be fairly large. The particular trade-offs of extreme flexibility must be evaluated against increased complexity of management and support.

It boils down to a consideration of scalability. In both situations discussed in this section, the placement of Authentication Servers and VLAN assignment, the complexity of the network is capable of affecting performance. Care must be exercised even in smaller, less complex networks to ensure that scalability is inherent in the design.

3.10   DESIGN RECAP

3.10.1   Section Summary

In the first section of this chapter, I discussed Design, or more appropriately, the stages of a design process. In that section, I also stated that the design effort would be revisited at the end of this book. Well, here we are. Unlike the first section on Design, this section will focus on specific issues that should be considered in a Port-Based Authentication design.

Every design is a multifaceted effort in which each of the aspects interacts with all the other aspects. A simple way to visualize this is to build a cube with three planes. These planes would be labeled Technology, Access, and Application. Evaluation of these planes individually and collectively through the four phases of a design process, Requirements Definition, Concept, Architecture, and Design will result in a complete definition for successful implementation. The three aspects of each plane stand alone in an evaluation and interact with each other as well as the aspects of the other planes, raising questions that will require resolution during the execution of a design.

The plane of Technology is devoted to the infrastructure of a network. Within an 802.1X design, consideration of the functionality of the various appliances is part of the plane of Technology. Evaluation of IOS releases and features is a fundamental part of the aspect of Transport. So is the actual placement of appliances. As an example, in an Airespace wireless environment the placement of controllers will have a significant role in wireless Port-Base Authentication. The analysis around the placement of these controllers is part of the aspect of Transport.

But the plane is not restricted to the evaluation of appliances. Appliances fall within the aspect of Transport, but there are also the aspects of Security and Management that must be considered as well. Thus, this plane includes the selection of an EAP-Method, additionally securing interlinkage of the network appliances that cannot participate in the traditional 802.1X Port-Based Authentication. The aspect of Security covers the appliances, the infrastructure, and the security of credential exchanges.

The aspect of Management also includes the dual role of managing the various appliances and the linkages among appliances, but it also includes management of the connectivity of client devices. In some cases, the client will be an 802.1X Supplicant and in others it will not. It would seem that non-Supplicants should be dismissed as not being a factor in 802.1X, but that is not reasonable. The consideration of what is not covered by 802.1X also refines the definition of what is covered. Therefore, management of printers, servers, and other appliances that may not be strictly part of an 802.1X design is absolutely necessary for a successful implementation.

The plane of Access is concerned with connectivity and traffic across a network. The three aspects: Client, Provider, and Support are categories of Access with each having a different personality. Client access is ultimately concerned with the conversations between Supplicant and Authenticator and between Supplicant and Authentication Server. Issues regarding the authentication process, in terms of access, are identified in this aspect. The final connectivity allowed a client, Supplicant, or non-Supplicant also is evaluated as part of this aspect. Provider access defines the connectivity for devices that are not strictly clients. This includes the Authentication Server, as well as other devices that behave in a similar fashion. This would include servers and printers. The way in which these devices connect and are controlled is covered in this aspect. A discussion of the intersection of this aspect with the aspect of Management was provided a couple of paragraphs earlier. Support access defines the interconnectivity of infrastructure appliances and how that connectivity is authenticated.

Application is the final plane in the cube. Application is concerned with what is transported across the network and the successful integration of network and function. Within an 802.1X Port-Based Authentication, most of the impact of this plane is peripheral in nature. This plane does have some significance in an Airespace implementation, but the majority of the impact is with the implementation of the wireless system, itself, and not with a SSID utilizing 802.1X. The three conversations in an authentication comprise the majority of the Application concerns. However, there are concerns that are fringe issues, like items such as the handling of certificates that may be required within a particular EAP-Method.

3.10.2 The Cube Revisited

Several sections ago, I presented a diagram that depicted interactions requiring consideration in the design process. The diagram was presented as a cube with three planes. The planes consisted of Technology, Access, and Application. There are specific aspects associated with each plane. The interaction of these planes—and the individual aspects with one another—forms the basis of a design.

The design of 802.1X, like any other network implementation, must be grounded in those interactions. The cube is shown below in Figure 3.7. The remainder of this chapter will deal with the consideration of designing an 802.1X implementation from the perspective of the interaction of the planes. Each plane will be considered individually and the aspects of each plane will be detailed.

3.10.3 Technology

Technology is a significant plane in most networking designs, but is especially important in 802.1 X Port-Based Authentication designs. Although

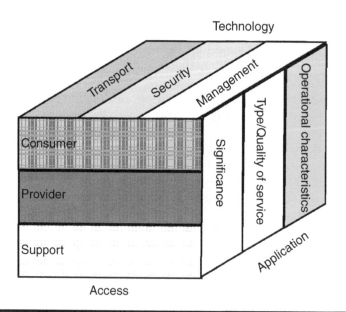

Figure 3.7 Design Considerations.

Technology is the infrastructure in a network, it is also Security and Management. All three of those aspects interacting form the foundation of the infrastructure.

3.10.3.1 Transport

Transport is one of the fundamental aspects in an 802.1X process. Primarily, this is viewed from the perspective of the Authenticator. The first question that must be resolved is: What portion of the infrastructure is going to be included in the authentication process? Will this include both wired and wireless?

Next an evaluation of the included infrastructure must be conducted. Are the appliances capable of supporting 802.1X? Are the appliances all from a single vendor? If not, do they support the same functionality? Which release of standards is supported? Are there any optional functions from the 2004 standards that are supported?

Consideration of the infrastructure itself, from the perspective of interconnectivity, is another issue. How are the connections between devices going to be authenticated? Is the implementation of mutual MAC filters a reasonable approach? How are trunks between devices going to be protected?

In short, what portion of Port-Based Authentication utilizing 802.1X can be implemented on the existing infrastructure—and how can it be done? After those questions are answered, the interactions of the infrastructure, or Transport, with other aspects in Technology and the other planes must be documented to determine what changes may be required to the physical implementation of the network.

3.10.3.2 Security

One of the primary considerations in the aspect of Security is the selection of an EAP-Method. The selection of an EAP-Method must be undertaken from dual perspectives. The first is the review of the current environment. An evaluation of current authentication and authorization techniques must be conducted. Is a Windows Domain utilized? Is a two-factor authentication process, usually based around tokens, implemented? Are certificates implemented? The second perspective to be utilized in the selection of an EAP-Method is a definition of the level of confidentiality required. What is the likelihood that an exchange of credentials can be captured? What is the likelihood that significant effort will be spent to capture and decrypt a credential exchange? Is the protection of credentials significantly exceeding the protection of the data flowing across the network?

Supplicant selection is also highly important. Many of the different Supplicants available offer a restricted subset of EAP-Method support. This means that the selection of a Supplicant and the EAP-Method go hand-in-hand. At this point, significant financial considerations may be introduced.

Of course, the EAP-Method is just the first consideration in the evaluation of Security. Consideration of what to do with the particular individual, based upon the state of authentication, is at least as important as figuring out how to authenticate the individual. This means that the definition of Guest VLANs, the determination of whether or not dynamic allocation of VLANs and access lists will be implemented, and the additional requirements of infrastructure configuration to support the intended access must be given consideration in the light of 802.1X.

3.10.3.3 Management

There are two parts to Management that must be evaluated. The first is the toolset used to support and control an implementation. The second is the manual support and intervention required.

The first issue is to determine which MIBs will be required to support the 802.1X functions chosen for implementation. Are all the functions supported within the 2004 specifications or are there proprietary functions involved? Given this information, a selection of tools to support and report can be made.

Actually, that paragraph is naïve. It assumes that automated management is limited to reporting for Authenticator activities only. Almost certainly, this is not the case. There are management activities regarding all three conversations that would include the Authentication Server conversations with the Authenticator and potentially with external databases, as well as the conversation between the Authentication Server and the Supplicant at the logical level.

The question of manual involvement with the management of the 802.1X processes is one that frequently is ignored, but probably is one of the most critical to a successful implementation. It is never correct, when discussing a failed environment, to state that the infrastructure was sufficient, but that the people charged with supporting it did not do so. Either the merging of manual and automated support is successful—is achieving the goals—or it is not. The two cannot be separated. Thus, the processes and training to understand the automation must be in place for changes to the network based upon an implementation of 802.1X.

3.10.4 Access

The plane of Access is primarily concerned with the implications of attaching devices to the network. The most obvious concern is that of communication from one device to another. There are two types of device that usually attach to a network—clients and providers. A client usually is proactive and communicates with a provider. The most common type of client probably is a user sitting at a computer that is connected to the network. Frequently, a provider is a server. However, a provider also may be some type of passive device like a printer.

Clients work with providers. Providers support clients. It is common for providers to be a group of devices that support the needs of clients. Providers also frequently use the services of other providers. Examples of this type of connectivity includes network backups and multi-tiered security implementations where data is separated from the application.

There is a third aspect of access that is included in this plane and that is Support. Infrastructure appliances often must communicate with one another for a variety of reasons. Some of the common reasons for this type of communication are network management and syslog. There is also the background communication that is required to make the network work. Support would include access for the exchange of Bridge Protocol Data Units (BPDUs), without which an Ethernet network can barely function, or the use of CDP in a Cisco environment.

It is easy to see that within an 802.1X implementation all three classes of access are present. Client access correlates well to Supplicant access and the exchange of credentials. Provider access relates well to exchanges between the Authentication Server and Authenticator. Additionally, there may be background exchanges between the Authentication Server and an external database such as the Windows Active Domain. Support exchanges are the heart of the 802.1X protocol itself—EAPOL. The communication on the link prior to Layer 3 being established, when either the switch or the client device has implemented 802.1X, is a Support access exchange.

In all three aspects, there must be identification and consideration of how devices that do not readily support the implementation of Supplicants will be placed on the network. Almost certainly, there will be devices that cannot support a Supplicant that must exist nonetheless in any given network. The network is not secured if there are ports available for connections that are not secured. This means that in a Port-Based Authentication design effort, the ports that cannot be secured via 802.1X are as important as those that can.

There is one type of access that is a little confusing within 802.1X: In situations where there are intermediate devices between the Authenticator and the Supplicant. The most obvious is that of a hub being inserted between a Supplicant and a switch. However, there is also the case of the type of connectivity in a wireless Airespace implementation. The access point and the controller are distinct appliances with significant considerations regarding placement above and beyond those associated with 802.1X. Yet, 802.1X is significant, even fundamental, in implementing wireless security. When designing 802.1X, the primary considerations are the three conversations that must take place. In this environment, the controller is really the Authenticator and the infrastructure between the controller and the Supplicant must be considered to be a single Layer 2 link. This includes the radio connectivity at the access point and all of the wired infrastructure between the access point and the controller.

3.10.4.1 Client

The client, or more aptly the Supplicant, has two conversations in the 802.1X process. The first is the physical conversation between the Supplicant and the Authenticator, and this is more properly classed as a Support conversation with one exception: Wireless. The other conversation is the logical conversation between the Supplicant and the Authentication Server.

In an authentication conducted over a wireless link, the "association" must be established before an 802.1X authentication can be conducted. The association is independent of 802.1X and, thus, can confuse the user. It is obvious that no communication can occur if there is no association. However, it is not obvious that communication still can be blocked when there is an association. Furthermore, there are security issues regarding the confidentiality of all communication that are defined in the configuration of the association that should be included in the definition of 802.1X. After all, it seems somewhat silly to secure the exchange of credentials without securing the exchange of information after authentication. Thus, consideration of the configuration for an association within an 802.1X implementation makes sense.

The selection and configuration of one or more EAP-Methods is the primary consideration of client-provider conversations as noted above. The synchronization of configuration on the Supplicant and the Authentication Server is the major consideration. But the use and support of certificates is another significant concern. It would seem that certificates should be considered to be a type of Support traffic. I have classed it as part of the client environment because the use, or non-use, of certificates has no impact on the configuration of the infrastructure between Authentication Server and Supplicant.

Another situation regarding client access is the maintenance of an authenticated session when moving from one access point to another within a wireless connection. In many ways, this process is exactly the same as that endured when originally establishing the authenticated session, with the added complication of ensuring that application connections are maintained while the Layer 2 link is moved from one point to another. The maintenance of application connectivity during mobility is actually a part of the wireless implementation and is not concerned with 802.1X at all. What is involved is the recognition and movement of an "authentication" from one access point to another. This movement must be accomplished quickly. This is a consideration when selecting both a wireless solution and an EAP-Method, as well as designing infrastructure paths for client access—Supplicant to Authorization Server.

3.10.4.2 Provider

Again, provider access is that access not directly initiated by a client. It can be the result of a client access or it can support a client access, but it is not a response directed back to the client. It is also not those accesses which can be classified as Support. The majority of the provider access is that access within the system being designed that is independent of infrastructure traffic or client/server traffic. Frequently, this type of traffic is server-to-server traffic required within an application.

The primary provider within the 802.1X model is the Authentication Server. There can be some additional considerations of "provider" access if the Authentication Database is separated from the Authentication Server. I will discuss that briefly in a moment. The largest concern in provider access is the placement of the Authentication Server with relation to the Authenticator. The length and complexity of the path between the two components is a significant design factor in 802.1X. As was shown in a previous section, the implementation and placement of redundant Authentication Servers can make a serious difference in the authentication experience for a user.

3.10.4.3   Support

As I stated above, EAPOL is entirely a Support type of Access. In all cases, this is the conversation between the Authenticator and the Supplicant. The vast majority of those conversations are involved in the exchange of credential information required to perform authentication. However, there are additional conversations within 802.1X that must be discussed. Remember that 802.1X is fundamentally concerned with Authentication prior to allowing access, and, as such, there are situations where access must be allowed in an unauthenticated environment.

There are at least two fundamental 802.1X—EAPOL—conversations that fall into this category. The first is the implementation of a Wake-On-LAN environment. This requires that certain types of communication be allowed between a device on the trusted—authenticated—side of the authenticator and the untrusted—Supplicant—side. The second is the reverse. Communication of certain types of alerts must be allowed from the untrusted into the trusted—ASF alerts. In both cases, the Authenticator must be specifically configured to allow this access.

There are additional considerations required to implement either Wake-On-LAN or ASF-Alert functions outside of the direct implementation of 802.1X. The entire functionality of either process must take into account that 802.1X has been implemented. In that sense, the classification of traffic in those applications might be that of provider and client rather than classification as Support. That is fine. 802.1X is not concerned with the success or failure of either application. It is only concerned with how those conversations will be "supported."

There are additional aspects of Support that must be considered. 802.1X is fundamentally an extension of Ethernet bridging. This expansion of functionality must be evaluated. The consideration of impact to bridging extends to the dynamic modification of VLANs. Depending on the implementation of Spanning-Tree, broadcast functions can be significantly altered. In some extreme cases, this can result in significant utilization changes on infrastructure links that do not appear to be involved with an 802.1X implementation. An evaluation of altered traffic patterns and the effect on the whole infrastructure is desirable and necessary.

The differences in wireless implementations, as illustrated by Cisco Aironet and Airespace, require different design approaches. In one, Airespace, the entire process is centralized with all traffic from all access points being collected and dispersed from a central point. In Aironet, on the other hand, each access point functions as an independent, intelligent entity. Because all information is automatically stored centrally in Airespace, it is easier to implement mobile authentication in it than with Aironet. Of course, the initial implementation of wireless is somewhat easier in a vanilla Aironet environment than with Airespace. There are always trade-offs.

In all three types of Access, understanding the flow of information through the infrastructure is of paramount importance.

3.10.5 Application

This plane is concerned with the functional aspects of Access. A client interacts with a provider to accomplish something. No network is implemented without the intent of accomplishing something. That something is Application.

Within 802.1X, Application is the definition of why Authentication is being conducted and what is being protected. It may seem that this has nothing to do with the Authentication process, itself, and that is true. However, just as with the selection of an EAP-Method, the consideration of Application on the network is significant in designing the implementation.

The requirements of the existing applications, as well as those that might be proposed as part of the package requiring implementation of 802.1X, must be carefully considered. A careful design of VLAN structures must be implemented. That is obvious. What is less obvious is that, because of the potentially highly dynamic nature of VLAN assignment, the particular access requirements of a given application have a much wider scope within the network than with some traditional implementations.

New and existing applications need to re-evaluate Operational Characteristics, Type/Quality of Service, and Significance in terms of this dynamic nature. The implementation of 802.1X must evaluate the placement of its components in the light of Application requirements of the network.

The Operational Characteristics of 802.1X have been enumerated in several aspects of several planes. These characteristics must function in an Application environment. While 802.1X has no Type/Quality of Service requirements in and of itself, the implementation could be affected by the previous implementation on a port as part of an Application. Also, the implementation of Quality of Service on a particular port can be sabotaged by the variable nature of VLAN assignments. It is important to identify how these parameters are applied. In a complex environment, where the network is heavily controlled, the Significance of traffic may be controlled in ways that have little to do with Type/Quality of Service. The directing of traffic across specific paths, and possible implementation of access lists, will be complicated further by the dynamics of 802.1X.

The following sections of this chapter will discuss some of the questions that should be asked when considering and developing an 802.1X Port-Based Authentication. Each stage of the process has different requirements that must be considered. The content in the next few sections should not be considered to be exhaustive. This is not a book that is dedicated to describing the design process. In some situations, what is presented may be overkill, and, in others, may not document all the right questions. But it should provide a solid understanding of the type of questions that should be asked at each point in the design process. The flow and gross responsibilities at each phase should become clear.

3.10.6   Requirements Definition

In this phase, the first in the project, the goals are defined and the basic information is gathered. The first step is to identify what is currently being done on the network, what applications are implemented, and what the infrastructure looks like.

The delineation of what currently is being done on the network is the best place to start the definition of what will be done on the network. What information is available on the network and what is the confidentiality associated with it? How is this confidentiality currently being enforced? The investigation must identify what security methods, including 802.1X, already have been implemented. Furthermore, what authentication information is currently utilized? Frequently, this will be Active Directory based.

The fashion in which logical infrastructure constructs such as VLANs must be documented. The way in which these have been implemented to support and restrict application access is an important piece of information. Also, the consistency across the network of VLAN numbering is an important piece of information. This will help in the definition of dynamic assignment of VLANs based upon authentication status. Also, any logical structures that restrict or expedite traffic flow should be documented. The most obvious of these would be access lists, but there are additional possibilities such as Layer 3 interfaces and routing, or implemented trunks that deny traffic from certain VLANs. Those are intended as examples and are not a complete list.

In addition to the logical definition of the network, in terms of applications, the physical network must be documented. The various makes/models of appliances, together with operating systems capabilities must be documented. The placement of any RADIUS servers and associated Authentication Databases likewise must be identified. The various links and data paths must be established. This physical documentation needs to be merged with the documentation of the logical network to provide a complete view of where and how traffic flows for applications.

One of the major aspects of the Requirements Definition phase is the impact of human organizations. They will both impact and be impacted by an implementation of 802.1X. It is obvious that the Help Desk will be impacted, but so will Network Management and the Security organizations. All the human organizations must be evaluated in terms of readiness to support this type of implementation, the availability of tools to support their role as impacted by implementation, and the general availability of processes and experienced personnel.

Several paragraphs ago, I stated that the definition of why 802.1X is being considered for implementation is one output of this phase—goals definition. It would be silly to attempt to design an implementation without having the objectives identified, but, unfortunately, I have been involved in some of those projects. Thus, as a final admonition, ensure that the goals/objectives are clearly written and review the information gathered as being pertinent not only to the documentation of the current state, but also as being supportive of analysis related to achieving the goals. If there is information missing or areas where it is incomplete, then go back and redo the job.

3.10.7 Concept

Concept is the marriage of goals and objectives to the environment. Once the information gathering has been completed, a concept of how the environment will be modified to implement the goals can be created.

The first step is to identify what constraints and limitations are going to affect possible scenarios. As an example, an environment that has not implemented certificates, and has a limited number of staff, might mean that selection of EAP-Methods that are certificate-based is not a good idea. Another might be the fact that VLAN numbering varies from site to site. VLAN 2 might mean access to payroll in one site and it might mean Internet only in another. This type of situation could put constraints on the dynamic VLAN assignment. Or it could mean that creative implementations of RADIUS will be required so that individual site idiosyncrasies can be addressed. Or it could mean that, concurrent with implementation of 802.1X, all VLAN structuring will be synchronized. All of these are possibilities.

Evaluation of the various options and alternatives available within 802.1X must be made and a subset selected. This will be affected by the infrastructure implemented. Identification of features available, based on whether or not the 2004 standards, including options, are supported, must be made. This will be the lowest common denominator in a mixed vendor environment or a mixed supported specification environment.

As noted above, the selection of an EAP-Method is part of the concept phase and is affected by a variety of factors. A clear understanding of the requirements of the various Methods must be achieved, and the ability to support those requirements in the network and various organizations must be documented.

By evaluating the information gathered, a solid concept of which options within 802.1X should be implemented, what peripheral changes will be required to support the implementation, how authentication will be performed, and where authentication devices, such as RADIUS servers, will be placed can be achieved. The concept identifies the changes required, including any upgrading of components or implementation of new infrastructure. This includes the logical constructs—VLANs, access lists, etc.—as well as the physical appliances.

3.10.8 Architecture

The architecture phase essentially takes the concept and reapplies it to the logical and physical network. 802.1X is described as a functioning entity in the proposed environment. The impact of the concept on the physical environment is documented in terms of traffic flows and patterns. In particular, the conversations within the selected EAP-Methods should be documented as flow diagrams within the individual networks or network segments.

Impacts of placement of RADIUS servers, along with the traffic pattern for conversations with Authenticators and Authentication Databases, are significant examples of this. The various RADIUS implementations should be documented as to the scope of applicability within the network. A single global implementation may be the most common implementation, but it is by far not the only possible one.

The documentation of the state changes associated with the authentication process at various points in the network is also a part of the architecture process. The possible VLAN states should be described for individual segments of the network, along with the implications for connectivity of each. This would include Guest VLANs, IPT VLANs, and the various dynamic VLANs available from RADIUS.

The various processes required to support 802.1X must be documented. Most of this would be in the area of management—either the Help Desk or Network Operations. Toolsets to support and manage 802.1X would have been identified in the concept phase. In the architecture phase, the traffic flows created by the toolsets and the methodology to utilize each tool will be documented. Training programs necessary for people involved with supporting 802.1X will be specifically identified, along with the numbers and type of job function to attend each.

3.10.9 Design

At this point, there is a significant amount of work to do. However, most of it has to do with the mechanics of implementing the 802.1X authentication defined. Most of what we are concerned with regarding 802.1X, itself, has been accomplished in preceding phases. The rest is simply mechanics. However, a brief discussion will be provided.

The design phase builds upon architecture by translating the architecture output into exact code. Authenticators and Authentication Servers is the obvious type of coding, but related changes to the infrastructure required by the implementation also must be coded. Any changes to VLAN structures, access lists, etc. required by this implementation and covered in the architecture are converted into actual coding to be implemented on the various appliances. From an organizational standpoint, the processes and scripts will be written that are to be used in supportin g the implementation. Similarly, training will be conducted.

And, finally, it is implemented.

Index